MW00855946

AVID

READER

PRESS

The LAST MANAGER

HOW EARL WEAVER TRICKED, TORMENTED, AND REINVENTED BASEBALL

John W. Miller

AVID READER PRESS

NEW YORK   AMSTERDAM/ANTWERP   LONDON   TORONTO   SYDNEY   NEW DELHI

AVID READER PRESS
An Imprint of Simon & Schuster, LLC
1230 Avenue of the Americas
New York, NY 10020

First Avid Reader Press hardcover edition March 2025

AVID READER PRESS and colophon are trademarks of Simon & Schuster, LLC

For information about special discounts for bulk purchases,
please contact Simon & Schuster Special Sales
at 1-866-506-1949 or business@simonandschuster.com.

The Simon & Schuster Speakers Bureau can bring authors to your live event.
For more information or to book an event, contact the Simon & Schuster Speakers Bureau
at 1-866-248-3049 or visit our website at www.simonspeakers.com.

Interior design by Ruth Lee-Mui

Manufactured in the United States of America

1   3   5   7   9   10   8   6   4   2

Library of Congress Cataloging-in-Publication Data

Names: Miller, John W., 1977– author.
Title: The last manager : how Earl Weaver tricked,
tormented, and reinvented baseball / John W. Miller.
Description: First Avid Reader Press hardcover edition. | New York :
Avid Reader Press, 2025. | Includes bibliographical references and index.
Identifiers: LCCN 2024033511 | ISBN 9781668030929 (hardcover) |
ISBN 9781668030936 (paperback) | ISBN 9781668030943 (ebook)
Subjects: LCSH: Weaver, Earl, 1930–2013. | Baltimore Orioles
(Baseball team)—History. | Baseball managers—United States—Biography.
Classification: LCC GV865.W38 M55 2025 | DDC 796.357/092/4 [B]—dc23/eng/20241016
LC record available at https://lccn.loc.gov/2024033511

ISBN 978-1-6680-3092-9
ISBN 978-1-6680-3094-3 (ebook)

For Mom, Dad, and Uncle Steve,

for taking me to ballgames, and my first ballplayers,

Jacob, Moe, and Davey; and Tom Mudd, RIP.

CONTENTS

SHORT NOTE ON STATISTICS

This is a book for everybody, not just baseball experts. Here's a key to the few statistics I use:

- .BA/.OBP/.SLG. When I cite three numbers in a row with slash marks, it's batting average/on-base percentage/slugging percentage. Example: .300/.400/.500. (Those numbers over a career would put you in the Hall of Fame. The American League average from 1968 to 1986: .256/.322/.378.)
- (W-L, ERA) Wins-Losses, Earned Run Average (earned runs per nine innings). Ex: 20-10, 2.84. (AL league average from 1968–1986: 3.69.)
- Defensive Efficiency: The percentage of batted balls a team turns into outs.
- OPS: On-base percentage plus slugging percentage.
- Wins Above Replacement: The number of wins a player adds to a team relative to a replacement-level player.

Part 1

DREAMS

Earl Weaver, king of managers when managers were kings, pantomimed throwing umpire Don Denkinger out of a game, August 25, 1977.

1

PART WIZARD, PART GENERAL, PART CLOWN

Baltimore, 1982

All life is six-to-five against.

—Damon Runyon

Earl Weaver was crying.

The crusty fifty-two-year-old Orioles manager with a sandpaper face, silver hair, and a scratchy voice had just lost the big game, but more than 40,000 Baltimoreans, stuffed with beer, hot dogs, and crab cakes, roared like they'd won the World Series.

The Memorial Stadium claps and cries echoed a passion that, for once in America, transcended winning and losing. Weaver had promised to retire after the 1982 season, which would have lasted longer if the Orioles had beaten the Milwaukee Brewers on October 3 with the American League East championship on the line. They lost, 10–2. The season, and Weaver's career, were finished.

On top of the pitcher's mound, Wild Bill Hagy, the paunchy, bearded cabdriver in ripped jeans, Baltimore's fan mascot, spelled with his arms: O-R-I-O-L-E-S. He signed an underdog city's love for its feisty baseball team and its manager, who represented Charm City as well as Mencken, blue crabs, and red-brick row houses. A tough little man with a chip on his shoulder standing up to the blue-blooded bullies from New York and Boston. Weaver broke character and joined the celebration. The cheers got louder.

Up in the TV booth, Howard Cosell, the legendary broadcaster for ABC Sports, could not believe his eyes. "You are bearing witness," he boomed, "to one of the most remarkable scenes maybe that you will ever see in sports."

The counterintuitive curtain call followed Weaver's first fourteen and a half seasons as uniformed dugout leader of the Orioles, during which he'd been so brilliant, colorful, and funny that he'd entered the pantheon of characters who'd marked baseball with their brilliance and quotable humor, in the same conversation as Yogi Berra, Pedro Martinez, and Baltimore's own Babe Ruth.

Orioles fans, whether they knew it or not, were celebrating the twilight of the age of the baseball manager, a mythical character plucked from the America of train travel, circuses, and vaudeville, springing from the nineteenth-century clubs in New York and other cities that turned an informal folk game into modern baseball, America's first mass entertainment.

The title of this book is not a statement of fact, but a slanted swing, exaggerated to make a point. Earl Weaver reigned supreme—the only manager to last with one team during the entire 1970s—when baseball managers were American royalty and powerful operators within the game, sometimes bigger stars than their players. In July 1983, Earl Weaver was the *Playboy* magazine interview of the month. ("Baseball's rowdy genius," the cover called him.) Other *Playboy* interview subjects in 1983 included writer Gabriel García Márquez, who'd just won the Nobel Prize for literature, media mogul and CNN founder Ted Turner, bestselling author Stephen King, actor Paul Newman, and photographer Ansel Adams. That was the level of fame, and cultural relevancy, that Earl Weaver, a baseball manager, occupied.

Part wizard, part general, part clown, the manager has been central to baseball and to its myth and represented an American cultural archetype—the tobacco-chewing mad scientist, as instantly recognizable as the cowboy, the astronaut, or the Elvis impersonator.

During the era of the baseball manager, fans and front offices believed you needed one of these larger-than-life leaders to build a great baseball team around. Managers inspired fans to dream of commanding their own team, a desire that fueled fantasy baseball, videogames, and a new literature of analysis.

After Earl Weaver's era, managers still had a tough job, and a good manager was better than a bad manager, but they were never as popular or as powerful. The centrality and certainty of data analysis, along with free agency, shifted control to general managers and to the players themselves. And unlike football's and basketball's head coaches, baseball managers can't design proprietary playbooks that transform teams into winners. In the twenty-first century, managers were no longer dominant forces; there were no more Earl Weavers.

While writing this book, I bicycled from my home in Pittsburgh to PNC Park on the banks of the Allegheny River, near the site of the first World Series in 1903, to interview current big-league managers visiting Steel City to lead their teams against the Pirates. They all professed envy for the power of their predecessors, and, in particular, admiration for Weaver. I found them polished, smart, well-rounded men, like the CEOs I interviewed when I covered global corporations for the *Wall Street Journal*.

They all conceded the game had changed. "Each manager, his ball club, it was *his* team, and everyone knew that, and now the mindset is it's *our* team," Dodgers manager Dave Roberts told me. "With that comes a lot more questions being asked, a lot more collaboration. I don't think it's a bad thing, it's just different." And then, as if to illustrate his point, Roberts jumped into a nearby line next to Mookie Betts, Freddie Freeman, Clayton Kershaw, and other members of the 2023 Dodgers—payroll $241.5 million—as they stretched to get ready for their game against the Pirates. Roberts, the most successful manager of this century, didn't yell or scream. Instead, he bantered, made jokes, and generally tried to make the men around him, most with annual salaries far above his paltry-for-big-league-baseball $3.3 million a year, feel good.

There was never any question that the Orioles were Weaver's team. The Bismarck of Baltimore drove his men forward, enforced high standards, and obsessively sought winning edges. Weaver invented new ways of building baseball teams, prioritizing a high on-base average, elite defense, and strike throwing. He was the first manager to use a modern radar gun in spring training, he pioneered the use of analytical data, and he helped make the first great baseball videogame for Electronic Arts, laying the groundwork for the megahit *John Madden Football*. He turned battles with umpires into legendary comic masterpieces. He campaigned to make Frank Robinson baseball's first Black manager and moved Cal Ripken Jr. to shortstop, where he reinvigorated the position. He even claimed magic powers, in the form of a gift for hypnotism.

More than any other baseball leader of his day, Earl Weaver saw straight into baseball's future. The Orioles manager was so good at his job and figured out so many things about baseball, without the benefit of a computer, that you could make the claim that he made his own job obsolete. Once computers came along, you didn't even need a manager anymore. You could just program them to think like Earl Weaver. That, broadly, is what front offices do now. They use powerful cameras and computers to develop game plans that look a lot like Earl Weaver's strategies and hire managers to implement them. They look for players with high on-base percentage, eschew the bunt, and value players much like Earl did.

Weaver's career is a pivot point in baseball history. He entered the old-time baseball world and, when he left, the game was modern. He was the only manager to hold his job during the five years leading up to, and five years after, free agency upended baseball in 1976.

The decline of the baseball manager in our culture has mirrored other technology-driven changes. The men and women of Earl Weaver's generation, from taxi drivers to schoolteachers, and musicians to doctors, practiced their craft without computers, giving more value to human experience and mastery. Earl Weaver's story stands out as an illustrative example of the last great leap forward of the human artisan without the assistance of the silicon chip. His passion, commitment, and craving for excellence burned a light by which we might measure what we've gained, and lost.

Of course, Earl Weaver's legacy only matters because he won, and his record is handy ammunition in one of baseball's great unresolved questions: Does the manager make a difference? His story suggests it does. Here's how the Orioles have done in their franchise history:

1901–1953 (in Milwaukee and St. Louis): 70 wins per 162 games
1954–1967 (Orioles before Earl): 81.9 wins per 162 games
1968–1982; 1985–1986 (Earl): 94.5 wins per 162 games
1987–2024 (after Earl): 76 wins per 162 games

In the twelve full seasons between 1968 and 1982, not counting the strike seasons of 1972 and 1981, Weaver won at least 90 games in 11 seasons, and averaged *97 wins*. The Orioles won more games, and recorded a better run differential, than any other team in baseball. No other franchise has had such an astonishing explosion of success and glory so directly linked to one manager. (You could make a case for the 1995–2005 Atlanta Braves, but unlike Earl Weaver, their manager, Bobby Cox, also had seven losing seasons with the Braves.) Of all the managers with 1,000 wins since Weaver started his career during the 1968 midseason All-Star break, here's who has the highest winning percentage:

Earl Weaver .583 (1,480-1,060)
Davey Johnson .562 (1,372-1,071)
Bobby Cox .556 (2,054-2,001)
Billy Martin .553 (1,253-1,013)
Charlie Manuel .548 (1,000-826)

Orioles fans on October 3, 1982, were cheering a winner, an iconoclast, and a complicated, funny, and flawed human being, who belonged to that rare class of originals of whom we can safely say: we'll never see another. Earl might terrorize umpires, fight his players, and cuss, drink, and smoke to excess, but he was also a curious, charming, and sensitive man who gardened, cooked, and played ukulele. He loved poodles and Elvis. And despite his abuse of the King's English, he was full of wisdom.

The tragicomic Shakespearean (and yes, he once quoted Shakespeare to an umpire) depth of Earl Weaver—Prospero (or maybe Falstaff) in cleats—touched everyone from Sparrows Point steelworkers to George Weigel, the biographer of Pope John Paul II, who likened Earl Weaver talking baseball to Homer reciting the *Iliad*.

When it came time to say goodbye after that last game in 1982, it was in a stadium full of love, tears cascading down the faces of thousands of fans and one craggy little man. "For people in Baltimore, Earl was one of us," said Greg Schwalenberg, a beer vendor that day. "He cussed, he smoked, he drank, he was funny, and he was always so good at managing, his teams always won."

Here's how Cosell wrapped up the scene: "Yes, the fans have stayed to cheer. They have stayed to cheer and honor the retiring manager of the Birds of Baltimore. A man who in fifteen years has become an absolute legend. . . . And Earl Weaver is crying. Very rarely if ever has there ever been a scene like this. . . . And Earl, you deserve it. You've been one of the greatest managers in the history of the game."

In 2013, when Earl Weaver died, the *Wall Street Journal* asked me to write his obituary. I watched the clip of the final game of the 1982 season so I could quote Cosell accurately. As I again observed Memorial Stadium rev up and Earl Weaver cry, I wondered: Where did this guy come from?

2

BRAT VS. BRAT

St. Petersburg, Florida, 1952

Not making the baseball team at West Point was one of the greatest disappointments of my life, maybe the greatest.

—President Dwight Eisenhower

You cannot understand Earl Weaver without understanding what happened in March 1952, the month he knocked on the door of his childhood dream and watched the baseball gods crack it open, and then slam it shut like a nightmare.

A fantasy looked like it was coming true. The hot ticket in St. Pete on March 8: Mickey Mantle and the New York Yankees versus Stan Musial and the St. Louis Cardinals. Before Superman and Captain America made their spring training debuts in front of 7,211 at Al Lang Stadium amid resort hotels, palm trees swaying in the salty breeze, and a harbor packed with sailboats, the first man to bat for the Cardinals was a stout twenty-one-year-old second baseman with a crew cut atop a high forehead, baby face, and devilish grin.

Now batting, playing second base: Earl Weaver.

What a triumph for this St. Louis street kid, leading off for his favorite baseball team, in a lineup full of ballplayers he had worshipped.

Earl was part of the elite, one of only forty players in the Cardinals system invited to big-league camp, and not one of those boring archetypes, like an over-the-hiller looking for one last chance, a veteran back for one more year, or a jaded superstar nobody liked.

Earl Weaver was a bona fide prospect. Across America, thousands of washed-up knuckleballers, phenom shortstops, and coal-league boppers would have killed to trade places. In 1952, throughout America, there were 43 minor leagues with 378 teams. (At this writing, there are 11 affiliated leagues and 120 teams.)

The kid had earned this chance. Four years earlier, in 1948, Weaver had graduated from Beaumont High School in St. Louis as a star three-sport athlete and signed with the hometown Cardinals. Initially a fringe prospect because of his short, stocky body, he'd proven scouts wrong with four fine minor-league seasons, including three team Most Valuable Player awards. He'd survived dead-end towns, rickety buses, lonely honky-tonks, and sleazy pool halls. His keen batting eye and sweet stroke had propelled him upward from West Frankfort, Illinois, to St. Joseph, Missouri, to Winston-Salem, North Carolina, to Houston, Texas, Omaha, Nebraska, and finally, here, a big-league spring training camp in Florida. On his first day, when he walked into the swanky Bainbridge Hotel in St. Petersburg, he thought he'd checked into heaven.

A "nice little jewel," the hometown papers called Earl, a "sure bet" for the future big-league second-base job. He could turn on a fastball, corral twisty infield grounders, and spin double plays with the agility of a ballerina. His batting eye was elite. Okay, let's not get too sentimental about young Earl. Already, he was rough around the edges. You would not have wanted him to date your daughter. Cranky and cantankerous, harboring streaks of pain and anger he could never master. There was a darkness that would never entirely vanish. A little seedy. He spit words like a never-ending firecracker exploding out of the gutter. He held court into the early morning, taking his teammates' money at poker and dice. As a ballplayer, he had shortcomings: he lacked speed and power, and was cursed with a mediocre arm that limited the impact of his soft hands.

Those hands and hitting skills, and his passion for baseball, though, were real. Fans rooted for Earl because he played with more fury, and loved baseball more, than anybody they'd ever seen. He took walks to help the team, broke up double plays like a linebacker, and threw punches to defend team-mates. He played baseball *right* and was the kind of player who fired up home crowds, gave people something to believe in, and got all the good nicknames. The Mighty Mite. The Omaha Flash. 100 Per Cent. He picked up that one in Omaha because, fans said, he never made mistakes.

On that first day of spring training against the Yankees in 1952, Earl, using a peculiar crouched wide-open stance, banged two singles in five at-bats. He played second base and made three assists. Up in the broadcast booth, the great Harry Caray broadcast the game to Earl's classmates and friends, family and fans in Skidmore and Springfield and St. Joseph and a thousand other Missouri towns, and millions from the Ozarks to Lake Michigan.

Almost every day that March, Weaver started and played the whole game. It was off-Broadway, but Earl for that month held his own. He blasted a couple of home runs, tied for second on the team in RBI, batted a solid .260, and fielded his position well. Among big leaguers for the first time, he *belonged*.

Bad luck for Earl: the man who would decide whether he'd make the big leagues was his manager, who wanted that roster spot for himself.

Eddie "The Brat" Stanky was a tough Polish kid from Philadelphia who'd scrapped his way to the big leagues. A short, hard-nosed second baseman who couldn't hit but drew walks in bunches, he was famous for performing feats of assholery other big leaguers never even dared to match, like waving his arms to distract the hitter when he played second base. Many described Weaver as "another Eddie Stanky."

On the 1952 Cardinals, All-Star Red Schoendienst would start at second base, and Solly Hemus at shortstop. The question: Who would back them up? It could be young prospect Earl Weaver. Or, if Stanky chose to be a player-manager instead of a "bench manager," as they called the job then, Stanky him-self would be the backup infielder.

Stanky, at thirty-five years old on the back end of his career, promised he would apply impartial scientific reason. "If I find out it will help the club for me to sit on the bench 154 games this season, that's where I'll be," he said. In a newspaper column, he wrote: "Our scouts are high on a kid called Earl Weaver. He was with Omaha last year. And guess where he plays? Second base."

Fred Saigh, the owner of the Cardinals, raved about Weaver. "Right now, the kid is better than some second basemen in the National League and the American, too." But he made it clear that the final decision would be Stanky's. The Cardinals hired Stanky to get them back to the World Series. Between 1926 and 1946, they had reached the World Series nine times, and triumphed in six. But they'd won nothing since 1946, so before the 1952 season, Saigh acquired Stanky from the pennant-winning New York Giants, where he'd been a hero under manager Leo Durocher, and gave him dictatorial powers over who would compose the team, and decide its practice plans, rules, lineups, offseason routines, and strategy.

Stanky ran spring training with an iron fist. He fined veteran Harry Brecheen $50 for being in the clubhouse during the national anthem. He penalized players a dollar for every pound over their playing weight, earning comparisons in the newspapers to Shylock demanding a pound of flesh in Shakespeare's *The Merchant of Venice*. Stanky set up Iron Mikes, pitching machines with slingshot arms that powered fastballs at hitters. He made players practice diving back to first and running into the catchers' ankles on plays at the plate. Weaver was the first one to raise his hand. He demonstrated diving and sliding until he was bruised up.

Earl feared Stanky. The first time he climbed into the batter's box, he was so nervous he screwed up a bunt. "Stanky simply could not accept incapabilities from any of his players, even though he had a lot of them as a player," recalled Earl. "In fact, he still had himself on the active roster when his own skills had diminished dramatically."

But the manager was king; Stanky's word meant everything. There was nowhere to appeal. Few players had agents, and there was no powerful players' union. There were no independent bloggers to raise hell if Stanky promoted himself over a better young player. Stanky served as his own public relations machine. He bragged about being only a pound overweight despite all those winter dinners at businessmen's clubs like the Kiwanis and the Elks and Moose. "If the records are correct, Eddie Stanky collected 127 walks and got 127 hits last season. That means I got on base more than 250 times," he wrote in an Associated Press column the week before spring training. "Somebody will have to hustle to beat out the Brat for that second base job."

Earl hustled, and got results. On March 13, he went 2-for-4. The next day, he again knocked two hits, including a home run. Playing with his childhood heroes was a dream. When Cardinals right fielder Enos Slaughter called him off on a fly ball behind him, like a good teammate, Earl yelled "Enos! Enos!" and remembered "those countless times that I had leaped to my feet in the stands at Sportsman's Park and shouted 'You got it, Enos! All yours!' as he ran down a line drive and speared it."

A month into spring training, things were still looking good for the home-town hero. On March 19, Weaver pinch-hit a single against the Red Sox. The starting left fielders that day were the other two future Hall of Famers in the game. Stan Musial went 2-for-3, and Ted Williams 0-for-3. "The more I see of him, the more I like" Weaver, Stanky told reporters. "He has impressed me more than any other individual in camp." If he doesn't make the big league this year, it'll be next year, Stanky insisted.

On March 21, the Associated Press ran a story headlined "Stanky Keeping Fans Guessing on Infield." Stanky, the story explained, "may know his plans for the infield this season but he still keeps a guessing game going." At that point, the story added, he had played only one game at second base. Stanky had told everybody he was battling a cold.

Cuts were coming. Everybody knew it. Players checked their hotel mail-boxes every morning. On March 23, Weaver started and drew four walks. The next day, Stanky said his cold was gone. He was ready to play again. It probably never mattered how well Earl played. The fix was in. The noose was coming.

Here's how the paper reported it:

ST. PETERSBURG, FLA. March 31—Manager Eddie Stanky lopped four Cardinals off his spring training roster today, sending a pitcher, an outfielder and two infielders to minor league farm teams. . . . Infielder Earl Weaver was released on option to the Houston club. The departures left 36 men in uniform on the roster.

The backup infielder for the 1952 Cardinals was player-manager Eddie Stanky. He batted .214 in 14 spring training at-bats, and during that regular season hit .229 in 83 at-bats, with no home runs.

On April Fool's Day, 1952, Earl Weaver left Florida for Houston. Back to the bush leagues. Instead of motivating him, the rejection drove him to drink and depression, set him on a purgatory through the minor leagues that lasted sixteen years. He threw in the towel, and would never again play as well as he had those first four seasons in the minor leagues, and never again share a locker room with Stan Musial.

We all fail at dreams, but there's a special pain when we run into bad luck, injustice, or the reality that there's always somebody better, and suffer a rejection that is explicit, painful, and personal. "When you're a twenty-one-year-old kid and you think you've come this close to realizing your unremitting dream, only to see it hook foul and out of play, it can do grave damage to your head and heart," recalled Weaver. "For the first time, I had doubts about my ability, serious doubts that occasioned the worst period in my life up to that point."

The moment when we hit bottom and must get up is when we start conjuring a true vocation from an alchemy of aspiration, talent, and circumstance. The humiliating failure of 1952 wired Earl Weaver for managing. When pressed to explain what made him a Hall of Fame skipper, Weaver often explained that he'd become an expert talent evaluator because of his failures as a player. He knew where the bar was. Because he was the bar. Any player better than Earl Weaver was a big leaguer.

His Orioles players ribbed him about his failures as a player. "The only thing Earl knows about pitching is that he couldn't hit it," said pitcher Dave McNally. That fit the cliché of Earl Weaver, the ranting, raving genius who pushed players to do things he never could.

The truth, like almost everything about Earl Weaver, was more complicated. Manager Weaver never told the version of his story where the newspapers called him a "a little jewel." Perhaps it hurt too much, or highlighted too acutely how he had had a legitimate shot at the majors, and then basically given up after failing to make the 1952 Cardinals. Or perhaps he didn't remember. He would always say his arm wasn't good enough, and that he wasn't as good as All-Star second baseman Red Schoendienst. That reasoning was easier to stomach than his own inability to cope with the injustice of Eddie Stanky stealing his job.

It is difficult to make a case that Earl was destined for a long major-league career. His arm wasn't good enough for short or third; backup second baseman is not a job. I ran his minor-league stats by two contemporary front-office analysts. They praised his high walk and low strikeout rates but said his weak arm, lack of power or speed, and small stature doomed him.

But Earl Weaver *had* been a high school stud. He *had* excelled for four minor-league seasons. He *had* earned a coveted big-league spring invite. He *had* played well enough to make the team. Most importantly, he had *thought* he was going to make it, and when he didn't, suffered a deep psychological bruise, on his way to learning that destiny is not a childhood dream but a complex mix of desire, ability, and reality.

As I reported for this book, I visited the Cardinals archives next to Busch Stadium in St. Louis. Amy Berra, the Cardinals' curator, had received Earl Weaver's 1952 spring training uniform. I invited Earl's daughter Terry and her son Mike Leahy, a St. Louis musician who goes by "Clownvis," to accompany me.

Terry brought along some mementoes she'd inherited from her dad. He'd left her a box that included programs, pictures, a 1969 American League championship ring, and a scrapbook.

The scrapbook was a pack of clipped newspaper box scores from 1952 spring training. At the top of the Cardinals lineup in almost every game, above stars like Musial and Slaughter, was written:

"Weaver, 2b."

"My dad was so proud of that spring with the Cardinals," said Terry.

Part 2

ST. LOUIS

The 1930s Cardinals won championships, played pranks, and carried musical instruments on the road, enchanting young Earl Weaver and his family. "I am possibly the only manager that carried an orchestra," said manager Frank Frisch.

3

MOUND CITY

St. Louis, 1930–1948

Your Holiness, I'm Joseph Medwick. I, too, used to be a cardinal.
—Former St. Louis outfielder Joe Medwick to
Pope Pius XII during a visit to the Vatican

During the Great Depression, working-class Americans survived in two ways: you could drive a truck, turn screws, or perform tasks for a paycheck—or you could hustle: work odd jobs, run bars, barbershops, or cleaners, or do favors for the illegal underworld. Earl Weaver came from a family of hustlers—and their main mark was baseball. Like all savants, from Mozart to Tiger Woods, as a child Earl bathed in his craft, watching, analyzing, and playing baseball.

It was less than a mile from Sportsman's Park, home of the big-league Cardinals and Browns, to the apartment in the smoky northern half of St. Louis, a crowded quarter of corner stores, barbershops, and saloons, where Earl Sidney Weaver was born on August 14, 1930, the second child of Earl and Ethel Weaver. Following the European tradition of naming daughters after fathers, they had named their other child, a girl born in 1926, Earleen.

To support his family of four, and an extended clan of parents and in-laws, Earl Sr. ran dry-cleaning businesses. In the mid-1930s, he earned contracts to wash the uniforms of the Cardinals and Browns. That made him an insider at Sportsman's Park, and one of Earl Weaver's earliest memories was walking through the boisterous and usually triumphant clubhouse of the 1930s St. Louis Cardinals. He could be forgiven for not remembering the Browns, perpetually stuck in last place.

When father and son walked to Sportsman's Park on summer afternoons, it was to watch one of the great acts in baseball history. The Cardinals' general manager, the prophetic Branch Rickey, hired the first public relations agent in baseball history to market the kind of baseball that Earl Weaver would come to love, with high drama, gut-splitting comedy, and athletic splendor. Rickey pushed his wild, winning squad with their nickname, the Gashouse Gang, after the rough portion of American cities devoted to storing fuel.

If 1920s baseball belonged to the New York Yankees and Babe Ruth, the first half of the 1930s belonged to the Gashouse Gang and their ace pitcher Dizzy Dean, a cotton picker's son from Arkansas with a gift of gab to rival the Babe's. Dizzy was the folksy hero Depression America needed. He didn't graduate from second grade. "And I wasn't so good at first grade either," he said. After he married a Houston party girl named Patricia, a sportswriter asked him if he was aware that Pat had been with most of the men in town. "Sure, I heard it," said Dizzy. "I'm one of 'em. And that's why I wanna marry her."

Earl Sr. loved the shtick, and taught his son to love it. He made Earl Jr. a replica Cardinals uniform and labeled it ME AND PAUL on the back, a reference to Dean and his brother, Paul, also a pitcher on the Cardinals. "Me and Paul" will win 45 games combined, Dizzy told writers before the 1934 season, in a quote celebrated for its bad grammar and good prophecy. (In 1934, Dizzy won 30 games, the last 30-game winner before Denny McLain in 1968, and Paul won 19.)

The rest of the Cardinals matched Dizzy. Third baseman Pepper Martin, nicknamed the Wild Horse of the Osage, raced mini-cars and carried spare auto parts in his trunk. Joe Medwick hated his nickname, Ducky, coined by a girl he met in the minors who said he walked like a duck. His preferred nickname: Muscles. Little Earl's favorite player was shortstop Leo Durocher, a dandy and ladies' man who prowled the night with gamblers in flashy suits. Durocher loved to fight with umpires and later managed the Dodgers, Giants, Cubs, and Astros, for twenty-four seasons.

Enchanting and entertaining Depression-era America, the Cardinals won five World Series before Earl turned eighteen, lit fires on the field, and planted black cats in opponents' dugouts. They drank, gambled, chased women, and started a cowboy band, the Mudcats, that was so good it played vaudeville circuits. They packed fiddles, harmonicas, guitars, and a washboard on their train trips to Chicago, Brooklyn, Cincinnati, Pittsburgh, Boston, Philadelphia, and New York. Their favorite tunes were "Rock Island Line" and "Wreck of the Old 97." "I am possibly the only manager that carried an orchestra," said manager Frank Frisch. "We traveled with more instruments than we did shirts or anything else."

The Cardinals were also America's team, because, until the Dodgers and Giants moved to California in the 1950s, St. Louis was the southernmost and westernmost major-league city, and hosted sports' widest radio network via KMOX's powerful 50,000-watt station. There were only sixteen big-league teams, eight in the American League and eight in the National League, all clustered in the northeast quadrant of the continental United States. The rest of America belonged to the St. Louis Cardinals.

Sportsman's Park, America's western cathedral of baseball, drew St. Louis steelworkers, Ozark farmers, and Mississippi boat captains, who sweated through boiling afternoons in straw hats drinking cold beer and soda pop. Red Smith, the great baseball writer, described the park as a "garish, county fair sort of layout." With American or National League games almost every day, crowds buzzed around Sportsman's Park and surrounding streets from April to October.

The shabby stadium smelled like sweat, tobacco, and beer. In the 1930s, they let a goat graze in the outfield. Steamy St. Louis summers baked the field hard like concrete. Infielders feared for their lives, but fans loved the pinball bounces. If they couldn't get tickets, they went across the street to Palermo's, one of America's first modern sports bars. It served food and played games on the radio. Until the park installed a public address system in 1937, ushers hustled around the perimeter of the field with megaphones to announce batters and other information to the crowd. A woman named Mary Ott, known as the Horse Lady, tugged at her ears and neighed to heckle.

Like most working-class families, the Weavers drank, gabbed, gambled, played cards (especially pinochle), and followed baseball by attending games in person, four blocks away, listening on the radio or reading the papers. At home, the entire family, including the women, Ethel and Earleen, argued and talked baseball loudly and incessantly. By 1930, St. Louis had three daily news-papers that covered both teams. The weekly *Sporting News*, the so-called Bible of Baseball in the twentieth century (it didn't cover other sports until 1966), was founded in 1886 in St. Louis.

St. Louis had never stopped being baseball-crazy since the modern ver-sion of the sport arrived from New York City around the time of the Civil War and replaced cricket as the most popular team game in St. Louis. (Yes, it's fun to imagine Earl Weaver, grandson of a native Englishman, as a crick-eter.) Sportsman's Park was built on a site laid out for a diamond used by the first St. Louis baseball club, founded in 1859. The first professional team in St. Louis, the Brown Stockings in 1874, was headquartered in a cigar store; their star was Jewish left-handed shortstop Lipman Pike.

When the Browns moved to St. Louis as the city's American League team in 1902, they took over Sportsman's Park. It had been built out of wood, a fire risk, so before the 1909 season, the Browns renovated it with concrete and steel, and added a second deck. It was the beginning of the era of the Classic Ballpark: Sportsman's Park, like Shibe Park in Philadelphia and Ebbets Field in Brooklyn, sat in the middle of taverns, factories, and crowded sidewalks. The Cardinals moved in as tenants in 1920.

Sportsman's Park then ran up the longest continuous stretch of two big-league teams playing in the same stadium, until 1953, when the Browns left for Baltimore and became the Orioles. The Browns kept offices at 2911 North Grand Avenue, and the Cardinals were around the corner at 3623 Dodier Street. Two quarters, two identities, quipped Branch Rickey. But even when the bad-news Browns played, it was still major-league baseball, featuring out-of-town stars like Babe Ruth and Lou Gehrig.

That was a lot of baseball for his dad Earl Milton Weaver to enjoy. He was born in St. Louis in 1901 to David Sydney Weaver, who was born in Glouces-ter, England, in 1858, and immigrated to Kansas in the early 1870s. David Syd-ney and his German wife, Anna Guettler, moved to St. Louis, where David worked as a carpenter, and had eight children. Their youngest son, Earl Milton

Weaver, married Ethel Wakefield in 1925, and they had Earleen, nicknamed Connie, in 1926, and Earl in 1930. One of Earl Milton's brothers, Arthur Sydney Weaver, was arrested in 1927 for smuggling booze during Prohibition and in 1930 for selling fraudulent race tickets.

Earl Weaver's mom, Ethel, had a difficult upbringing. Her dad died when she was a child, and her mom, Gertie, put Ethel and her three siblings in the St. Vincent German orphanage while she went looking for a new husband. After she found and married Fred Zastrow, she recovered her children. This was not uncommon. Orphanages often took in children during times when their parents couldn't care for them.

The children suffered damaging trauma. Ethel's sister Irene drank too much and ran with bad men, and one of Ethel's brothers, John Wakefield, "Uncle Red" to Earl, was a petty thief. He spent years in prison for stabbing and killing a man. Earl remembered his grandparents Gertie and Fred taking him to a prison in Detroit as a child to visit Uncle Red. Later, when the family referred to Uncle Red as "living in Detroit," Earl challenged them. "Is Uncle Red in jail?" he asked, moving his grandmother to tears.

At home, Ethel cooked and cleaned, and served German dishes like spaetzle and red cabbage salad, or English roast beef and potatoes. Grandmother Gertie also helped with the cooking. Earl liked Fred Zastrow, his grandmother's second husband, but thought he was austere. "When he died, the only blessing was that she was allowed to smoke in the kitchen," Earl said. "He was a strict Dutchman." The family attended Lutheran church services and sent Earl to Sunday school for nine years.

Even during the Great Depression, as unemployment soared, St. Louis was a vibrant river-port city and manufacturing hub. Thousands of factories produced almost everything, most famously shoes and beer. "First in booze, first in shoes, last in the American League," Browns fans joked. The nation's biggest ice cream cone factory baked 150 million cones a year. Hundreds of factories churned out cars and car parts. Before Roosevelt brought back beer in 1933, Anheuser-Busch sold soap, yeasts, and a malt drink called Bevo. After Prohibition ended, they rehired thousands of workers.

St. Louis emerged as America's preeminent frontier city in the nineteenth century amid so many Native American mounds it was still nicknamed

Mound City in 1930. Amplified by steamboats and railroads, it had become the biggest city between the Great Lakes and the Gulf of Mexico. "The City Surrounded by the United States" was the official slogan printed on official documents. By 1930, St. Louis had nineteen trunk rail lines, so called because they could carry passengers' long-haul baggage, with an aggregate track mileage of over 95,000 miles. Over 50,000 passengers a day went through downtown Union Station.

Earl Sr. hustled from the time he could earn a dollar, as a teenager selling newspapers on packed streets between corner stores, dive bars, and soda fountains, and then getting into the laundry business. It's not clear how he got those contracts to clean the teams' uniforms, or how often he got them. During World War II, he worked construction on a plant that made TNT explosives. When I visited St. Louis, the Cardinals' archives had no records. He may have secured the contracts because he sold newspapers as a young man with Bill DeWitt, then the owner of the Browns. Mike Weaver, Earl's son, recalled going on a Cardinals uniform run in the 1950s; the plant smelled like kerosene.

Phone books from the 1930s show Earl Sr. changing cleaning companies every year. By 1934, he owned his own company, North End Cleaning. Four employees sued him, demanding "an accounting and for the appointment of a receiver." They alleged that "the company is dominated by the principal stockholders, Mr. and Mrs. Earl Weaver." They were upset about not getting paid enough, Weaver Sr. said. "Weaver, who is president and manager of the company, said the plaintiffs are employees, who are disgruntled over salary differences."

Earl Weaver later said he was proud of his dad's connections to big-league teams, even if it was only to wash the uniforms. He loved trailing his dad to pick up uniforms from day games right before supper, taking them to an industrial cleaning plant, and then delivering clean uniforms the next day. Sometimes his dad sent him along to deliver uniforms. "It was my job to deliver them and get them from the park," he said. "That was a thrill. I would walk into the locker rooms and see the ballplayers. My eyes would grow really wide. I was a Cardinals fan. I loved the old Gashouse Gang."

Later in life, Earl Sr. offered a portrait of himself as an ascendent

American business owner. In 1951 he ran for alderman in St. Louis's Twentieth Ward as a Republican. The *Post-Dispatch* described him as "operator of a glove-cleaning business" and ran a short profile of him as a candidate: "A native St. Louisan, he attended public elementary and high schools and Rubicam Business College. He has been in the cleaning business for 25 years. Weaver is 50, married, with two children, and lives at 4713 Northland Avenue. He has been active in youth organizations." He ran unopposed in the Republican primary, and lost in the general election.

Young Earl was a baseball addict who sought refuge from his packed house at the ballpark. "See that little guy?" he once remarked to a reporter before a big-league game, pointing at a young fan. "That was me at the ballpark with my parents back in St. Louis. My folks were big fans and would take me to Cardinal games and Browns games. The Cardinals had the Gashouse Gang then. Durocher, Frisch, Pepper Martin, the Dean brothers. I'd be hanging over the rail watching them just like that little guy." Earl told lots of stories of himself as an enchanted fan. Joe Medwick signed a scorecard for Earl, who walked home and wrapped it into a bat to hit a paper ball with. The scorecard fell apart.

In the stands almost every day, Earl Weaver watched and studied baseball. During World War II, while people in St. Louis planted victory gardens and went to work in factories, the Cardinals and Browns kept playing. Weaver saw his first night game in 1940, when Sportsman's Park installed lights. The Cardinals and Browns segregated fans by race until 1944. That year, when the Cardinals beat the Browns 4 games to 2 in the World Series, Earl bought tickets to all six games. In 1945 Earl watched Pete Gray, a one-armed outfielder, play for the Browns. A couple of years later, in 1947, the Browns were the third team, after the Dodgers and Indians, to sign Black players when they hired Hank Thompson and Willard Brown.

Managers fascinated young Earl. As baseball boomed in popularity in the twentieth century, pushed by mass-market newspapers and radio, journalists and fans celebrated managers as the voices of their teams and sport.

The job of baseball manager had existed since outfielder and pitcher Harry Wright in 1869 captained the Cincinnati Red Stockings, the first team to recruit mercenaries from far afield and mold them into a professional team. Wright, who was born in Sheffield, England, had been a cricket star. Once he became an ace baseball player and was given control of a team, he started teaching his teammates to be better baseball players. As the team fight song went:

> Our Captain is a goodly man
> And Harry is his name;
> Whate'er he does, 'tis always "Wright,"
> So says the voice of fame.

Wright rewarded his players with bouquets of flowers when they performed well. He invented training drills to teach baseball and get players in shape. "Harry Wright in a poetic sense was the first manager because he was the first to be puppet master of a team," said nineteenth-century-baseball historian Thomas W. Gilbert. When an aspiring player asked for advice about playing professionally, Wright advised that he "eat hearty—Roast Beef rare will do," and that he live moderately and learn to be "a sure catch; a good thrower, strong and accurate; a reliable batter and good runner; all to be brought out, if in you, by steady and persevering practice."

The next star manager after Wright was Adrian "Cap" Anson, who got his nickname for leading the White Stockings. These early managers were more like golf or tennis pros, there to teach players how to play a constantly evolving sport. They usually played too, and often served as business managers, scheduling games, ordering uniforms, and paying players.

Ned "Foxy" Hanlon revolutionized the sport by managing the Baltimore Orioles in the 1890s with strategic control and cutthroat in-game aggressiveness. He pioneered practices like hand signals, spring training, bunting, hit-and-runs, and the "Baltimore chop," slapping the ball hard into the ground so it bounced too high to throw out the batter or any runner.

One of Hanlon's ballplayers, John McGraw, carried forth his style of play into the twentieth century. McGraw was the first manager to frequently substitute for players—for example, pinch-running—during games. Little Napoleon managed thirty-two seasons and won ten NL pennants and three World Series for the New York Giants. During McGraw's era, before the invention of the farm system, managers operated a bit like college football coaches do today, recruiting players from the country's vast network of amateur and semi-pro teams. In the 1920s, one of McGraw's players on the New York Giants was Billy Southworth, who resolved to manage more empathetically than his mentor. The Cardinals' skipper from 1940 to 1945, Southworth was elected to the Hall of Fame in 2008.

In the stands, young Earl studied Southworth. He also observed Yankees skipper Joe McCarthy, statistically the greatest manager in baseball history, and three other Hall of Famers: Connie Mack, the "Tall Tactician," who, rather ridiculously, piloted the Philadelphia Athletics during ten presidential administrations, from Cleveland to Truman, from 1901 to 1950, while wearing a suit and bowler (and as he got older, boater) hat; Bill McKechnie, who managed the Pirates, Cardinals, Boston Braves, and Cincinnati Reds; and Bucky Harris, who skippered the Senators, Tigers, Red Sox, Phillies, and Yankees over twenty-nine seasons between 1924 and 1956. Like many managers before World War II, Harris, like the Cardinals' Frisch, started as a player-manager.

Like fans and writers of the day, Earl evaluated if managers made good decisions about sacrifice bunting, changing pitchers, and lineup selection. Bunting, the strategy popularized by Orioles manager Ned Hanlon in the 1890s, was of particular interest. The sacrifice bunt—the batter deadening the ball to guarantee the advancement of runners on base even if he made an out—was a popular strategy, but even then a source of controversy.

In 1944, Weaver watched as, in the third inning of game 1 of the Cardinals-Browns World Series, with the score 0–0, nobody out, and two runners on, Southworth made Stan Musial sacrifice-bunt. The Cardinal slugger tapped the ball as commanded, making the intentional out and advancing the runners. With runners on second and third and one out, the Browns then intentionally walked Walker Cooper, loading the bases. The next two batters made outs. The Cardinals failed to score and lost the game 2–1. "Did Southworth blunder when he called on Musial to bunt?" asked one newspaper, complaining of the skipper's "one managerial flaw."

It wasn't Earl Sr. who usually took Earl to ballgames. He attended some by himself, joining other youngsters in the Knothole Gang program, which gave them free admission. He often walked from school, or his own ballgame, to catch the last few innings. No choirboys, Earl and the Knothole kids trolled the chaperone, a mean one-armed man named Wingy; threw melted snow cones; and rolled empty bottles down the steps, competing to see whose could roll farthest before smashing into pieces.

For weekend and evening games, Earl had another companion.

In 1931, Ethel's sister Irene married a small-time mobster and bookie named Edward "Bud" Bochert. Irene and Bud tied the knot on a trip to Terre Haute, Indiana, a popular mob hangout in the 1930s. It was the second marriage for both. Irene, who liked to drink and hang out with bad men, had married and divorced a World War I vet. In 1925, Bud's twenty-year-old first wife, Mabel, had died of gas poisoning. Bud told police she committed suicide.

Uncle Bud, as Earl always called him, had no children of his own. But he loved baseball, and he took a liking to his nephew.

4

GANGS OF ST. LOUIS

St. Louis, 1930–1948

The gambling known as business looks with austere disfavor upon the business known as gambling.

—Ambrose Bierce

Young Earl Weaver didn't just watch baseball; he *analyzed* it, via the sport's daily roulette wheel of precise, probabilistic outcomes.

Earl usually attended games at Sportsman's Park with his favorite uncle, Edward "Bud" Bochert, a character straight out of Damon Runyon's wiseguy tales, the basis for the 1950 musical *Guys and Dolls*. Bud was a bookmaker from the St. Louis underworld with connections to Al Capone's Chicago mob. As in other large U.S. cities, gangs in St. Louis controlled swaths of the city's economy, unions, and politics, ran betting rings, and collected protection money. Gambling was everywhere, in corner craps games, tavern number rackets, baseball, boxing and horse-racing books, and blackjack, poker, and pinochle. On packed city streets, gangs clashed for dollars with tricksters, cheats, and con men. In the 1930s, mobsters loved baseball because it was part of their gambling business, but they were also simply fans.

One of their foot soldiers, Bud, was a thick, heavyset man who in a Weaver family picture arched his eyebrows and wore an expression of

Earl's favorite uncle, illegal bookie Bud Bochert, and his wife, Irene.

controlled menace as though he were deciding what to do with you after you've run out of words. Bud ran a city gambling den, the Parkview Buffet, which was frequently raided by cops, forcing him to grab his betting sheets and scram. He'd been born into a St. Louis crime family in 1902. In the 1920s, Bud hooked up with a powerful St. Louis gang, Egan's Rats, one of six main outfits battling each other for liquor markets during Prohibition. In the late 1920s, after Egan's Rats disbanded, Bud associated himself with the Cuckoo Gang, which started out as a baseball team, named after Cuckoo-brand soda pop.

The Cuckoos, violent gangsters who drove a maroon automobile with armored plating, bulletproof windows, and machine guns mounted on the rear doors nicknamed the "Death Car," were big baseball fans. Boss Herman Tipton and his goons were always regular visitors at Sportsman's Park. Once, when police were looking for a gang member suspected of a murder, they found him at the ballpark. "An elastic bunch of punks," a police captain called the Cuckoos.

Bud and other bookies roamed the grandstand at Sportsman's Park behind first base and the right-field bleachers. Earl admired Bud, whom he called shrewd and good-natured. Bud shared with Earl how things were going in the bookmaking business, and Earl relished his occasional windfalls. The Weavers hustled, but, with Bud around, they were never poor. "Uncle Bud was the well-to-do member of the family," Earl recalled.

During a time Bud was living with the family, Earl once saw him pull $70,000, fifty times the average annual American income in 1940, out of an ottoman in the family living room. "He was always handing out cash" to family members, said Mike Weaver, Earl's son.

In telling Bud's story, Weaver shielded his mentor and his rogue's den of thieves, pimps, bookies, boxers, and bartenders. But he and newspaper and police records have revealed enough to see the man's lingering effects in Earl's wiseguy humor, street hustler's craving for an edge, skill at cards, love of a good wager, and contempt for authority. If Earl Sr., who tolerated but did not appreciate his brother-in-law, was an attentive and caring dad, Uncle Bud was a darker force, whose spirit Weaver channeled every time he threatened to knock an umpire "right on your ass."

In a moment of candor in 1982, Earl Weaver told a reporter that a "psychiatrist friend" had blamed his "combativeness" on Uncle Bud. "When I was just big enough to crawl, if I inched up a little, Uncle Bud would pull me back," Weaver said. "We used to play ball in the backyard—one-on-one. He never let me win. I fumed." One can only guess at how many times Uncle Bud, sober or not, pushed or pulled young Earl Weaver, but it's easy to imagine why he started fuming. He carried a fast temper through high school, the minor leagues, and his career as a big-league manager, never quite shaking feelings of anger and rejection, and the darkness that went with them.

Weaver and Uncle Bud watched games in a culture saturated with gambling. Americans wagered as much as $5 billion a year on baseball in the 1940s. The sport's pitch-by-pitch beat of precise, often binary outcomes has always fit gambling like a ball in a glove. In fact, it's unclear if baseball would have become a popular professional sport without the interest of gamblers. The first game to charge admission, between New York and Brooklyn in 1858, drew a crowd of 10,000, trailed by a small army of gamblers. "People think the NFL invented sports betting, but in the industry we all know it started with baseball," said Raphael Esparza, an oddsmaker with Doc's Sports, a Las Vegas–based gambling company. Fans now bet tens of billions of dollars a year legally on baseball games via companies like FanDuel and DraftKings, and TV announcers openly tout betting lines. Once again, ballplayers are embroiled in betting scandals. Front offices pass around books on poker and blackjack and hire analysts who cut their teeth winning fantasy baseball leagues run by gambling companies, which recruit front-office analysts and invest in the same predictive algorithms as teams.

In the 1940s, bars, saloons, clubs, and hotels carried Western Union tickers that spit out scores. Newspapers printed odds and quoted bookmakers on big games. "You will see them everywhere if you know where to look—'finger' bettors, they are sometimes called in the trade," reported John Lardner in *Newsweek* in 1944. "The gentlemen occupy the same seats daily, and offer odds and take bets by hand signals on balls, strikes, hits, whether there will be a score that inning, etc. That payoff is outside the ballpark after the game." In 1949, casinos in Los Angeles offered "television baseball gambling." Croupiers stood in front of a televised ballgame singing out odds. "Will the batter fly out, strike out, single, knock the ball out of the park? Will the runner on second go on the next pitch? What will the next pitch be, ball or strike?"

St. Louis was a hotbed. Bookies in town handled $1.5 million a week in wagers on baseball. Uncle Bud and his associates at Sportsman's Park offered prop bets on pitch counts, runs, hits, and a dozen other categories. The Cardinals sometimes cracked down, under pressure from Judge Kenesaw Mountain Landis, the baseball commissioner tasked with cleaning up the game's image after gamblers were caught fixing the 1919 World Series. After the Black Sox scandal, baseball imposed an omertà on discussing the booming gambling industry surrounding its ballgames. The talk died down. The action didn't.

In 1940, Cardinals owner Sam Breadon hung a sign that said GAMBLERS EX-PELLED AND DENIED ADMISSION TO PARK. It was in vain. The gamblers kept coming. Breadon took down the sign. Teams opposed the betting halfheartedly. Just like today, wagering buttressed the bottom line. Gamblers are "good customers of a ballclub," said legendary team owner Bill Veeck.

Earl Weaver's relationship with his favorite uncle went beyond baseball. When Earl was a teenager, Bud taught him golf, a favorite mob pastime of the 1930s. When he was in his twenties and looking for work during offseasons, Bud used his mob and union connections to get him jobs.

All the while he was taking care of young Earl, Bud got himself and others into trouble. In 1937, Irene was riding in the passenger seat when Bud ran his car into an oncoming vehicle on U.S. Highway 40 opposite a gambling hot spot, the Madison Kennel Club near St. Louis. She fractured her left arm and ankle and suffered lacerations in her body and head. Seven years later, Bud got drunk and shot her in her right hip and then disappeared before turning himself into the police. No charges were filed. In 1941, Bud and an accomplice roughed up a former U.S. congressman and prosecutor named C. Arthur Anderson. This was not a random assault. Anderson had served as prosecuting attorney of St. Louis County from 1933 to 1937, working on high-profile mob cases. In 1934, gangsters ran his car off the road, forcing him to walk with a cane. Police often arrested Bud for running books on horse racing and big-league ballgames. It appears he never spent significant time in prison.

A wake-up call for any ballplayer associating with gamblers came in 1947, when Commissioner Happy Chandler banned Brooklyn Dodgers manager

Leo Durocher, the former Cardinals shortstop and one of Earl's heroes, from baseball for a year because of his connections with mobsters. Earl Weaver continued to associate with Uncle Bud in the 1950s, but by the time he had reached the major leagues, Bud was out of sight. Ballplayers and managers could be suspended for associating with known gamblers.

Bud retired to the suburbs and was getting out of the gambling business in the 1960s and 1970s, according to people in the family who knew him. A cousin recalled him as a docile old man who liked playing cards with his wife and other family members. He once gave one of Earl Weaver's cousins a pony he won in a card game. Bud died in 1977; Irene in 1985.

A world saturated by gambling was the perfect place for young Earl Weaver to hone his analytical skills. The betting public Uncle Bud and other bookies sought in the 1930s and 1940s were the people they called the "squares," baseball fans who wanted to wager a few dollars on the home team. Bookies were more careful about taking money from the "sharps," professional gamblers who paid closer attention to the games.

I found betting guides from the 1940s to the 1970s, published as books and as stories in magazines like *Esquire* and *Playboy*, that laid out systems for betting on baseball games. They're not sophisticated compared to modern sabermetrics, but they were using the data they had more creatively than most teams and fans, and it's not hard to see the analytical edge Earl Weaver might have picked up from his mentor. Baseball, John Davenport reported in *Esquire* in 1956, "has proved more profitable to bookies than any other sport" because "the baseball bettor unknowingly permits his emotions to temper his judgment." He quoted a bookie: "You don't have to be a ballplayer to know all about the game. I'd bet my bankroll that the guys who figure our daily 'line' could show [then Yankees manager] Casey Stengel or any of 'em a thing or two."

In 1942, a Youngstown, Ohio–based bookie named Samuel J. Georgeson published *Pitchers Record Guide*, a book with pitcher statistics from the previous season, breakdowns versus specific teams, and charts that allowed gamblers to track the performance of pitchers against individual teams during the current season. "It can be of extreme value to know that a certain pitcher is almost always successful against a certain team, but seldom wins against another," Georgeson wrote. Over a quarter century later, Earl Weaver introduced to big-league dugouts an awareness of the variability and complexity of matchups of his team's hitters against specific pitchers, and vice versa.

In the 1956 *Esquire* article, Davenport described a baseball betting system based on a 1–10 rating system for evaluating pitchers that relied on earned-run averages, strikeouts, and bases on balls, while disregarding win-loss records. "A pitcher, after being hit hard, can leave a game at the end of the fifth inning with the score 8-to-6 in his favor and be credited with a victory because his team eventually won the game," he noted. It is "the ratio between his strikeouts and his [walks]" that bookies look for, he wrote, preceding the insights of modern analysts by decades.

As Bill James and others advanced their study of baseball in the 1970s, the gambling community kept pace. In 1979, Jim Jasper, a bookie who'd worked on baseball since the 1950s, wrote in his book *Sports Betting* that any manager who made a nonpitcher bunt was "an idiot" because "the idea is *not* to make an out. To make outs on purpose is crazy. They will argue that they are playing for one run. This only makes sense if that one run wins the game right then and there. The big inning wins games." He added: "The intentional walk is another piece of bad strategy, especially early in the game. Again, the idea is to get the other side out, not put them on." Not wasting outs was at the core of Weaver's thinking as a manager. "Your most precious possession on offense are your twenty-seven outs," he wrote as his Fourth Law in his 1984 book, *Weaver on Strategy*.

As research, I performed an experiment in how betting can clarify your vision of baseball strategy. In March 2023, I attended a World Baseball Classic contest in Phoenix between USA and England. The spread—the minimum number of runs the favored team has to win by—was 8.5 in favor of the home team. I bet $100 on USA. It felt like a safe bet: The USA team included stars Mookie Betts, Mike Trout, and Trea Turner. England was headlined by Vance Worley, Ian Gibaut, and Harry Ford. The U.S. won, but only 6–2. I lost $100. The promise of easy cash slipping away changed how I watched the game. If I hadn't bet money, I would still have rooted for USA, but I wouldn't have cared how many runs they scored. But because I needed USA to cover the spread, I paid close attention to their offensive strategy. I wanted them to take pitches, draw walks, and hit home runs. I was mad if a player swung at the first pitch and popped up. Paying attention to run spreads like a gambler basically forces you to endorse a modern, Earl Weaver–style offense.

The *Esquire* piece made another recommendation that reveals an insight 1940s and 1950s gamblers had about baseball, the same one I had when I lost $100 betting on USA at the World Baseball Classic: if there's a run spread, bet on the team that plays for big innings instead of the team that bunts a lot and plays for one run at a time. "This is the first time," John Davenport concluded in 1956, "that a formula has been conceived which is able to defeat the daily baseball 'line' during an entire season's play."

There's no evidence Earl Weaver ever bet on the outcome of a Major League Baseball game during his professional career in the game, but like a lot of managers and players, he loved to wager, at horse and dog tracks and at cards, and made bets on everything from golf to growing tomatoes. Like others in the game, he tracked Vegas's assessments. "You look at the daily gambling odds over 162 and see how many times the Orioles are underdogs on any given day," he said in 1979. "Almost never . . . The reason is starting pitching."

His betting philosophy: "I'm a conservative man, and I bet favorites at the racetrack." He and the beat writers who covered the Orioles often engaged in daily wagers over who would hit a home run in the next day's game. If the writers wanted to bet on baseball, he sometimes gave them tips.

Like the Italian Renaissance polymath Gerolamo Cardano, who developed mathematical theorems by playing dice, Weaver grasped probability theory through the prism of gambling. "Earl talked like a bookmaker," said Dan Duquette, who hired Weaver to instruct his manager and coaches when he was general manager of the Montreal Expos in the 1990s. Weaver peppered his postgame comments with gambling analogies. "Sometimes the ground decides the game," said Weaver, comparing baseball to a dog race. "You don't want to lose your money on some fucking pebble. I had money on two dogs once who were leading the field. They bit each other." After one loss, he said: "If we had been at a crap table tonight, we'd be broke. If we were playing blackjack, we would have had 12 every deal. If we had been betting on the horses, the things would still be running, and if we were betting on the doggies, those things would have got stuck in the box."

After losing the 1969 World Series, Weaver said: "All the time people tell me, 'I lost lots of money on you guys.' One day I see a guy I sort of know and he says, 'Hey I lost $400.' I mentioned the name of a friend we have in common and he said he must have lost $10,000. Then this guy says, 'That's nothing: I lost a lot more than that.' He started off telling me he lost $400."

Little Earl Weaver bats in his St. Louis backyard.

5

COACH WEAVER

St. Louis, 1934–1948

Throw to second, not first. Second is the one in the middle.
> —Aleksandr Adatov, Soviet national team coach,
> teaching the game to Russian beginners in 1989

If Earl Weaver had just watched baseball games with bookies, he would have become a bookie. He became Earl Weaver because he learned to *play* baseball better than almost anybody else in America. As a boy, baseball was life; he was always swinging or throwing. A family picture of Earl aged four shows him in child overalls, poised with a bat, front shoulder coiled, weight expertly on his back foot, facing the camera with a stern, focused expression.

Like almost every baseball story, this one started with family in local parks and backyards. Almost every day, Earl Sr., Grandpa Zastrow, or Uncle Bud pitched to Earl in the yard on Northland Avenue. He clenched his teeth and swung hard and often sent balls flying, sometimes shattering glass panes in the garage.

In St. Louis, as in other American cities before the suburbs began sprawling in the 1950s, Earl could find ballgames in every neighborhood. Children played stickball in the street and on vacant lots. Fathers pitched to sons in tiny backyards. Schools, church groups, and youth associations organized regular games. There were eighty-nine public baseball fields scattered throughout the city, and after school and work, Earl walked or took trolleys to go play baseball in organized games. He was an "average" boy with "not a great deal of desire to study," he said.

The economic boom of the 1920s had given American men leisure time to coach baseball. In the nineteenth century, previous generations had codified and fine-tuned baseball, and now that its rules were set in stone, baseball claimed its place at the heart of American culture. For the first time, adults founded youth leagues that mimicked big-league baseball, with uniforms, fields, and umpires. In 1926, the American Legion founded a program for teenagers that became a pillar of youth baseball development. In 1939, a man named Carl Stotz in Williamsport, Pennsylvania, founded Little League Baseball. Both organizations aimed to instill patriotic, anti-communist values via the National Pastime.

Every city in America fielded thriving independent youth leagues. In north St. Louis, Earl Sr. coached a team sponsored by Woltman Jewelers. Earl Jr., already pushy at age eleven, badgered his dad to enter his squad in a St. Louis city league. Weaver Sr. recruited the best players he could find by organizing tryouts at Fairgrounds Park, a sprawling sculpted urban park with baseball diamonds and a lake. The team won three straight city titles, going 53-2, a feat the St. Louis *Globe-Democrat* called "breath-taking." The near certainty of victory during this formative time may have contributed to Earl Weaver's desire that his epitaph be "the sorest loser who ever lived." Imagine the arrogance of a teenager who's played for his dad as a coach and gone 53-2. Scouts followed them around, signing several players to pro contracts. Earl was one of the team's stars. In one game at Sportsman's Park, fifteen-year-old Earl blasted a home run over major-league fences. When asked by a reporter what the secret of the team's success was, Earl Sr. said: "It's the old hustle—that's all." It was hustle merged with skill, talent, and toughness, honed on the streets and vacant lots of St. Louis. The boys all played baseball almost every day. Young Earl wasn't afraid to get into it. "He was a real scrapper," said Joe Monahan, a Cardinals scout. "Earl used to surprise fellows twice as big as he was by licking them in fights."

Coaching a winning youth team gave Earl Sr. credibility with St. Louis's baseball establishment. Rich Woltman, the jeweler who sponsored the team, threw a party at the Fairground Hotel after their 1946 championship. The toastmaster was Cardinals scout Water Shannon. Earl Sr. loved baseball and played hard, and sometimes dirty. In August 1948, after his son had left home to play professional baseball, the league suspended Earl Sr. for using an ineligible player under a false name on the Schweiss Pastry team. He'd pulled a player out of the stands who was better than the boy he replaced, but ineligible. Schweiss Pastry's victory over Kennedy Chevrolet was overturned.

Earl Weaver's true baseball education came from high school. After attending Benton Middle School, he enrolled at Beaumont High, the all-white public high school for his north St. Louis district, housed in a Gothic fortress across the street from Fairgrounds Park. The city opened Beaumont in 1926 on the site of the Cardinals' old stadium, Robison Field. When Beaumont finally desegregated in 1954, a knife fight broke out. Charles Guggenheim made an Oscar-nominated short film about the school's painful integration.

Weaver did fine in class, looked preppy in his coat-and-tie uniform, and even memorized enough Shakespeare to quote it accurately thirty-five years later to an umpire. Later, when he came into his own as a quasi-public intellectual quoted in the country's leading newspapers and magazines, he regretted not having paid more attention and learned more in school. But baseball was his whole identity. His senior yearbook quote said: "Pitchers be careful when you hurl / The baseball to our player, Earl."

In any case, Beaumont wasn't known for academics but for its champion sports teams. Baseball coach Ray Elliott based his philosophy on tough discipline—he made all his players get regular haircuts—and a rigid enforcement of fundamentals such as bunting, team defense, and throwing strikes. In seventeen seasons, Elliott won 308 games and lost 138, for a .691 winning percentage, and coached fifty-four future pros, including seven big leaguers, such as All-Stars Roy Sievers and Bobby Hofman. They played on the same American Legion team as another St. Louis kid, Lawrence Berra. Hofman, Weaver's teammate, nicknamed him Yogi because of the cross-legged way he sat.

Earl enrolled at Beaumont in January 1944, when he was only thirteen years old. He presented himself as a tough street kid, teaching other students to swear like a sailor. ("He taught my dad to say 'cocksucker,'" the son of a classmate told me.) Hofman, a future world champion with the 1954 New

York Giants, was a senior. Sievers, who was named American League Rookie of the Year in 1949, was a junior. Two other teammates, Bobby Wiesler and Jimmy Goodwin, became major-league pitchers.

Immediately, Weaver achieved his goal of starting for the celebrated Blue Jackets. Multiple newspapers covered high school sports for a wide audience in a baseball-crazy city. One story from April 1944 mentions that Earl played third base and went 3-for-4 with a double. In 1945, he made headlines by hitting a game-tying home run in the ninth inning. "A hard-hitting second baseman," one paper called him. Earl was a three-sport star, cocaptain of the football team, and a state champion in basketball. "He was a stud, such a good ballplayer that people were talking about how good he was in the 1950s," said Bob Hardcastle, who played for Beaumont a decade later and, after graduation, was signed by the Orioles and cut by a minor-league coach named Earl Weaver.

Coach Elliott was a tough taskmaster. "The first thing I remember about him was that he was always on us to get haircuts," said Earl. "In fact, a lot of us were convinced his brother was a damn barber." Elliott's reasoning: "You can't field a baseball with all that hair in your eyes." The coach made players do 50 or 100 push-ups if he didn't think they were trying hard enough. He rigged up strike zones with strings tied between volleyball poles, made pitchers throw at the targets until their fingers bled, and kept a notebook where he collected data on how many strikes each pitcher threw at practice. Only the top performers would earn assignments in games. Earl inherited Elliott's obsession with strike-throwing.

In Elliott's view, teaching young men to win baseball games required, more than any special strategy, setting their sights on executing tasks, such as throwing strikes, making all routine defensive plays, and putting pressure on defenses with plate discipline and hard contact. Elliott never let up. During St. Louis winters, he organized indoor practices with tennis balls in the school gym, a rare exercise at the time, and invented drills to improve the team's fundamentals. In the coach's version of "pepper," an informal game where a half-circle of players flip balls to a hitter 10 feet away who chops it back, the fielders stood 60 feet away and threw hard strikes. Elliott called it "long-distance pepper".

Coach Elliott loved his little infielder. "A fighter all the way," he called him.

"And a good one. He succeeded Hofman at second base after playing third for a year. He was just in the wrong place at the wrong time as far as making the majors." Once Elliott took his son Pat to watch Earl manage a spring training game in Florida. Something triggered Earl. He exploded and tore up a rule book at home plate. "I looked over at my dad and I said, 'For heaven sakes, did he behave like that in high school?'" said Pat Elliott. "Dad said, 'Heavens no, he kept his yap shut.'"

Earl wrote up the 1946 season for his school yearbook, revealing a young mind contemplating how baseball teams fit together. He struck a tough tone, reporting that "Coach Elliott has had a hard time with the catcher" and "there was much trouble trying to find the infield that would work together." In the end, there was a happy resolution to that situation, Earl reported: "Finally, Coach Elliott selected Harley Beavers to hold down the hot corner [third base], Michael Kickam to play short, Earl Weaver to manage second, and Bob Reed at first to make the put-outs." Like a good leader, teenage Earl praised bench players: "Capable substitutes for this infield were Bart Mantia, Carl Runge, Bill Jenkins, and Norm Newman." He concluded: "The champions would like to thank Coach Elliott for all his help and the time he has spent in [sic] our behalf."

While at Beaumont, Earl played four summers for a St. Louis American Legion team called Stockham Post, where Yogi Berra had starred five seasons before him. Earl's Stockham team won two state championships. Between high school and his other leagues, Earl played almost a hundred games a year, melting his shoes during St. Louis summers. Later, when he was sweating it out in bush-league towns, he said he was thankful for the training he received in St. Louis, where he learned to take the heat.

Baseball scouts took an interest. Earl was small, but he had good hands and hammered the ball. Earl Sr. received his first call from a scout when his son was only thirteen years old. During World War II, big leaguers enlisted, or were drafted, to fight Hitler, creating a scarcity of high-quality prospects. Joe Nuxhall pitched for the Cincinnati Reds in 1944 when he was just fifteen.

"Would your son Earl be interested in playing professional baseball, Mr. Weaver?" asked a Brooklyn Dodgers scout named George Sisler, in a conversation reported later by Earl himself.

"Yes, he would, Mr. Sisler, but Earl won't be fourteen years old until August."

"Oh, I didn't realize he was so young. Obviously it's too soon to talk about signing him, but I'll be keeping an eye on that young man."

Besides the war, another reason major-league teams had started recruiting fringe prospects like Weaver was the expansion of so-called farm systems. Branch Rickey had pioneered the concept in 1919 while manager and general manager of the Cardinals. Frustrated at being outbid by richer clubs, he acquired interests in minor-league teams in Houston and Fort Smith, Arkansas. By 1939, the Cardinals controlled 32 teams and 650 players.

The business model was simple: Sign as many ballplayers as you could afford, and then turn the best into stars for your team and/or currency to barter with other teams. Get rid of everybody else. There were no sophisticated scouting methods, just a Darwinian test of survival for those who signed on. Quality out of quantity, Rickey called his method. It was exploitative and relied on the "desk contract." The scout signed a player and kept the contract in his desk, so that the player didn't know what his rights were.

Earl Weaver was good enough to get a desk contract. He hit .430 as a junior and .444 as a senior. There was never any question of doing anything else. Earl told *Prom*, a widely read magazine that catered to St. Louis youths, that his favorite pastime was "juggling baseballs." When he filled out a questionnaire given to professional baseball players at age eighteen, he wrote that he had no other hobbies.

Earl Sr., in the eternal tradition of daydreaming baseball dads, worked his network. Among his connections was Freddie Hofmann, a colorful big-league catcher nicknamed "Bootnose" who played for the Yankees in the 1920s and roomed with Babe Ruth. Now a coach for the Browns, Hofmann took time out of his schedule to throw Earl batting practice and hit him ground balls.

Earl Sr. wanted his boy to sign with Freddie's team, the Browns. He and Browns owner Bill DeWitt had sold newspapers together when they were teenagers in north St. Louis in the 1910s.

Walter Shannon, the Cardinals scout whom Earl Sr. had befriended, was also scouting Earl, setting up a duel for the hometown kid. Shannon attended most of Earl's high school games. When Earl got a big hit, Shannon found him after the game and told him, "You're gonna be hitting like that for the Cardinals in a few years."

The Browns were circumspect. Browns minor-league director Jim McLaughlin liked Earl's defense and bat, but said he couldn't throw or run. "An Eddie Stanky–type player," he determined. "Who beats you more with his guts than his ability."

A few days before graduation, Earl Sr. called his pal Freddie to ask him if the Browns would sign his son.

"You really want to know, Earl?"

"Yes, I want to know what you honestly think of his potential in pro ball."

"He's a class-A player, tops."

Earl Sr. hung up on his buddy. They didn't speak for a year. Like any good dad would, he went behind Hofmann's back and took his son to Sportsman's Park to meet with his other Browns connections, McLaughlin and DeWitt.

"Earl, as far as we're concerned you don't play very well," said the Browns owner. "Your arm is average; it's a second baseman's arm, period, which means you can't play the other side of the infield. Now you hit over .400 in high school but we don't know if you can hit on the professional level. The competition is that much tougher."

Still, the Browns offered Earl $175 a month, plus a $2,000 bonus if he survived a round of midseason cuts and was still on the team on June 15.

Earl looked at his dad, shook his head, and led him to the Cardinals' office, down the corridor at Sportsman's Park, where Shannon gave Earl the sweet-talk treatment. He walked him over to a window overlooking the big-league diamond and pointed at second base. "You'll be playing here in a few years, Earl," he said.

Who knows if Shannon believed what he was telling his recruit, but it suited his interests. One more desk contract gave the Cardinals another chance at a potential big leaguer or a trade chit, with no risk to the organization. Scouts from the Yankees, Red Sox, and Dodgers also made offers, but they were all under $1,000.

Weaver signed with the Cardinals for $175 a month, the same level as the Browns, and got an unconditional $1,500 bonus up front. Some players got less. Roy Sievers, Earl's Beaumont High teammate, signed for a pair of shoes.

As he shook hands with Shannon on the deal, seventeen-year-old Earl Weaver almost broke the older man's wrist. He was a professional baseball player.

On February 18, 1948, the *St. Louis Star and Times* reported:

> Earl Weaver, second baseman for the Woltman's team, which won city intermediate baseball championships for three years, and a January graduate of Beaumont High School, has been signed to a 1948 contract with the Cardinal-owned Lynchburg (Va.) Club of the Piedmont League. Weaver's signing was announced today by Joe Mathes, director of Cardinal minor league clubs. Weaver played four seasons with the Stockham American Legion team which won the state championships in 1945 and 1947. As a student at Beaumont he was co-captain of the football team, a member of the 1946-47 all-state basketball team and a four-year baseball letterman. The new Cardinal is 17 years old and resides with his parents at 4713 Northland av.

In the spring of 1948, after graduating from high school and winning a state championship in basketball, Earl Weaver was ready for his first trip far from home. The Cardinals had assigned him to attend their minor-league spring training camp in Albany, Georgia, a small town 730 miles away in the Red Hills of southern Georgia. The Weavers threw Earl a going-away party. They gave him a suitcase and a shaving kit and wished him well. In 1948, America's train network covered the country like kudzu, and there was a direct train route from St. Louis to Albany. Earl's parents took him to Union Station and waved him off, along with Harley Beavers, a center fielder for Beaumont and the Jewelers who had also signed with the Cardinals. The boys were nervous and worried they wouldn't get off at the right stop. Beavers paid a porter two dollars to wake them up in Albany.

They arrived at Albany's red-brick train station around midnight.

"You ballplayers?" a man asked them.

"Yeah."

"Follow me."

The man led them to a school bus that was taking ballplayers to private homes, where residents had agreed to lodge young Cardinals.

"Weaver and Beavers, your stop. The people are expecting you. Report to the YMCA downtown at ten tomorrow morning." Weaver was so excited he barely slept.

The next morning, the boys from St. Louis walked into town and found the YMCA. There they joined hundreds of uniformed apprentices, each hoping they'd survive long enough on $1.25-per-day meal money to make the big leagues. Earl turned to his pal and wondered: "My God, Harley, where the hell are all these guys going?"

Part 3

BUSHES

Earl Weaver was a "gem" in the St. Louis Cardinals'
minor-league system, 1951.

6

LETTUCE DAYS

West Frankfort, Illinois; St. Joseph, Missouri; Winston-Salem, North Carolina;
Houston, Texas; Omaha, Nebraska, 1948–1951

Mr. President, you can tell those Russians we're having an awful good time
over here playing baseball.

>—Orioles catcher Rick Dempsey to President Ronald
Reagan after winning the 1983 World Series

On the first pitch of the first at-bat of his pro career, Earl Weaver picked up a
hefty 36-ounce bat, coiled his 155 pounds, and exploded into a ball that sailed
over the wooden left-field fence in the small coal-mining town of West Frankfort, Illinois.

The improbable home run helped his class-D Cardinals affiliate West
Frankfort beat Marion, 5–2, in the first game of the Illinois State League
season. Rounding the bases, Weaver joked to himself: "Just 59 to go." At the
time, Babe Ruth held baseball's single-season home run record with 60. Earl
didn't homer for another two months, but the leadoff dinger soothed his
nerves.

The West Frankfort crowd, miners whose families had migrated from Po-
land and Ukraine, howled for their new seventeen-year-old infielder and stuck
dollar bills through the fence. In a minor-league tradition known as "picking

the screen" or "picking the lettuce," Earl grabbed as many bills as he could and walked back to the dugout with $40 in his pocket.

In the late 1940s, as men returned from World War II, almost every town in America had a minor-league baseball team. In West Frankfort, population 15,000, boosters built a field on a part of the mine site that had been used to store dynamite to blast away at the earth. The stadium groundskeepers planted rosebushes before the 1948 season. The West Frankfort team lasted only from 1947 to 1950 and then folded as the U.S. military recruited men for the Korean War and the public lost their enthusiasm for minor-league baseball, besieged with nightly television and preoccupied with new cars, highways, and houses.

But in 1948, minor-league baseball was hot. There were 58 *leagues*—divided since 1902 into class-A, -B, -C, and -D teams—and 430 teams. Attendance at minor-league games topped 40 million in 1948, up from less than 10 million in 1945. In those days before interstates and suburbs, Americans walked out their front door for entertainment—to the circus, the theater, or ballpark. The biggest news in small towns, people said, was if the bank was robbed or the ball club won the pennant. They cheered their home team because it was the only baseball they could watch, and celebrated their players as heroes.

Earl earned that West Frankfort assignment the month before at the Cardinals' minor-league spring training camp, in Albany, Georgia. The Cardinals had commandeered an abandoned air force base that was part of the emergency infrastructure the U.S. military had built to defeat Hitler. After the war, these facilities attracted baseball teams looking for ready-made barracks and fields. The Albany site had seven baseball fields.

On his first day in Albany, Earl Weaver walked onto a ballfield with over 500 players trying out for the Cardinals' twenty-one affiliated minor-league teams. Earl recalled that he could barely see the outfield grass, it was so packed with young men. "I felt like crying," he said. He fought the urge to quit and go home to St. Louis. The first number pinned to his back was 521.

The fear of getting cut attached itself to every player's stomach. Every ground ball felt like life or death. Every morning, a coach read the name of the players getting whacked. "If your number came up, you were told to go to a certain place and that was the last you ever saw of that player," said Weaver. "He was gone."

So began Earl's education in the painful psychology of professional baseball. He noted his own fear and jealousy, and how players looked at each other, hoping the other men would screw up, giving them a chance. "Come on, you jerk, throw it in the dirt," he found himself muttering to teammates.

Luckily, Earl wasn't one of the limp-armed high school dreamers. He was, in fact, a ballplayer. He hit everything thrown at him and made every play. The only question for the Cardinals was where to send him.

Weaver was lucky to not make the Dukes, the Cardinals' Class C team in Duluth, Minnesota. That summer, the Dukes' bus crashed, killing five players, including two of Earl's buddies from St. Louis. Cash-strapped teams made young, tired, and sometimes drunk players drive rickety buses. Future Hall of Famer George Kell was such a good bus driver that it delayed his ascension to the major leagues.

The Cardinals assigned Weaver to Class D West Frankfort, where there would be less pressure and more playing time. The teenage second baseman boarded a bus, driven by manager Hal Contini, for the twelve-hour trip from Albany to the coalfields of southern Illinois.

Once settled in West Frankfort, Earl rented quarters in a rooming house at a special rate of $5 a month because he was a ballplayer. Every day, with his $1.25-a-day meal money, he ordered two eggs, bacon, toast, grits, and coffee for twenty-nine cents at the Little Egypt, so named because southern Illinois reminded nineteenth-century white settlers of what they had read about the Nile delta. The Little Egypt also gave pitchers free cakes when they pitched shutouts.

The Illinois State League, which lasted only two seasons, sat at the bottom of the bushes. Players traveled to mosquito-infested fields in bulb-nosed buses, ate on Formica tables at country diners, and battled constant boredom by drinking, playing cards, and chasing women. Boosters built West Frankfort's ballpark, Memorial Stadium, in a few months out of local lumber. Money in the league was so tight that pitchers on their off days were assigned to chase foul balls into the crowd. When it rained too much, clubs poured sawdust and gasoline and lit the field on fire. There were infields where the rock-hard dirt turned ground-ball outs into triples, and outfields where singles turned into home runs because outfielders couldn't find the balls in the uncut grass. One locker room was a twenty-foot-round hut with a bench on the perimeter, surrounding a concrete pit where a single pipe dispensed showers of cold water. Earl struggled to scale the cold, wet concrete floor to hang up his clothes.

But in towns like West Frankfort, minor-league baseball was not a lesser version of the sport. Players spent entire seasons with their club, and towns fell in love with their players. Teams lifted civic spirits and morale in places sustained by dirty, dangerous jobs. In West Frankfort, a disaster in 1951 killed 119 coal miners. "Before television, before air conditioning, before backyard barbecue—the best place you could go on a summer night was the ballpark," said 1940s minor leaguer Walter Buckel. "It was the era of minor-league baseball where communities adopted the team. They adored their baseball players. They'd take you into their homes and restaurants. It was just beautiful. You were a celebrity in the town."

West Frankfort's blue-collar fans adored Earl. He made flashy plays in the field and ran the bases hard. Earl wasn't afraid to jaw with umpires and opponents. Teammates thought he was a little too sparky, and complained when the Cardinals gave him the team's Most Valuable Player award. For the season, Earl played all 120 games, hit .268, and scored 96 runs. Most impressively, he drew 92 walks and struck out only 24 times. In the league's all-star game, he tripled in the only run in a 1–0 win. West Frankfort went 85-35 and won the Illinois State League championship.

West Frankfort's manager was a cerebral career minor leaguer named Hal Contini. Like many minor-league skippers, he was a player-manager, and bus driver. He kept detailed statistics on his team's pitchers and batters, including, in some cases, how they fared against specific opponents. It was Weaver's first taste of an analytical approach to managing a team.

Contini also liked to let the boys have some fun. After West Frankfort clinched the pennant, he let his players choose random positions that were not their regular spots. Earl suited up at catcher. The team lost 21–8. The league president fined Contini $200 for disrespecting the game. The Cardinals' brass in St. Louis sent him an angry note. Weaver was one of their prized prospects; Contini shouldn't be endangering his health by playing him at catcher, they said.

Before games, players walked up and down West Frankfort, gazing at the female clerks and housewives wandering around. They walked into the five-and-dime stores and the soda fountains. There were few phones. They would grab a copy of the *Sporting News*, their bible, and compare their stats with players in teams above and beneath them. After games, they drank or played cards. If they were lucky, they found a date.

That summer, a St. Louis girl named Jane Johnston was visiting her grandparents in West Frankfort when they proposed taking her to a ballgame to see the young second sacker from Beaumont High. They invited Earl for dinner. He liked Jane's looks and her grandmother's cooking. After the season, when he returned to St. Louis, he and Jane started dating.

There was no such thing as a full-time professional baseball player in the 1940s. Even big leaguers took offseason jobs. Earl found work as a warehouseman with the Inland Steel Company for $60 a week. With his bonus money, he bought a new Chevrolet for $1,400. Still, he was mindful of staying on top of his game. He played basketball and worked with a track coach to improve his running speed. The Cardinals believed he might get taller than 5'7". He and Jane dated throughout the winter, and in February they announced their engagement for the end of the 1949 season.

Earl reported at Sportsman's Park for the 1949 season. There were seventy players, just from St. Louis, waiting to take the bus to the Cardinals' minor-league camp in Georgia. Once at spring training, Earl felt lonely. He partied with his teammates but didn't join them in their womanizing. He and Jane talked on the phone or wrote every day and moved up their engagement date.

After spring training, Earl was assigned to a class-C team in St. Joseph, Missouri, and given a raise to $275 a month. His first priority was to get married. He arranged for a church, a reception area, and a tiny apartment, and married Jane on May 7, 1949, with his family, and Jane's father, mother, and stepfather present for a 3 p.m. church ceremony. They ate dinner at the reception and received $400 in gifts. By 5:30 p.m., he was at the ballpark. Whoever submitted the newspaper wedding announcement noted that "Earl and Jane Ann planned the wedding so that the former Stockham American Legion junior baseball star would not miss a St. Joseph game." Michael Weaver, Earl Weaver's first and only son, was born in 1950, and Rhonda, his first daughter, in 1952. The couple's third child, a daughter named Terry, was born in 1957.

St. Joe was an outpost of the Western Association, a league of sweaty bus rides linking Muskogee, Oklahoma; Fort Smith, Arkansas; Salina, Kansas; and Joplin, Missouri. The hotel rooms were so hot that players soaked their bed-sheets with water, hoping ceiling fans would spread the moisture around.

Earl thrilled the fans at City Stadium and again outperformed his peers, batting .282, knocking in 101 runs, drawing 75 walks, and earning another Most Valuable Player award. St. Joseph went 96-42, winning Weaver his second pennant. Earl learned something about himself as a player: in both his pro seasons, he had walked a lot, and he noted how that often led to big innings.

Weaver also noted the despair and resignation in minor-league baseball. Toward the beginning of the 1949 season, two St. Joe teammates walked into the locker room so drunk they could barely stand. One fell down, and the other flung himself over a railing and vomited. "I was only eighteen and thought that if this is the way things went as you got closer to the major leagues, I was going to have to quit," Weaver remembered. "I later realized that both guys were twenty-six years old. They had been through the mill and were on their way down. An occasional drunk probably kept them their sanity."

In 1950, the Cardinals promoted Weaver to a class-B team in Winston-Salem, North Carolina, a town of 100,000. The eight-team Carolina League included the Durham Bulls, which would one day be made famous by the movie *Bull Durham*. For the first time, Earl played with big-league prospects, led by left-handed pitcher and future Republican congressman Wilmer "Vinegar Bend" Mizell, named after the town in Alabama where he started pitching. Vinegar Bend later won 90 games in the major leagues and made an All-Star game.

Back then, Vinegar Bend wore bib overalls down to his knees and ankles, and shirts with sleeves that hung just below his elbows. He liked to toss a wad of paper and try to hit it with tobacco spit, jolting the paper in the air. At Earl's prod-ding, he would then try to spit again and hit the paper with his saliva a second time, while it was in the air. It looked like so much fun that Earl felt compelled to chew tobacco. Surprisingly, that habit lasted only a few years, until a dentist talked him out of it. Nobody could ever talk him out of cigarettes. Once, Vinegar Bend rode in on a mule and sang for the crowd at home plate. One night, the team hired an orchestra and organized a massive square dance.

Earl owned the Carolina League that summer of 1950. He was hitting around .300 and Winston-Salem had an 18.5-game lead when he broke his thumb trying to stop a wild throw with his bare hand. "Things won't be the same without Weaver making his hits and defensive plays together for the club," wrote the *St. Louis Globe-Democrat*. "The Cardinal front office is high in its praise of the former Beaumont High School all-star." After recovering from his injury, Earl finished the season with a .276 average, led second basemen in fielding percentage, and made the league's all-star team. Again, his team dominated the league. Earl Weaver, it seemed, was a stud and a winner.

It was Weaver's luck that season to be paired with twenty-nine-year-old Winston-Salem manager George Kissell, one of professional baseball's legendary teaching gurus. Kissell, who worked for the Cardinals from 1940 until his death in 2008, is credited with inventing the "Cardinal Way," St. Louis's systematic method of building winning baseball teams. Baseball men from Branch Rickey to Tony La Russa would rave about his instruction. "He could teach a snake to box," said Hall of Fame manager Sparky Anderson.

Kissell was one of the first instructors to take the teaching of baseball as seriously as he took the playing. He got a master's degree from Ithaca College, and wrote a senior thesis on instructing young baseball players. In Weaver, he found a young player who took baseball, if not personal discipline, as seriously as he did. Kissell taught Weaver systems of cutoff and relays that Weaver would later use with the Orioles. "I went to school with George Kissell," Weaver recalled. "He was a great fundamentalist, but he was also a grating perfectionist, a manager who had rules for everything imaginable, and who assessed fines for the least infraction."

Kissell, a devout Catholic, imposed bed checks on single players and called the married men at their homes. Discipline was a problem for Earl, a night owl who drank and played poker. Like most minor-league managers of his day, Kissell coached third base, but stayed on his players, sometimes catching Earl for smoking in the dugout and fining him $10 per infraction.

In the winter of 1950–1951, the Cardinals promoted Weaver to their Double-A team in Houston, the Buffaloes. He negotiated a contract that would pay him $600 a month and headed for Texas. In spring training, he won the starting second baseman's job, even though eight of the team's players were over thirty. In the spring of 1951, Earl took his first flight on an airplane when the Buffaloes flew to Panama to play a game. The DC-3 plane shook all the way down. Earl was scared to death and threw up.

For the first time, in 1951, Weaver struggled, hitting .233 in his first 13 games in Houston. The Cardinals demoted him to class-A Omaha, where the team used cow-milking contests and appearances by Miss Nebraska to draw fans. When the team tried to cut his pay to $400 a month as part of the demotion, the hotheaded Weaver threatened to quit and drive home to St. Louis. Management agreed to restore his salary. Fortunately, in Omaha, Weaver was reunited with Kissell. When the 1951 season had ended, Weaver had hit .279 and made another all-star team.

As in other minor-league towns, fans in Omaha fell in love with Earl. "Omaha's Stanky," one newspaper wrote, "has never played a game at Muny stadium in which he didn't give 100 per cent. He's all heart." The papers also called him "Tiger" or "The Brat." Nicknames were a way of forging relationships, and establishing identity. If you were a smart guy who read books, you got called Deacon or Professor. If you didn't drink, Lady. Peach Pie Jack O'Connor was named after a pickup team he played for in St. Louis called the Peach Pies. Players were named after their habits, or what they looked like when they played baseball: Fidgety Phil Collins, Pretzels Pezzullo, Twitchy Dick Porter, Jumping Jack Jones, Herky Jerky Horton. Or after their character: Sunny Jim Bottomley, Mysterious Walker, Smiling Mickey Welch. Or what they liked to eat: Sweetbreads Bailey, Oyster Burns, Spud Krist. There was a whole category of players named after animals—Turkey Tyson, Bullfrog Dietrich, Goose Goslin, Ducky Medwick, Hippo Jim Vaughn, Harry (The Cat) Brecheen—and another for little players: Flea, Bitsy, Bunny, Shorty, Scooter, Skeeter, Peanuts.

On August 16, the *Omaha World-Herald* called Weaver "probably the league's finest competitor" and "the answer to any manager's prayers." A few weeks later, the same paper gushed: "Was [Chicago White Sox All-Star second baseman] Nellie Fox any better with Lincoln three years ago than Earl Weaver now?"

At the end of the 1951 season, Weaver had accumulated enough minor-league time that by the rules of the day, he would have to be promoted to the major-league roster, or made available to other major-league teams in the annual draft. The Cardinals didn't want to lose him. On October 15, they announced the addition of "four promising youngsters" to their forty-man roster. One of them was Earl Weaver. He was over the moon. This was what he had dreamed of since walking through the Cardinals clubhouse in the 1930s and idolizing Dizzy Dean, Ducky Medwick, and Stan Musial.

But in December, the Cardinals made another move that spelled doom for those dreams. The team traded two players to the New York Giants for second baseman Eddie Stanky, and named Stanky as the Cardinals' new manager. The repercussions for Weaver were obvious. It wasn't fair, baseball writers noted, that after all Weaver's hard work, and four excellent seasons, he would have to compete against his own manager. "What is happening to the Earl shouldn't happen to a rookie second baseman just about to have his first chance at the big time," the Associated Press wrote. "Until now, Earl has been billed 'the Eddie Stanky' of the Cardinal organization. Since the Redbirds have the original Stanky who has served notice he intends to keep right on playing, Earl's unofficial title—and his plans—may require some revision."

Earl said he was confident things would work out. "After all," he said. "I'm only 21. I have lots of time."

7

THE BUFF GOAT

Houston, Texas; Omaha, Nebraska; Denver, Colorado;
New Orleans, Louisiana; Montgomery, Alabama, 1952–1956

Oh, Lord, give me a bastard with talent.
—Inscription on pillow George Steinbrenner gave to Howard Cosell

Earl Weaver went through two phases in his career as a minor-league ball-player: one from 1948 to 1951 when he was headed up, and one beginning in 1952, when he went down, and down, and down.

Getting cut after his glorious 1952 big-league spring training in St. Petersburg wrecked twenty-one-year-old Earl Weaver. Instead of batting ahead of Stan Musial at Sportsman's Park, he reported to Houston, to sweat it out as second baseman for the Houston Buffaloes.

The Texas League was the last place Earl Weaver wanted to be. There was no big-league baseball anywhere near Texas. "I reported to Houston with bitterness camped in my throat and indecisiveness swirling around my head," recalled Earl. "I played miserable baseball." He drank himself into oblivion every night, and entered a vicious cycle of worse baseball and more alcohol. He found Houston overwhelming and unwieldy. It was hard to find lodging and hard to get around.

On April 13, Weaver lost the Buffaloes both games of a doubleheader—in game 1, he missed a throw, allowing the winning run to score all the way from first, and in game 2, he committed an error that allowed the winning run to get to third base, setting up a game-ending sacrifice fly. "The Buff second baseman, Earl Weaver, was the goat," the *Freeport Facts* bluntly reported. (That's goat as in the animal that symbolizes failure in sports, not the Greatest Of All Time.)

A month later, Earl booted a grounder with two outs in the twelfth to cost his team a game against Fort Worth. The fancy nicknames were gone. Now the sportswriters simply called him "Little Earl Weaver." In his first half of the season at Houston, Earl Weaver hit .219 in 57 games.

On June 10, the unimpressed Cardinals demoted Earl back to class-A Omaha and cut his salary to $400 from $600 a month. In denial and angry, Earl once again refused the assignment and drove back to St. Louis. The holdout lasted a day. The Cardinals agreed to reinstate his salary. It was a bargain he accepted, but in a newspaper picture published June 21, he wore a sad, tired face.

At least in Omaha, Weaver was once more back with his mentor Kissell. He was happy to be back in Omaha, where he was beloved, and one of the team's best players. Weaver, the *Omaha World-Herald* said, "is a steady, poised second baseman and has fine competitive instincts. Any manager in the Western League would be glad to have him." In early August, with Omaha in the middle of a 21-8 streak, the *World-Herald* called Weaver "the best player in the Western League for his pounds (160) and inches (5-7)."

Weaver got his act together and cut down some on the drinking. He'd seen "guys in their late twenties who were on their way down" who'd "come to the ballpark with so much booze in them that they were only marginally ambulatory." Those men weren't going to the major leagues, Earl knew. "I now realized I wasn't either if I kept beering up."

By the end of the season, he'd picked up enough pieces to hit .279 for Omaha with a .403 on-base percentage. In future decades and with some other organizations, Weaver might have gone back to Cardinals spring training to get another shot with the big club. He was only twenty-two. But for the 1953 season, he was headed back to Omaha. He had become what in front-office slang is known as an "org guy," whose purpose is to provide teammates for players in the organization who have a shot of making the big leagues.

Earl Weaver was a twenty-two-year-old has-been. After the 1952 season, the Cardinals left him unprotected in a draft that would have allowed any major-league team to sign him. Not one did.

There is an alternative path here, where Earl, instead of tumbling into alcohol and acedia, fights back by making adjustments to his game, improving his conditioning, and laying off the booze. He earns another spring training invite or two and makes the big leagues. In this other path, he really has given it his best shot, and doesn't have to blame his lack of talent, or Stanky.

He didn't have it in him.

After a winter in St. Louis doing odd jobs and playing basketball to stay in shape, he went to minor-league spring training in February 1953 hoping to impress Johnny Keane, the manager of the Cardinals' AAA team, Columbus. Keane didn't want him either. So it was back to Omaha, where he had his first bad season as a player, hitting .243.

Often Earl wasn't even starting anymore, and as his role as a player shrank in stature, he started to fight and get thrown out of more games. When he got tossed, teammates often had to walk with him off the field so he didn't get into more trouble. He played hot, and it didn't help his performance.

In September, he was hitting .237 in 136 games when Omaha sold him to the Denver Bears, a Pittsburgh Pirates class-A affiliate, for the 1954 season. A couple of days later, the *Omaha Evening World-Herald* analyzed the state of their fallen hero: "Can Weaver reach the top rung as a ball player? Probably not. He's had his three shots in the Cardinal chain."

Now Earl Weaver was truly a busher. It didn't matter that in 1954 for the Denver Bears he hit .283 with a .403 on-base percentage and 124 runs scored. Pittsburgh only wanted Earl to replace Curt Roberts, a Black second baseman playing for the Pirates in 1954. As talented Black players took their well-deserved places in big-league baseball, there would be even less room for marginal white players like Weaver.

In Denver, Weaver found a second mentor to complement George Kissell in the Bears' manager, Andy Cohen. Like Earl, Cohen was a short, scrappy middle infielder. He'd played for the legendary John McGraw and was smart and savvy. Cohen was born in Baltimore to Jewish immigrants but raised in El Paso, Texas. In the 1920s, McGraw signed Cohen to draw more Jewish fans in New York City; the Giants were trying to compete with Babe Ruth and the Yankees. Cohen, who performed on the vaudeville circuit with an Irish ballplayer, played 1,878 games in the minor leagues and 262 in the majors. "Andy was a genius as far as handling his players on and off the field," said Weaver. "He knew how to talk to a person and how get them to play ball," even if that meant leaving them alone.

Weaver needed help from a wise baseball lifer like Cohen. Playing minor-league baseball can crush a person psychologically. You make no money. You eat dog food. Often you have no real prospect for advancement. In 2023, I met up during spring training with two career minor leaguers at a bar on the outskirts of Sarasota, Florida. The two men had spent a combined nineteen seasons in the minor leagues and had received eight total big-league spring training invites, but had yet to taste as much as one at-bat in the Show. They told stories of drinking and chasing women and getting screwed over by front offices. "Man, I love baseball," said one. "And I hate baseball."

Cohen engaged constructively with young Earl Weaver. After Earl got thrown out for calling an umpire every name in the book, Cohen barked at him to "get your ass in the clubhouse or it's gonna cost you a hundred dollars."

"You know what would have happened if you'd called that man those names off the field?" Cohen asked.

"We'd have fought," Weaver said.

"You're damn right," Cohen said. "And you know he can't punch you without losing his job."

In 1955, the Pirates' class-A affiliation switched to the New Orleans Pelicans, and that's where Weaver and Cohen both went. The season in Louisiana was a slog. Fans nicknamed Earl "Doodles" after TV comedian Doodles Weaver, which drove Earl crazy. In early August, a fastball drilled him in the head, crushing the bones beneath his left eye and landing him in the hospital for eleven days.

In desperation, Weaver cheated by illegally swinging a tampered bat. A bat mechanic drilled six-inch holes in the Pelicans' bats, packed them with ground-up cork, and topped off the holes with plastic wood and sanded them smooth. "When you swung the bat, it whipped around so much quicker than normal that balls literally leapt off it," remarked Weaver. "We had the man cork bats for everyone on the team and instantly went on a homer binge." After a teammate broke his bat, the league put out word that it would start inspecting bats, and the Pelicans threw away the dirty sticks. For the 1955 season, Weaver batted .278 with 6 home runs and 59 RBI.

That was good enough to get him an invite to play winter ball for Santiago in the Dominican Republic. The money was good, and winter ball with other pro players would keep him in shape. But that winter, when Weaver wrote to the Pirates and asked for a chance to try out for the team at major-league spring training, they didn't answer.

"Now I had to deal with the reality that had finally and irreversibly damaged my dream," recalled Weaver. "I was never going to make it to the major leagues. No way, I thought, as scenes from sandlot ball and high school ball and Legion ball and games at West Frankfort and St. Joseph and Houston and Omaha and Denver swept through my head like ghosts of wonderful moments past. I was heartbroken."

He would have to think about alternate career paths. Like other ballplayers, Weaver always worked offseason jobs. Usually they came via Uncle Bud, who had connections in St. Louis throughout city politics, unions, and the mob. Weaver was, like his father and uncle, a hustler.

During his first few offseasons, Weaver had worked as a warehouseman in Teamsters Local 688 in St. Louis, handling galvanized steel. The job paid well but banged up his hands.

In the winter of 1950–1951, Uncle Bud got Weaver a soft job on a government contract installing parking meters. All he had to do was slap yellow paint over an X, chalked up by a pal of Bud's, marking the spot for engineers to install meters.

The following winter, Weaver hooked up with the maintenance crew that serviced all the meters. He checked and fixed them if they were broken. It took him two hours to check half of the five hundred meters. He then took four hours off before checking the other 250.

A year later, in the winter of 1952–1953, Weaver worked as a city tax agent, collecting duties on jewelry and automobiles. You couldn't get a new license plate unless you paid the tax. People would come grouchily into his office. "I was empathetic to everyone," Earl remembered, "except those who showed up with a $1,200 assessment and handed me that amount in single dollar bills or coins—which I had to count."

The next winter, Earl asked Bud to get him a union card as a common laborer. He could make $420 a month as an apprentice. On the first day, the foreman took him into a room with sand piled up the ceiling. He told him to move the sand to the opposite corner. He finished the job in three hours.

When he reported on Wednesday, a couple of days later, the foreman assigned him to carry mortar up ladders to bricklayers. Inexperienced in carrying mortar up a ladder, Earl dropped it on a bricklayer's foot. The man scooped up the mortar and threw it in Weaver's face. He wanted to kill the guy, but he held back. Manual labor bored him, but he needed the money.

In the winter of 1954–1955, he got a job as a stonemason's helper. "I was a definite menace until I learned how to operate a jimmy pull to raise and lower into place huge blocks of cut stone, granite, and polished marble," Earl said. "I lost a slab of marble that would've killed somebody on the floor below if anyone had been standing where it landed."

The way Earl saw things, 1956 would probably be his last year in baseball. He'd make his $800 a month and then go look for a real job after the season ended. He had two children, and his marriage to Jane was going about as well as his baseball career. In 1955, Earl lived part-time in an apartment next to Uncle Bud's, according to the St. Louis phone book.

After a respectable performance for New Orleans in 1955, again any team in baseball had the chance to claim him, for $25,000. Again, not one did.

Weaver went back to Louisiana and bombed, hitting .228. On May 12, 1956, the Pelicans sold him to the class-A Montgomery Rebels, an independent minor-league team in Alabama and another rung lower on baseball's ladder. For the first time, Weaver was playing outside the orbit of major league–affiliated baseball.

A story in the *Alabama Journal* described Earl how a has-been at the bar might tell his best war story: "His all-around ability caught the eyes of the St. Louis Cardinal moguls and he was directed to report to the Cards' spring training camp in 1952. It was there that Weaver experienced his greatest base-ball thrill, collecting more hits than any other Cardinal aspirant, including the great Stan Musial."

In June, the Montgomery Rebels announced they had been purchased by investors in Knoxville and would move to Tennessee.

8

THE EARL OF KNOXVILLE

Knoxville, Tennessee, 1956

A baseball manager is a necessary evil.

—Sparky Anderson

In the mid-1950s, Earl Weaver's Beaumont High classmates started lucrative careers in banks, traveled the country as salesmen, or finished up medical school. They contributed babies to a boom and bought new suburban homes. In 1956, President Dwight D. Eisenhower created the Interstate Highway System.

Life wasn't so simple for failed ballplayers. The minor-league baseball constellation was shrinking. Americans drove new cars on fresh highways to their air-conditioned houses and lost interest in trooping to the local ballyard. It was easier to stay home and watch *I Love Lucy*. By 1953, Americans had 52 million TV sets, and 15 of the 16 major-league teams had television contracts. A 1950 survey found that 53 percent of Americans living in minor-league towns would prefer to watch a big-league game on TV rather than go to their local ballpark.

The baseball recession paved the way for Earl Weaver to secure his first managing job. The class-A Knoxville Smokies stunk, couldn't draw fans, and lost money. Team owners blamed their manager, Dick Bartell, one of those elite players who fail at managing because they can't relate to struggling ball-players. Joe Torre and John McGraw are the rare big-league stars to turn them-selves into Hall of Fame managers. More common is the fate of Ted Williams, Ty Cobb, Frank Robinson, and other Hall of Fame players turned unsuccess-ful managers.

Like Weaver, Dick Bartell was a small, quick infielder famous for his intensity and temper. Rowdy Richard, they called him. But unlike Earl, he had played in over 2,000 big-league games, appeared in the first-ever All-Star Game in 1933, and gone to three World Series. A big leaguer, and he let you know it.

Bartell quit a job as a scout for the Cincinnati Reds in early 1956 to man-age the Smokies. Knoxville was excited to get Bartell, a star well-connected throughout the sport. A working agreement with the Cleveland Indians was falling apart, and the Smokies' owners hoped Bartell could secure a new con-tract with the Yankees. Without a working agreement to supply players and sometimes equipment, independent baseball teams like Knoxville struggled.

The city had potential, and a stadium with 8,000 capacity. But after draw-ing 21,279 fans in their first six home dates, the Smokies were attracting under 2,000 people a game, not enough to stay in business.

When the team moved to Knoxville, Weaver had thought about quitting. Without any degrees or qualifications, he would have a hard time making more then $800 a month during the summer. It was still baseball or bust. He went to Knoxville. The team was bad. Couldn't hit, couldn't field, couldn't pitch. Bartell couldn't manage, and couldn't accept that he couldn't manage—only bark at players to play as well as he had. "He wanted nine Dick Bartells on the field," one player moaned.

Bartell made weird controlling decisions, like ordering his players to stop throwing the ball around the infield after outs, a routine baseball practice. He said he wanted to save time. He kicked front-office guys out of the clubhouse. As the team kept losing, Bartell got madder and madder. Off the field, he was a gentleman. On the field, he ranted and raved. Like Jekyll and Hyde, said a reporter who covered the team.

Bartell was also earning $1,400 a month, almost half of what the owners had paid for the team, and after a strong start, the Smokies weren't drawing well. In August, the Smokies fired Bartell. To everyone's surprise, they replaced him with their brash second baseman, twenty-five-year-old Earl Weaver, "for the good of the team and for the fans," a spokesman said. "My dad realized they could save some money by making Earl the manager," said Jimmy Duncan, a former U.S. congressman whose father, John J. Duncan, headed the owner-ship group that brought the Smokies to Knoxville. Weaver had initially turned down the assignment. He thought he was too young to give up on his career as a player. An extra $200 a month changed his mind.

The Smokies called a press conference. An official read a statement: "We have appointed Earl Weaver, second baseman, the new manager. We have every confidence in his ability. He is a steady, level-headed ball player who hustles all the way. He is well liked by every member of the team." The team had already put Weaver in leadership positions, sending him to lecture the South Knoxville Rotary Club when Bartell got sick.

The players backed him. "Earl is the best possible choice on the team," said catcher John Malangone. "He would have been a unanimous winner if the players had selected the field boss." Pitcher George Aitken said "the fellows all like Earl and will do their best for him." Outfielder Jacques Monette: "The pressure is off the players now. We'll look better now because we won't be afraid of making a mistake. Manager Weaver should do great. He sure knows his baseball. Mr. Bartell treated me okay, but he thought we should win every game. He never conceded defeat."

Bartell lashed out with a dig that mocked the manager's importance. "I am quite sure that in making this change and the naming of Earl Weaver manager, pro tem, who is a fine boy and a good little hustler, that every player on the club will now hit .350, field 1.000 and not make any mental mistakes, and that the pitchers who have pitched the low-run game will now pitch shutouts," he said.

Earl, showing he'd already learned something about the diplomacy of handling the media, advised reporters that he wouldn't be working any mira-cles. Like a winning politician, he praised his defeated opponent. "Dick Bartell is a good baseball man who is bound to succeed in various baseball capacities," he said. "He has my sincere best wishes for his baseball future." Bartell never managed again. Typically, Weaver downplayed his big-league opportunity in the 1952 spring training with the Cardinals. "It's hard to get Weaver to tell you," one paper reported, "but his home run off Washington's Bob Porterfield in an exhibition game that spring was one of his big moments."

Before Earl Weaver's first game as a manager, he posed for a picture with Jane, Mike, and Rhonda. Five-year-old Mike looked at him with a mischievous glint. Weaver later recalled that he sent his family back to St. Louis when he went to Knoxville, but the picture proved they attended some games. Weaver also placed a request in a local newspaper advertising his need for a two-bedroom apartment or a house.

The Smokies won the first game Earl Weaver ever managed, 5–0. "The new Smoky skipper looks like a youngster just out of college," a beat reporter wrote about Weaver. "His boyish grin and his flat-top haircut belie the fact that he's a veteran who is in his ninth season of pro ball." In a picture in the *Knoxville News-Sentinel*, Weaver sits at a desk with a pen, writing out his lineup. He looks too young to be in charge of anything. In that first game, Weaver batted second and played second base. He went 0-for-4. That's when he realized he needed to start benching his weakest link: himself.

The day after Weaver took over, the Smokies got a visit from a man who worked for a Major League Baseball team on a mission to find talent. Harry Dalton didn't know it, but he was looking for Earl Weaver. He was a young assistant farm director for the Baltimore Orioles, aka the ex–St. Louis Browns, who had moved to Maryland only two years before. Dalton was hired by the Orioles after earning a degree in English from Amherst College and serving as a U.S. Air Force public relations officer in Japan and Korea during the Korean War, where he had earned a Bronze Star. He loved his job with the Orioles, but it still paid so poorly that he drove a cab on the side. Dalton would work in the Orioles front office for the next sixteen years, and play a pivotal role in making the team, and Earl Weaver, winners.

The Orioles' move to the Chesapeake Bay followed the Browns' abysmal record in St. Louis. In 1953, the Browns had drawn only 300,000 fans in 77 home games in St. Louis as they lost 100 games and finished last. The franchise was a mess. They sometimes ran out of baseballs and had to use dirty batting-practice balls. Owner Bill Veeck had tried to move the Browns to Baltimore the year before, but the other team owners had rebuffed him. They hated Veeck's circus promotions like Grandstand Managers Day, when fans were given placards saying "bunt," "steal," and "swing," giving fans free beer and ladies' stockings, hiring forty-four-year-old Negro Leagues legend Satchel Paige, and sending a little person to bat in a big-league ballgame. (Weaver, of course, loved Veeck's antics. *Did you hear the one about the fucking midget?*)

Tommy D'Alesandro, the mayor of Baltimore and Nancy Pelosi's dad, pushed a consortium of Maryland investors to raise a million dollars to buy the Orioles and move them to Baltimore. After a couple of false starts, the deal was done. Veeck was out of baseball and the Browns were headed to Baltimore, becoming the Orioles, and giving the birthplace of Babe Ruth a Major League Baseball team for the first time since 1902. A year later, the Philadelphia A's moved to Kansas City. In 1958, the Dodgers moved to Los Angeles, and the Giants to San Francisco. By 1977, 26 big-league teams stretched from sea to sea.

The Orioles' new owners were determined not to let the team suffer the same devastation as the Browns. The only employee they kept was farm director Jim McLaughlin, who had scouted teenage Earl Weaver in St. Louis. He hired Dalton as his assistant. McLaughlin was a Shakespeare scholar and a humanist, able to think about ballplayers as more than hired horses. He invented a circle graph to evaluate players, with physical tools on top and mental tools on the bottom, and pioneered the use of a cross-checker, a second scout to back up the opinion of the first, and hired FBI investigators to perform background checks on players. He sent minor-league managers to communications and leadership seminars.

After a brutal 54-100 start in their inaugural season, the Orioles in 1955 hired Paul Richards, a sharp-chinned savant with a track record rebooting teams and a sterling reputation for handling pitchers, to serve as their manager and general manager. He replaced the Orioles' first manager, a soft-spoken big-league lifer named Jimmy Dykes who chain-smoked cigars and was fond of one-liners like "when I leave I'm going to have mistletoe hanging from my belt in the back."

When Richards arrived, McLaughlin told him the truth about the Orioles farm system: it was "horseshit." Richards set about remaking the organization according to his firm baseball beliefs, especially a reliance on pitching, defense, and fundamentals, and commanded his minions to scour the country for players, coaches, and managers.

In Knoxville, Weaver's intensity caught Dalton's eye. "I coached third base and apparently made a good impression on Dalton," Weaver said. "He gave McLaughlin a good report on me, he later confided, because he dug into back issues of the local newspaper and read that I was a hustler, a guy who was always in the game, and something of a character who excited fans."

When Dalton returned to Baltimore, he mentioned the young Smokies manager to McLaughlin. Jim recalled his time in St. Louis and told him about Earl and Earl Sr. Maybe this little guy in Knoxville should be managing with us, they agreed.

In Knoxville, Earl realized he would have to grow up—at least a little. He'd been in the habit of playing poker, and taking his teammates' money, until three or four in the morning. "I wanted to see how I could do as a manager, even for a few weeks," he said. "I guess somewhere in the back of my mind it had occurred to me that managing a ball club was something I could do pretty well." McLaughlin dispatched Jim Russo, one of the great baseball scouts of the twentieth century, to Knoxville. Russo was impressed. Weaver didn't shut up. The players liked him. The fans adored him.

The Smokies still stunk, and went 10-24 under Weaver, but in his remarks to reporters we can discern a managerial gift for positive, constructive, and team-aware discourse. "Each man is an individual and will be treated as a separate person," he said, already sounding like an older version of himself. "Some fellows need help and others will help you. I believe they'll all give their best to win."

Of course, Earl still clung to the dream that he might still make it as a player. In St. Louis phone books, where Weaver still had entries in the late 1950s, he listed his occupation as "baseball player, Baltimore Orioles." He had a few more hurrahs. In August, he hit a three-run homer to beat Savannah, 5–4, and break the Smokies' 8-game losing streak.

And he was still learning about baseball strategy by *playing* baseball, not just watching it. Weaver hit .237 for Montgomery and Knoxville in 1956, but he noticed how well he hit a brilliant Puerto Rican lefty named Juan Pizarro, who later won 131 games in the major leagues. Against Pizarro, Weaver saw the ball perfectly and could lay off pitches outside the zone and hammer strikes. As he recalled: "We'd get on the bus, and everybody would be worrying, 'Oh Jeez, Pizarro's pitching,' and I'd be thinking, 'Duck soup, three-for-four for me.'" A review of clippings confirms Weaver's memory. On June 16, 1956, Pizarro beat the Smokies, 5–3, but Weaver went 2-for-4. The lesson that a mediocre hitter like himself might star against a superior pitcher stayed with him.

Weaver said: "I expected to be a player instead of a manager next year but, of course, when you have a family, you're looking for the best offer. Just say I'd be available." He didn't get any new offers to play, and went back to St. Louis that autumn, where he took a job with a loan company. It wasn't manual labor, but again it was a hustle job for a tough, scrappy man on the margins of polite society. An outfit called "Liberty Loan Company" paid him to assess applicants and chase down defaulters. There weren't many, Weaver bragged. He could read people, look 'em in the eye, and tell if they were lying about money.

In December, McLaughlin called Weaver with a better offer. How would he like to manage a class-D team in Georgia for the Orioles, and keep playing? After initially offering him $3,500, they agreed to match the $4,000 salary he'd made as a player. And just like that, Earl Weaver was the new player-manager of the class-D Fitzgerald Orioles in the Georgia-Florida League, and an employee of the Baltimore Baseball Club Inc.

The season would start at minor-league spring training in Thomasville, Georgia. In their attempt to reverse decades of losing and disrupt the Yankees' hegemony, the Orioles had taken over a World War II military complex in the Deep South and were running a regimented baseball training camp. The Cardinals and Dodgers had their "systems" for triaging talent and building winning baseball teams. Paul Richards wanted a system for the Orioles.

To enforce his system, he wanted rugged, determined baseball men like Earl Weaver.

Earl Weaver's first job for the Orioles was to
triage young players like Cal Ripken Sr.

9

BIRD'S NEST

Thomasville, Georgia, 1957–1965

I'm superstitious, and every night after I got a hit, I ate Chinese food and drank tequila. I had to stop hitting or die.

—Tim Flannery

Earl Weaver reported in March 1957 to a swampy, snake-infested military hospital base in Thomasville, Georgia, which in the previous decade had hosted German prisoners of war.

The Orioles occupied eight long barracks with beds and two with equipment and uniforms, as well as sliding pits, batting cages, three practice fields, and a tiny ballpark. In the Jim Crow South, the Orioles, like other teams, kept Black and white players separated until 1965, and when they played games, seated Black fans down the right-field line, farther from the action.

The U.S. Army built Finney General Hospital in 1943 to house soldiers wounded on the battlefields of Europe and, occasionally, enemy captives. After the war, the army turned over Finney, a mini-village that included a chapel, theater, bowling alley, and canteen, to what is today the U.S. Department of Veterans Affairs (VA), which housed homeless survivors of the Spanish-American War, World War I, and World War II, and, in the spring, baseball teams there.

The main practice field, known as "the hole," was sunk below the barracks and the rest of the base, and copperhead snakes sometimes interrupted play. When one tried to ensnare outfielder Dave May, he threw his glove into the air and sprinted off the field.

Every spring, the Orioles shipped in over two hundred young men from all over the U.S. and Caribbean countries, and triaged the best into their minor-league teams. Cutting players was Weaver's job, earning him the nickname "The Hatchet." After getting stung by Eddie Stanky five years before, he now had to break other young men's hearts. Over the next eight years, he honed his skills as a professional baseball coach and manager, and helped the Orioles develop a rigorous method for winning baseball games. The Oriole Way joined the Dodger Way and the Cardinal Way as one of the three great organizational philosophies of the era.

In Thomasville, Weaver, who was drawn to men who might teach him his craft, got to know Paul Richards, his third great role model. George Kissell, the father of the Cardinal Way, had taught Weaver to be an organized and detail-oriented coach. Andy Cohen, his manager in Denver, had shown him a better way of relating to players. Now Richards would teach him to be daring and disruptive.

The first combined manager/general manager since John McGraw, Richards systemized instruction and turned Thomasville into a baseball school, a precursor to the academies that major-league teams later founded in the Dominican Republic. It was Spartan but high-tech for its time, geared up with Iron Mike pitching machines and walkie-talkies for the coaches.

Like Weaver, Richards was a smart, foulmouthed baseball lifer who clashed with umpires. Richards was born in Waxahachie, Texas, thirty miles south of Dallas. His dad taught him to read box scores. Big-league teams often played in the area as they barnstormed north after spring training, and Richards often went to watch Tigers, Reds, and White Sox at Jungle Park, a stadium near his house.

In 1926, he took a train ride to Brooklyn at age seventeen to play for Wilbert Robinson's Brooklyn Dodgers. Robinson managed Brooklyn from 1914 to 1931 and was elected to the Hall of Fame in 1962. Like McGraw, he had played for Ned Hanlon's Orioles teams in the 1890s. Richards, who only got eight big-league at-bats from Brooklyn, preferred the manager he later played for on the New York Giants, Bill Terry, who emphasized fundamentals and making every play. Terry believed that most games are lost, not won, an assessment Richards adopted.

After a sporadically successful big-league playing career—for the Tigers, he hit a three-run double in game 7 of the 1945 World Series—Richards became a manager, picking up the nickname "Ol' Rant and Rave." The Wizard of Waxahachie managed four seasons for the White Sox before the Orioles signed him in 1955 to turn their franchise around.

Richards was part of a new generation of cerebral baseball managers and coaches. In the late 1940s, for example, Richards started collecting a new statistic he called "batting average with bases on balls." It was on-base percentage. He loved teaching and encouraging pitchers to use the changeup, and he was the first manager to count pitches to protect pitchers' arms. Like Weaver, he was a pioneer. When Orioles catchers couldn't handle Hoyt Wilhelm's knuckleball, Richards designed a comically large catcher's mitt.

In 1955, Richards published a book he termed a "postgraduate" course in baseball called *Modern Baseball Strategy*. Pitching, he wrote, is the backbone of any baseball team. The most important problem "facing a baseball manager is the handling of pitchers," he wrote. "Your team's strength begins with the pitching staff. Its failure can mean disaster—its success can hold an average club in a pennant race for an indefinite period." Rest was key. "You must remember that any pitching program will be subject to immediate change and must be altered to prepare each individual pitcher," he wrote. "One man may need four full days' rest with only light throwing in between, coming one or two days before he starts again."

Led by superscout Jim Russo, the Orioles pioneered the use of "cross-checkers," scouts who would verify players recommended by area scouts. The Orioles gave any player a scout liked a contract and a bus ticket to Thomasville. If a kid could play, he stayed. Otherwise, he got a bus ticket home. "If we expect to improve our player strength, we must sign slightly more prospects each year than our competition," wrote Harry Dalton in a memo. "We can only do this if we approach each major case in an aggressive manner and stay in active competition to the point where our judgment on ability indicates we should stop." The Orioles were setting themselves up to win games in 1960 and 1965 and 1970, years down the road. This aggressive recruiting of young talent followed by sculpting and polishing is how the Orioles found Hall of Famers Brooks Robinson and Jim Palmer, and stars like Davey Johnson, Mark Belanger, and Boog Powell.

Living on a military base only a dozen years after the end of World War II, the young Orioles ate, practiced, and played together, and slept in tight quarters. When one farted, his teammates threw pillows at him. Every morning, a coach blew a reveille. After breakfast, the players changed into uniforms and ran to the fields. They played baseball until noon and ran back to the barracks. After lunch, they ran back to the fields for ballgames. They dined in the mess hall and attended chapel on Sundays.

Richards made all his coaches teach the same way of playing baseball. He believed you could win baseball games by not losing them, that if you tightened up your pitching and defense, you would outlast the opponent. Richards lectured players for hours, explaining baserunning, defensive positioning, pitching, hitting, relays, cutoffs, and pickoffs. If a pitcher made a bad throw in practice, he'd admonish him in a nasal Texas twang: "See, you didn't set yourself to throw the ball, that's the thing, big inning right there, five runs." One spring, the Orioles let a CBS camera crew follow him around for a "deep, intense look into the mind and methods of Paul Richards." (The episode was sponsored by L&M cigarettes. Slogan: Let your taste come alive.) "Spend your time on fundamentals, not trick plays, and you find something for yourself that works every day," he said. People "who glorify the triple and the home run are more in demand, while actually it is the defense that wins or loses the games."

There was also a lot of sliding practice. If you watch footage of spring training from the 1950s and 1960s, you'd be forgiven for thinking sliding was as important to baseball as pitching or hitting. Coaches were obsessed with teaching sliding properly, because it was considered one of the main sources of possible injury. Jim Palmer explained that coach Barney Lutz, one of Earl's best buddies, liked to demonstrate how to slide on cement "to illustrate [that] if you slid the proper way, cement, dirt, whatever would not be a problem." The Orioles also used a recycled bazooka from the military to shoot high practice pop-ups for their catchers.

Every day, Weaver hit ground balls, threw batting practice, and barked at players with his raspy voice. He played when he could, but that was no longer the point. He was now a teacher. The coaches, men like Billy Hunter, who was so strict the players nicknamed him "Little Hitler" (another coach who came along later, Gene Woodling, would be called "Big Hitler"), battered players with Richards's rules: Make the simple play. Never beat yourself. Run out every ball. Throw strikes. The coaches soothed players who cursed themselves: never wear your emotions on your sleeves.

The Orioles gave Weaver a house, and he brought Jane, Mike, Rhonda, and Terry, a second daughter born in 1957, for parts of his stays in Thomasville.

In the evenings, Weaver joined other coaches in a little building on the hospital grounds the Orioles had converted into a meeting room. They called it the Bird's Nest. A contractor named Marvin Coram got a veteran to paint an Oriole logo and drilled a hole in the bird's mouth, where coaches could chuck their beer cans. "Daddy also put in two fridges with refreshments," said Ken Coram, Marvin's son. Refreshments, he emphasized, "meant beer."

Marvin used to drink with Earl and his coaches, and took his son with him. "They'd cuss," said Ken, "and somebody said there's a kid here, and Daddy said don't worry about it."

Weaver wasn't that friendly, Ken recalled: "He was all business, like he knew he had a job to do."

Every day, the coaches performed the same routine.

"Let's have today's nominations for cuts," Dalton said.

The coaches graded players on a scale of 1 (excellent) to 4 (poor) for hitting, pitching, running, and throwing.

Any player with multiple 4 ratings was in danger of getting whacked.

Every day, the names of the players cut were posted in the mess hall with a note that said, "After eating, will the following please report to Mr. Weaver."

Some players, not that much younger than Weaver, got angry. "Why the hell are you cutting me? I can outplay half the guys in this goddamn camp." Some refused to leave camp. Some burst into tears. "Oh no, Mr. Weaver, you can't do that . . . you can't send me home already, not without giving me a chance. What am I gonna tell my mom and dad? What can I say to my high school coach? He said I had the ability, that I'd go all the way to the majors."

Weaver learned that when a kid started crying, he'd best be silent, or the player might break down. It broke Earl's heart, but he couldn't show it. "The decision had been made and it was my job to be honest and ease the kids out in the most painless fashion possible," he said. "And I had to be the truthful rotten little bastard." That instilled a lesson Weaver would remember for the rest of his managing career. "You're always going to be a rotten bastard, or in my case, a little bastard, as long as you manage," he said in 1982. "To keep your job, you fire others, or bench them or trade them," he said years later. "You have to do the thinking for 25 guys, and you can't be too close to any of them."

The manager, coaches, and scouts, fueled by unlimited alcohol, went back and forth. "Get rid of that SOB, he can't play." The scout who signed the player would rise to his defense: "Wait a minute! The kid's only eighteen and he's had trouble at home. But he hit .480 with power in high school, and you guys are gonna run him outta here in three fucking weeks?" If there was a dispute, Weaver, who could outdrink and outtalk the rest of the staff, usually had his way.

In the Bird's Nest, Weaver hardened. "The Hatchet," he recalled, "never faltered." The first few weeks, they cut ten players a night. Nervous players crept under the window by the Bird's Nest and listened to the coaches in terror at hearing their names called. "It was Baltimore's version of Russian Roulette," recalled pitcher Tim Sommer.

After a first round of meetings at the Bird's Nest, the coaches ate dinner in the canteen, and then returned to the Bird's Nest. One of the stars of the late-night bull sessions was Freddie "Bootnose" Hofmann, Earl Sr.'s old buddy from St. Louis. At night, over beers, Bootnose told stories about his old roommate Babe Ruth. The other scouts and coaches loved it. Richards gave all the scouts cameras. Bootnose turned his in with no pictures. He'd never taken off the lens cap.

Weaver and his buddies also drank at the American Legion or Elks Club. It was a dry county, but private clubs were exempted, and everybody loved the baseball guys. They drank, talked baseball, and teased the young Dalton about finding him a local girl.

Weaver and the other coaches figured out a way of gaming the slot machines. They stood by the machines with a handful of coins and waited for a machine to go through a long stretch of never paying out. When they were confident they had waited long enough, they shoved half-dollars into the machine until it paid out. They'd buy drinks for everybody or play bingo. One night, Earl and a buddy hauled twenty-seven drinks from the bar to the bingo table. Ten for him, ten for his buddy—and seven for their friends.

The coaches golfed on Sunday mornings. The loser paid for a five-dollar dinner at the Elks Club. Earl traveled with a set of wooden-shafted clubs Uncle Bud gave him after teaching him to play golf.

In 1961, Dalton named Weaver director of the Thomasville camp. From then until 1965, Earl's last season before he moved to Triple A, it was his show. Dalton began collecting coaching tips. When they later translated into major-league success and were written down, these methods, pioneered by Weaver & Co. in swampy southern Georgia, became the official "Oriole Way" manual. There's a copy in Dalton's papers at the National Baseball Hall of Fame in Cooperstown, New York.

The Oriole Way prepared the great teams from 1966 to 1983, 1950s.

10

CLIMB THE FLAGPOLE

Fitzgerald, Georgia; Dublin, Georgia; Aberdeen, South Dakota;
Fox Cities, Wisconsin, 1957–1961

I'd rather ride the buses in Triple A than be a lawyer.

—Tony La Russa

When I visited Fitzgerald, Georgia, the storefronts were mostly empty and the downtown quiet, but in the middle of the twentieth century, factories and a thriving business community supported professional baseball. The town had been carved out of 50,000 acres of pine forests in the 1890s as a utopian settlement for Civil War veterans from both the North and South.

Fitzgerald was part of the old Georgia-Florida League, a minor-league glory-days satellite of Major League Baseball's minimum-wage empire. The league folded for good in 1963, but from 1935 onward it offered thrilling summer nights watching professional baseball from wooden benches on a concrete grandstand covered by a tin roof. Weaver might have been showing promise in his new role, but he was still stuck in the bushes, the dark underbelly of pro baseball. He bought his girls a poodle, which he walked around on his off-days while smoking cigarettes.

Even as a father, the focus of Earl's life was the ball field and his tribe of merry men. In Fitzgerald, he and his players favored a restaurant, the Spotted

Pig, that was shaped like a long railroad car that could seat over one hundred people. It was so big that it had to be set on the outskirts of town. The players would try to finish their games by 10:30 p.m., in time to make last call at the Spotted Pig. Pitchers would hurry their pitches and hitters would swing at everything. Frequently, Earl arrived with teammates right round closing time and pleaded with the servers and cooks to let them in. They ate their cheeseburgers and giggled like little boys.

It was a difficult season. Fitzgerald went 65-74. The team drew 18,046 fans—for the season. Earl didn't have another losing season until 1986. (There's an elegant simplicity to his record: one losing record in his first full year as a manager, twenty-six straight winning seasons, then one losing season in his final year, and then done.) Weaver got 469 plate appearances in 1958 and hit .288, preserving some shred of hope that he might still make the major leagues. But he was eating and drinking and putting on weight.

He had also made a mistake in selecting his team. He picked an older group. "My club had a hell of a first half, and then the teams with the kids started to come on, and my team started to drop back and back and back," he recalled. Fitzgerald finished fourth. Not one of Weaver's players made the big leagues. From then, he resolved to pick younger, more talented players, even if they were inexperienced and made mistakes. He would trust his eye for talent and the capacity of talent to evolve. "Players in their second season of D ball don't improve," he realized. "Those with ability improve and pass the vets." The experience helped instill in Weaver a healthy beginner's mindset. He would look at himself critically and admit his mistakes.

From the beginning, Earl Weaver combined brains and brutishness. From his first season onward, he was ejected from six to eight games a year. In Waycross, Georgia, one night in 1957, Weaver grounded out to second base. The opposing dugout had been heckling him. It was a steamy, hot August night at a ballpark famous in the league for its infestations of roaches, snakes, and mosquitos. Weaver was ready to lash out.

After being called out at first base, he took a right turn and jogged back to his dugout.

"Nice hit, clown."

"Watermelon Head."

Weaver lost it. He charged into the opponents' dugout by himself with his fists flying. Ten players on the other team grabbed him and pushed him down. Falling backward, he covered his head and crouched on the ground as they beat him senseless.

When it was over, his teammates carried him to his clubhouse. He sat on the training table, unable to move the right side of his upper body. The team called an ambulance, which took Weaver to the hospital. He had suffered a concussion and couldn't remember his own name, where he was from, or what his job was.

The doctor taped his arm to his chest and said he'd have to stay that way for six weeks. The next day, Earl was managing with one sleeve empty. A fan brought a pair of crutches and heckled him: "Hey, Weaver, pull up a wheelchair and sit down." The experience traumatized him. He never launched another brawl.

In 1958, again Earl managed and played, this time in Dublin, Georgia. The Orioles weren't drawing enough in Fitzgerald, so they moved to Dublin, a small industrial town of 18,000. Reporters started using a new set of words to describe Weaver. A common one was *colorful*, as in he was "one of the biggest and most colorful little men in minor-league circles." One paper described him as 5'7", 175-pounds "of baseball energy."

In the low minors, Earl often had to scramble to keep his team together. Over the first three seasons of his managing career, he *pitched* in eight games. On June 27, 1957, Weaver pitched four shutout innings for Fitzgerald and earned the win in a 9–7 triumph over Waycross, his only career win. There is no record of his career ERA.

The Dublin team won 12 of its first 14 games. Weaver might still be a busher, but within the Orioles organization, word was spreading about this hot young manager. One thing was clear: he had star power. In May 1958, Dublin made an announcement. After pulling in 1,256 on Opening Day, it was drawing fewer than 500 fans a game. It needed at least 750 to pay "actual expenses." You could buy fifteen tickets for $10. The club advertised the Weaver Show as a reason to come watch: "We have a good manager full of pep and 'argument' with umpires! The boys are working and fighting hard, trying their best to win every game."

In Aberdeen, South Dakota, the Orioles' class-C team was 2-20. Harry Dalton wanted to move Weaver to South Dakota and Aberdeen manager Barney Lutz to Dublin. Word got out. Fans flooded the Dublin front office with phone calls. They all wanted Weaver to stay.

Dalton changed his mind. "The deal's off," he said. "We can't go against the wishes of the Dublin directors." Newspapers in Georgia celebrated the triumph of the underdog. "The heartening tale of a town which fought to keep its fiery baseball manager," wrote the *Atlanta Constitution*. "And the town itself is proud of its directors who, though not stubbornly unyielding, sounded off loudly and clearly where they stood. Minor league baseball cannot be dead." Earl Weaver the manager was a drawing card.

Earl still had a few playing pops left. In July, he hit a three-run homer to help Dublin beat Valdosta, 5–3. In August, he hit a two-run dinger against Brunswick. But for the first time, newspapers were writing stories where Weaver was a teacher. For the season, Dublin went 72-56 and finished third. It drew 31,704 fans. Earl got excellent reviews from the Orioles, but a warning about his temper. W. T. Anderson, the president of the Georgia-Florida League, a southern gentleman who dressed in a coat, tie, and hat every day, learned to expect regular reports of this new young manager kicking dirt on home plate or getting in the face of an umpire. He complained to the Orioles. "Mr. Dalton, can't you do something about your man Weaver? He gave my umpires such a bad time last night." When Dalton tried to talk to his young skipper, Weaver would insist the umpire had blown the call and he was a victim.

The Orioles didn't want their young prodigy to get stuck in Georgia. In 1959, the team promoted Weaver to Aberdeen, where he met the first piece of his future dynasty, a blond beast from Florida with a sweet power stroke, John "Boog" Powell. The team went 69-55 and finished in second place. His behavior with umpires was starting to spawn tales that burned through baseball's gossipy clubhouses. According to one of these stories, Earl got so mad at an umpire who tossed him from the game that he climbed the center-field flagpole and watched the rest of the game from the top of it. After the game ended, he couldn't get down. Stadium officials had to call the local fire department, as if he were a cat.

In 1960 and 1961, Earl managed a team in Appleton, Wisconsin, Fox

Cities, of the Three-I League. Fox Cities was the only team in the league not in Indiana, Iowa, or Illinois. In August 1960, his catcher, Cal Ripken Sr., was hitting .320 when his wife, Vi, had to go home to Maryland to give birth to their first child, future Orioles Hall of Famer Cal Ripken Jr. Cal went into a slump, which Weaver said was because he missed his wife. If Vi hadn't gone home to have Cal Jr., Earl teased Cal Sr., he might have become a big-league catcher.

When Cal Jr. was born, he was, according to his mom, a "big, full-faced kid with no wrinkles." Ripken Sr. got the news on a road trip, via a telegram announcing the birth of his boy at 9 pounds, 2.5 ounces. "He must have been born with his catcher's gear on," said Boog Powell. In Wisconsin, Weaver worked with Hall of Fame pitcher Burleigh Grimes, the last legal spitballer, and an Orioles scout.

In 1960, Fox Cities won the league with a 82-56 record. It was Weaver's first pennant as a manager. He wanted to win so bad he defied Dalton's orders to not play a prospect named Pete Ward at third base. Dalton wanted Ward to play outfield because Brooks Robinson had cemented his hold on the position in Baltimore. Weaver simply lied to Dalton and played Ward at third.

One of Weaver's stars at Fox Cities was Dean Chance, who won 128 games in the majors. "I remember Earl Sidney Weaver well," he told author Terry Pluto. "God, how he hated to be called Sidney. We did it just to piss him off. In fact, his three favorite words were *shit, fuck*, and *piss*." One night, Weaver ordered Chance to lure the next day's opposing starting pitcher into a poker game. Chance wasn't scheduled to pitch, so it didn't matter if he didn't get any sleep. He kept the card action going until 4 a.m. and Fox Cities won the baseball game. "You have to love playing for a guy like Earl," said Chance. "He gives you 150 percent, is a great guy, and he never misses a trick."

In 1961, Fox Cities went 67-62, slipping to fourth place, but the Orioles front office still raved about Weaver. His players learned one of the key rules of Earl Weaver: his temper was outrageous, but he didn't hold grudges. Once, at Fox Cities, Weaver walked out to the mound to remove a right-handed pitcher named Dick Hunt. The hurler threw the ball into Earl's chest. After the game, Hunt was on his sixth beer when Weaver walked into the clubhouse and started throwing fists. They knocked over the food table. The next day, it was forgotten.

At the end of the 1961 season, Dalton gave Earl his biggest promotion yet, to manage the Pioneers in Elmira, New York. Major League Baseball was instituting its first major reform of the minor leagues in over sixty years, creating four classifications: Triple A, Double A, Single A, and Rookie. The Elmira Pioneers were classified as the Orioles' Double-A team. Whatever his assignment on Opening Day, every March Earl was back in Thomasville for spring training, talking baseball and drinking beer deep into the night, and gambling at poker, golf, or slots at the Elks.

11

BULL DURHAM

Elmira, New York, 1962–1965

I could manage Adolf Hitler, Benito Mussolini, and Hirohito. That doesn't mean I'd like them, but I'd manage them.

—Billy Martin

Two rungs below the majors, Earl Weaver moved to Elmira to manage the Orioles' best prospects. For the first time, Weaver settled down, far from his parents and Uncle Bud, in a river factory town of 32,000 in south-central New York State that made typewriters and fire trucks.

Elmira was the first place where Weaver didn't feel broke. He bought a house and, in selling cars, figured out a new job he would enjoy if baseball didn't work out for him. His marriage with Jane reached a breaking point, and he resigned himself to spend less time with his children, but he found community and made true friends in Elmira, including a new woman. He also met an accountant named Jack Crandall, who encouraged him to keep detailed statistics about opposing players.

The Elmira Pioneers played at Dunn Field, a stone-and-steel ballpark built in the 1930s by the federal government's Works Progress Administration, close to the grave of another Mississippi River original, Mark Twain, whose wife, Olivia Langdon Clemens, grew up in Elmira. The Pioneers ran promotions to turn out the town, and Earl cooperated in the nightly vaudeville show of blind wheelbarrow races, egg tossing, pipe smoking, and fungo-hitting contests. He played ukulele for the "Earl Weaver Ukulele Trio," a country band with two of his players.

As was always the case in bush-league towns, Elmira was full of eccentrics, like the fan who yelled: "Put some zookum on the ball," prompting chants of "Zoo-kum, zoo-kum!" Announcer Bob Bolger drank too much and rambled and belched and left his mic on when he shouldn't. After the umpire ruled a foul ball on a ball down the line, he muttered, "That son of a bitch is blind."

The diamond was one of the best in minor-league baseball, with a pool table surface, luscious green grass, and rich brown dirt. The field was curated by the groundskeeper Pat Santarone, who would become one of Earl's best friends, a rock who grounded Earl and tempered some of his self-destructive impulses. Weaver loved Santarone's epicurean perfectionism. The man sculpted infields with the same care with which he made wines and hunted for mushrooms. His family had lived in Elmira since arriving from Italy shortly after 1900. Santarone's father had been a farmer in Italy and a professional groundskeeper in Elmira, rearing Pat and his brothers twenty feet past the right-field fence. The three boys accompanied their dad to sweep the stadium and shag balls. The family controlled a herd of a dozen goats that pastured at the ballpark. The players bellyached about the droppings, which they sometimes had to clean up before batting practice. When Santarone was twenty-two, his dad died; he took over groundskeeping duties.

For Earl Weaver, Elmira was an opportunity to prove that he could help the Orioles' best prospects reach the majors. Atop that list was pitcher Steve Dalkowski. The great Ted Williams said the 5'11" left-hander slung a baseball harder than anyone he'd ever faced. One of Dalko's catchers, Cal Ripken Sr., estimated his fastball at over 110 miles per hour, faster than Walter Johnson, Satchel Paige, or Nolan Ryan. Because Dalko played before radar guns and video, we'll never know. The stories of Dalkowski's freakish left arm are part of baseball lore: He fired a ball through a wooden backstop, and heaved another one over the center-field fence 410 feet away from home plate. He broke an umpire's mask. He beaned the mascot. He is baseball's Paul Bunyan, a mythical hero trapped forever in Elmira—with Earl Weaver.

The stories inspired Orioles minor-league infielder turned Hollywood director Ron Shelton to invent the character of Ebby Calvin "Nuke" LaLoosh for the classic baseball movie *Bull Durham* (1988). "That is what haunts us," Shelton wrote of Dalkowski. "He had the equivalent of Michelangelo's gift but could never finish a painting." The tall tales surrounding Dalkowski are debatable. His potential as a major-league superstar is not. "As forty years go by, a lot of stories get embellished," said Pat Gillick, a teammate in Elmira who became a Hall of Fame general manager. "But this guy was legit. He had one of those arms that come once in a lifetime."

There were two catches. First, Dalkowski had no idea where the ball was going. And second, he drank. But the potential always made the problems feel surmountable.

The Orioles signed Dalkowski out of New Britain, Connecticut, for a $4,000 bonus in 1957. He wore Coke-bottle glasses and looked unintimidating, but his freakish flexibility allowed him to whip the ball ferociously to home plate. In high school, his fastball was so electric that classmates called it the radio pitch. "He had long arms, big hands, and his delivery was nice and fluid," said high school coach Bill Huber. "He had that whipping action you want." With the stands packed with scouts, he once struck out 24 batters in a high school game, setting a state record.

In his first season, pitching for Kingsport, Tennessee, in the Appalachian League, Dalko struck out 121 and walked 129 in 62 innings. The next year, 203 strikeouts and 207 walks in 104 innings. Ridiculous feats of wild power.

Orioles coaches drove themselves crazy trying to turn this divine talent into performance. They made Dalko throw a 75-pitch bullpen before starts, hoping the fatigue would improve his command. Gave him new glasses. Had him practice with hitters in each batter's box. They fiddled with his pitching motion, his arm movement, his leg kick, and his follow-through. They told him to concentrate. They told him to not concentrate.

Steve's reaction was to overreach, try too much, throw too hard, worry about the game ahead, and thus slip back into old habits and old results. Nobody thought to ask Steve how he was doing, or tried to get him meaningful help for his alcoholism.

Weaver believed the Orioles were confusing Dalko, and simplified his mission. He told him to take some juice off his fastball, throw sliders instead of curveballs, and focus on throwing strikes. Weaver, who was still drinking plenty himself, said he understood the need to hit the bottle but begged Steve to not drink before he pitched. "You won't live to be thirty-three," he warned him.

Steve came from a family of alcoholics and started boozing in ninth grade. Weaver took midnight phone calls telling him Crazy Steve was sleeping on somebody's lawn or was in the drunk tank downtown. Dutifully, he would crawl out of bed and go after him. Four times in three seasons, Weaver bailed Dalkowski out of jail.

Steve had an iron constitution and was capable of drinking all night and running wind sprints in the morning. When Steve was intoxicated, he resented Weaver as an authority figure, referring to him as "that friggin' midget." In sober moments, he praised his manager as the best he'd ever had. "He handled me with tough love," recalled Dalkowski. "He told me to run a lot and don't drink on the night you pitch. Then he gave me the ball and said, 'Good luck.'"

In 1962, Weaver said, he "finally made Dalkowski understand one thing when I told him for the millionth time: 'Steve, if you don't throw the ball over the white thing and the batters don't swing—you lose.'"

Weaver's message worked. In 1962, Dalkowski ended the regular season at Elmira with a 7-10 record, including 6 shutouts, 8 complete games, and a 3.04 ERA. For the first time in his career, he walked fewer batters than innings pitched: 144 walks and 190 strikeouts in 160 innings. Elmira celebrated the new Dalko. Reporters asked Steve what happened. What was he doing differently? "I wish I knew," he told them after a shutout. "I think I'm throwing the same but I'm not pumping as hard as I used to. Maybe that's good. . . . Maybe that's the answer. . . . I just don't know. . . . I wish I did."

Dalkowski helped Elmira rebound from a slow start and win the playoff title in 1962 for the first time since 1943. Dalton was delighted. Part of the Oriole Way was winning in the minor leagues. If young prospects could learn to win together at lower levels as *teams*, the thinking went, they could do it in Baltimore. The town buzzed with excitement. Each player received a playoff bonus of $50, funded by a twenty-five-cent surcharge on playoff tickets. "I feel great, great, great," Weaver told reporters.

At Moretti's, an Elmira watering hole where Earl drank after games, he befriended a Pioneers director named Jack Crandall, who kept team statistics. Crandall proposed sorting out box scores and compiling data on how each Elmira pitcher and hitter fared against every team in the league. "I started keeping the box scores, then decided I'd compile the figures—just to see how they compared," Crandall explained. Eventually, Weaver used the reports to make lineup and pitching decisions. "But can I trust a Yankees fan?" he sometimes joked as he accepted Crandall's files.

Crandall's numbers fed Earl's strategic imagination and hunger for an edge. When Crandall died in 2021, his *Star-Gazette* obituary noted: "He helped Earl Weaver in Elmira and Baltimore make decisions on best player and pitcher matchups using the analytics he developed, which was a precursor to the analytics commonly used in baseball today." That's overstating the case. Crandall's numbers were crude by modern standards, but they planted a seed in Weaver's mind. What looks like genius to later generations is usually a master craftsman with a sharp eye for great ideas.

After the 1962 season, Weaver got an offer he couldn't refuse: $3,600 to manage three months in Venezuela, for an owner named Antonio Harerra, who wore a big white hat and a white suit with baggy pants, "like a fugitive from an old Warner Brothers movie," Weaver recalled. "Harerra didn't speak English, but his GM translated. There were only seven Americans on the club, the rest were local players who couldn't understand me."

Meanwhile, Steve Dalkowski seemed headed to the Show. In March 1963, he dominated the star-studded Yankees in a spring training game, striking out Roger Maris and Mickey Mantle. "After the game, the Yankees stars all yukked it up in the clubhouse, imitating each other's bailout moves," said George Vecsey, who covered the game for the *New York Times*.

But in that game, Dalkowski felt his left elbow snap after a pitch. Injured and depressed, he drank beer for breakfast and behaved even more erratically. Weaver stopped bailing him out of jail.

The Pioneers finished second in 1963, another strong showing for a Weaver team. Dalko sat out most of the season. In 1964, Earl Weaver arrived in Elmira toward the end of February. Again, Dalko dominated the conversation. "Let it suffice that he is the greatest unharnessed pitching talent ever to set foot on the mound," lamented Weaver. He remained unharnessed.

The Orioles released Dalkowski. He moved to California and worked as a migrant farmworker picking grapes, oranges, and lemons, digging potatoes and chopping cotton, and hit the bottle. He developed alcohol-related dementia and finished his life in a Connecticut nursing home. He died at age eighty of COVID-19 in 2020. His career numbers: 46 wins and 80 losses, 1,324 strikeouts, and 1,236 walks in 956 innings.

The fall of Dalkowski wasn't the only loss Weaver suffered in Elmira. Like many baseball marriages, his union to Jane had always been fraught. They were apart ten months a year, and when they had to manage anything together, they ended up screaming at each other. The divorce sent Earl down the drain emotionally. "I had to really buckle up and watch the beer because I was depressed and feeling a ton of guilt about the loss of my three kids," he recalled. The experience matured him, somewhat. Later, Weaver reflected: "You must remember that anyone under 30—especially a ballplayer—is an adolescent. I never got close to being an adult until I was 32."

After games in Elmira, players partied at bars like Moretti's and at a place called Sheiks Oasis on nearby Seneca Lake. Earl met a fun-loving secretary who was also divorced named Marianna Osgood. Soon they were dating. In 1964, they married. Pat Santarone was best man. With Marianna's daughter, Kim, they formed a new family. Earl bought his first house, for $6,000, a mile from the stadium. It was still standing when I visited in 2021, a tiny working-class bungalow with plastic siding.

In the fall of 1963, Earl gave baseball a break and returned to St. Louis. He stayed with his parents and picked his kids up after school to take them for a hamburger or movie. They bowled on Sunday afternoons. Weaver took a four-week training course in selling insurance. Maybe he would stay in St. Louis to be closer to his children. That life was not for him. "By the time I finished I didn't believe in any of the malarkey," he said. "I wasn't about to go out and lie to old people for a buck. Or young people, either." Faced with a choice between family and baseball, Earl Weaver could only pick baseball.

He returned to Elmira to manage the Pioneers—and sell cars. Working an offseason job for the Elmira Chrysler-Plymouth dealership suited Weaver's chatty, smart-alecky, bantering persona, and his skill at reading people. Weaver realized that, if he could keep conversations going, they'd hang in there with him and become more likely to buy a car. "You know, I think we're gonna put together another pennant winner this season. You like baseball, I hope," he'd say. Once the relationship was anchored, once Earl had engaged their trust, he could put on the hard sell. "This car was made for you! You gotta have this car! I wouldn't sell it to anyone but you! Get behind the wheel . . . yeah. You want this car, and you're definitely gonna have it."

Marty Chalk, a former public address announcer in Elmira, bought a 1964 Plymouth Sport Fury convertible off Weaver for $4,000. "He was very persuasive, a hell of a car salesman," said Chalk. "He called me a few times to make sure I was satisfied."

Weaver's quick, curious mind latched on to the pop psychology of the 1950s and 1960s. Managers, after all, were gurus in their own way. Weaver read Dale Carnegie's business classic *How to Win Friends and Influence People* (which was passed around the Orioles front office much like hit business books are today), Morey Bernstein's *The Search for Bridey Murphy*, about an Irishwoman who regressed to a previous life, and the books by Edgar Cayce, a midcentury psychic and clairvoyant known as the "Sleeping Prophet."

Weaver was likely also inspired by the St. Louis Browns hiring a psychologist and hypnotist named David F. Tracy in 1950. The St. Louis papers and *Sporting News* covered Tracy as a brave new experiment in managing baseball players and teams. The doctor, who was more like an Old West traveling con man than a proper psychologist, was a bust. Two months into the 1950 season, with the team at 8-25, the Browns fired him. They finished the season 58-96.

In 1951, Tracy published a book about his experiences with the Browns, *The Psychologist at Bat*. He recommended a lot of yelling. "The fellow who's hollering encouragement to his pitcher and teammates can't be worrying about himself at the same time," he wrote. "While he's releasing nervous tension through his vocal cords, he's simultaneously directing his teammates' attention away from themselves. That's why a pepper pot like Eddie Stanky is such a great asset to the Giants, or any team he plays with."

Weaver claimed to have a gift for hypnosis, and to have hypnotized hundreds of people. As a manager, he never hypnotized any ballplayers. But, he said, "I have tried to reach the subconscious by planting suggestions in any manner, shape, or form I could come up with." With baseball players, he said, "you have to plant the belief that *he can do it*." Whether he was selling cars or coaching young baseball players, Weaver was fascinated by what made people tick. "I would have a million messages to convey to youngsters," Weaver recalled. "What made a great teacher was his or her ability to reach a student's mind."

In one successful month in Elmira, Weaver sold twenty used cars and earned $1,700 in commissions. For the first time, he no longer felt broke. Instead of driving an old Chevy without a reverse gear that he sometimes had to push to park, he drove a company car. "I had that job two winters and loved it," Weaver recalled. "I knew I'd found a profession I could step right into if I had to leave baseball."

But he wasn't leaving baseball. Not with the way the Pioneers kept winning. The team finished 83-55 in 1965, just one game behind Pittsfield, an affiliate team of the Boston Red Sox. The players called Earl "Popeye." Ron Stone, an outfielder, recalled that "Weaver would stand in the dugout chain-smoking and yelling 'Jesus Christ, oh fucking mighty,' but he was a guy who would always fight for you, a very intelligent manager."

On May 8, 1965, Weaver managed a twenty-seven-inning game, then a professional baseball record. It broke the Eastern League record by six innings. The game against Springfield started at 3 p.m. in front of 386 spectators, although a hundred wandered in around 7 p.m., in the eleventh inning, thinking it was the start of a night game. The game was scoreless for twenty-five innings. Both teams scored a run apiece in the twenty-sixth, before the Pioneers walked it off on an infield ground ball in the twenty-seventh for a 2–1 win. Miraculously, the whole thing took less than seven hours.

At the end of the 1965 season, the Orioles promoted Weaver to Triple-A Rochester. Weaver wrote Elmira a thank-you letter: "Never in all my travels in baseball, which includes 40 states, the Dominican Republic, South America and Panama have I enjoyed a community as much as I have enjoyed Elmira," he wrote.

As he prepared to climb the final rungs of the Orioles' minor-league system, Weaver was only thirty-five. He had managed winning teams in nine straight seasons. But there were concerns in Baltimore about the young manager's temper.

One night in Elmira, Weaver got so mad he threw a bunch of bats onto the field. Another time, Weaver, ejected from a game, yanked third base out of the ground on his way to the clubhouse. There were no spare bases, and Weaver returned the base only when the umpires threatened his team with a forfeit. He made a habit of covering up home plate with dirt. Once, he lay on top of the plate. The umpires weren't paying any attention to it, he pointed out. Another time, he sat atop the plate like a Buddha.

Dalton took his manager out after a game and tried to talk some sense into him

"You just can't keep badgering the umpires the way you are."

"They're wrong."

Despite his chronic contrarianism, Earl had found stability and happiness in Elmira. One of his players, Frank Peters, recalled talking with Weaver at a motel in Connecticut. He asked his manager what his ambitions were. "Make it to Triple-A Rochester and sell Chryslers in the offseason," Weaver responded.

That's not how Dalton saw things. Weaver was incorrigible. He antagonized umpires and sometimes drank too much, but Weaver was a winner, maybe a genius, and in Elmira, his protégé had proven he could be a big leaguer. Weaver was dealing with "guys who, in some cases, weren't going to make the majors and weren't happy about it," said Dalton. "Earl took those guys and won. And when he starts doing *that*, taking castoffs and misfits and making a championship club out of them, you had to have respect for what he'd been doing."

Earl Weaver first managed his famous frenemy
Jim Palmer in Rochester.

12

PRINCE HAL

Rochester, New York, 1966–1967

Thou hast the most unsavory similes, and art indeed the most compara-
tive, rascalliest, sweet young prince.

—*Henry IV, Part 1*, Act 1, Scene 2

In Rochester, a thriving industrial city that was home to Kodak, Xerox, and
Western Union, Earl Weaver first managed the hot young pitcher with whom
he would form one of the most volatile, iconic, memorable relationships in
baseball history. They had encountered each other in minor-league spring
training in Thomasville, but this was their first time working together on a
team.

What made the famous frenemies' bickering compelling was that they
were so successful. From 1969 to 1982, Jim Palmer won the most games of any
pitcher in the American League. His manager, Weaver, won the most games
of any manager. Their fights begged the question you always had to ask about
Earl: How could there be this much drama—and also this much winning?

Palmer, tall, handsome, born rich, was everything little Earl was not.
Palmer didn't cuss like a sailor, get hammered, or gamble at dog tracks. He
pursued alternate careers as an underwear model and silk-tongued broadcaster. Born in New York City, he was adopted as a baby by a wealthy garment

executive named Moe Wiesen and his wife, Polly. The family lived on Park Avenue, and Palmer learned to play baseball by playing catch with his butler in Central Park. Wiesen died when Jim was nine years old. Polly moved to California and remarried a Hollywood actor named Max Palmer. Jim took his name.

After excelling at football, basketball, and baseball in high school, Palmer signed with the Orioles at age seventeen in 1963 and made his big-league debut in 1965. In 1966, at age twenty, he starred in the Orioles' World Series win over the Dodgers. But when he went to spring training in 1967, he couldn't pitch without pain. He believed he had developed biceptal tendonitis from painting a wall in his house. His arm had been bothering him since before the World Series, but cortisone injections had seen him through.

On June 19, 1967, the Orioles sent Palmer to Rochester to rehab. The official diagnosis: a pinched tendon, to be treated with heat, cortisone shots, and other medication. And instead of resting on an injured list, the plan was for Palmer to go down to the minor leagues and pitch himself out of pain.

During Palmer's first game, against the Reds' farm team, the Buffalo Bisons, Weaver walked to the mound and told him to challenge future Hall of Fame catcher Johnny Bench with the bases loaded. "Throw the ball over the middle of the plate," said Weaver. "This guy's nothing." Bench blasted a grand slam. In his major-league career, Palmer had never given up a grand slam, and he never would. He blamed his young manager. "I learned a lot from Earl Weaver," he recalled. "The first thing I learned was that he didn't know a thing about pitching."

Rochester has a rich baseball tradition. Frederick Douglass, the famous abolitionist, played semipro there in the nineteenth century. The Red Wings had been a Cardinals farm team from 1929 to 1960; Stan Musial played there in 1941. In 1957, the St. Louis Cardinals sold the Red Wings to Morrie Silver, a thriving local record and appliance store owner who is still a hero in Rochester for keeping Triple-A baseball in the city. In 1961, he contracted with the Orioles for Rochester to serve as their farm team, a relationship that lasted until 2002.

The Red Wings were struggling. Silver was delighted with Weaver's appointment—the screaming banty rooster was a minor-league owner's dream.

All summer, fans relished the sight of Earl rushing out to fight for his troops. He was the star of the show. In two seasons with Rochester, umpires ejected Weaver 21 times. Pitchers would "sit in the bullpen and wager a dinner or a beer on the inning we thought Earl would get tossed," said Rochester relief pitcher Paul Knechtges. "Sometimes we felt sorry for the umpire because we knew what it was to have Earl get in your face. Believe me, it wasn't a pleasant experience." Knechtges thought it was part of a wider strategy. "That was Earl. Always looking for any edge he could find. It was all part of his competitiveness. I don't care if it was baseball, golf, or cards."

One edge: a complete intolerance for poor control on the mound. When pitcher Jerry Herron didn't throw strikes, Weaver screamed at him: "If you walk the next guy just pack your bags and go back to Elmira. I'm not even going to come out to the mound. Walk the next batter and you're gone. Just get the hell out and go to Elmira." Herron didn't throw strikes. The Orioles demoted him to Elmira. The players didn't love Weaver, but he didn't care. "He was trying to win a pennant, not a popularity contest," said Carl Steinfeldt, an assistant general manager at Rochester.

Managers have always been essential to a minor-league franchise's success. "The ideal manager for us is an outgoing, great baseball guy who knows how to win ballgames," said Dan Mason, general manager of the Red Wings in 2023. That was Earl. Getting thrown out of games can be a popular move, said Mason. "It's entertainment. I like to tell those guys if you put on a good show, don't worry about it."

Weaver's fame spread to cities around the league. In Richmond, Weaver got so irate at the organist playing during his hitters' at-bats that he ordered the umpire to make him stop. On the Red Wings' next trip to Richmond, on August 3, 1966, Richmond organized "Earl Weaver Music Appreciation Night," booking a Dixieland jazz band and offering free admission to anybody who brought an instrument. Weaver thought it was hilarious. "The noisiest night I've ever been through in baseball," he said. "Since then, I have been dear to the hearts of the people in Richmond."

Weaver guided the 1966 Red Wings, a powerhouse team starring future big leaguers Mark Belanger and Mike Epstein, to a tie with one game to play. On the final day, the Red Wings led 10–2 against Syracuse when Weaver walked out to coach third base in the bottom of the eighth. The fans gave him a thunderous ovation. He hadn't heard anything like it since he was a spectator himself at Sportsman's Park.

Syracuse scored four runs and almost came from behind to win. The score was 10–6, and the game ended on a dramatic catch in center field. The Red Wings were champions. After the game, the fans summoned Earl for a curtain call. The failed minor-league second baseman was overwhelmed. "When I stepped out of the dugout on that empty field and heard that noise and, waving my arms, looked around into all those ecstatic faces, for a moment I couldn't breathe," he recalled. "It was as if all the oxygen had been sucked out of that ballpark, but it didn't matter. I was inhaling pure joy."

The Red Wings weren't the only winners that year. The Orioles, twelve years after moving from St. Louis, rebuilt by Paul Richards and his army of coaches like Earl Weaver, swept the Los Angeles Dodgers 4–0 to win the 1966 World Series.

After the 1966 season, Hiram Cuevas, the owner of Puerto Rico's Santurce Crabbers, hired Earl for $6,000 to manage his team. The stacked Crabbers, led by Hall of Fame slugger Orlando Cepeda, finished second in the regular season and then won the playoffs. An impressed Cepeda put in a good word for Weaver with the Orioles at the winter meetings.

In Puerto Rico, his third Caribbean assignment after the Dominican Republic in 1955 and Venezuela in 1962, Weaver discovered future Orioles catcher Elrod Hendricks. "For God's sake, draft him, Harry," he pleaded with Dalton. "We ain't gonna find nobody like this SOB—a catcher who can hit over twenty home runs a year. If Hendricks doesn't make the Orioles, he'll hit a pile of home runs for me in Rochester with that 310-foot fence in right."

In the four-team Puerto Rican winter league, Crabber fans cheered for Earl's feisty, fighting style. They called him Mickey Rooney, a nickname Weaver despised. "This was Earl's first chance to manage big-league ballplayers," said Larry Haney, one of his players. "He wasn't intimidated. Earl was a quality manager wherever he managed and the players had to adjust to his style of play." The Orioles developed a working agreement with Santurce. It was Roberto Clemente's home club, but in the 1971 World Series, against Clemente's Pirates, Santurce fans supported the Orioles.

In 1967, Earl returned to Rochester to manage the Red Wings. They kept on winning. Morrie Silver organized "Earl Weaver Day." Over 10,000 fans watched Silver give Earl a check for $5,000 and make a speech calling him "the finest manager and one of the finest men I've ever known." Earl gushed back. "No major-league manager has better fans than I," he said. "I am the luckiest man alive." The team finished tied for first but lost a playoff.

After the season, Earl was awarded the Orioles' Fred Hofmann Award for "service and dedication to baseball." Weaver's performance had helped save minor-league baseball in Rochester. After losing money in 1965, the Red Wings turned a profit of over $100,000 in 1966 and over $150,000 in 1967. In 1968, after Weaver left, it dropped to $45,100. Attendance increased in 1967 to an average of 4,616 per game, from an average of 3,245 in 1965. Earl Weaver wasn't just a winner; he was something just as exciting for a big-league team: a drawing card with stage charisma.

In Baltimore, the Orioles were struggling with a losing record after their World Series season. In late 1967, Harry Dalton ordered his superscout Jim Russo to spend a few weeks on the road following the major-league team. "You could see they were not in good physical condition," said Russo. "After winning the Series, they had become complacent. Even Brooks Robinson, as great and as dedicated as he was, had gotten overweight. The problem was obvious, but the coaches and manager were too close to see it. This was the first time we thought about making Earl the manager."

After the 1967 season, Hiram Cuevas invited Earl back to Puerto Rico and gave him a $1,500 raise. Weaver won a pennant thanks to the hot bat of Hendricks, whom the Orioles finally signed after the season.

After Earl and his family returned to Elmira from Puerto Rico, Dalton phoned Earl and invited him to drive down to Baltimore. Earl met Orioles owner Jerry Hoffberger. Later that day, Dalton called Earl and told him they had named him first-base coach on the 1968 Baltimore Orioles. Earl hugged Marianna and shouted, "I'm finally going to the major leagues!"

Older fans in Rochester still remember Weaver as one of the city's all-time baseball legends. Along the concourse of what is now called Innovative Field, his likeness still adorns a banner hanging from the rafter, next to his childhood hero, Stan Musial.

Part 4

BALTIMORE

13

BIG LEAGUER

Baltimore, 1968

There comes a time in every man's life, and I've had plenty of them.

—Casey Stengel

Twenty years after he homered on the first pitch he saw in the coalfields of southern Illinois, Earl Weaver, a big-league first-base coach, arrived in Baltimore as the city reeled from the murder of Rev. Martin Luther King Jr. Before the season, Earl rented an apartment at the Colony Apartments in Towson, Maryland, north of Baltimore. The suburbs beckoned to Americans of Earl Weaver's class and race. Over 200,000 white residents had left Baltimore city since World War II, shuffling into ranch houses and two-car garages, getting away from the narrow streets occupied by Black Americans who had fled the lands in the South where white farmers in the century before had violently enslaved their families.

Baltimore had once been the second-biggest city in America. Babe Ruth was born in 1895 into a dense metropolis, where people still spoke German in the streets, corner grocers sold local vegetables, and bookies took bets at local taverns. Just as the Mississippi River molded St. Louis, the Chesapeake Bay gave Baltimore a distinctive character, blowing salty air on humid nights, drawing residents into its sleepy coves, and laying a mouthwatering bounty of crab cakes and oysters.

Since its beginnings, Baltimore, Washington's Brooklyn, had embraced its second-city status, and the chip on the shoulder that went with it. Because it wasn't New York or Washington, D.C., Baltimore had the freedom to deplore, as H. L. Mencken wrote, "American piety, stupidity, tin-pot morality and cheap chauvinism in all their forms." In other words, an ethos to fit Earl Weaver. In Baltimore's row houses and side-street taverns, pool hustlers and Sparrows Point steelworkers drank beer, bet the ponies, and cheered the baseball Orioles and football Colts.

But in the spring of 1968, people in Baltimore found it hard to focus on baseball. On April 4, James Earl Ray murdered King in Memphis, Tennessee. That day, Washington erupted. A day later, Chicago. Baltimore exploded on April 6, and the unrest lasted a full week. Angry Black residents marched in Baltimore streets. Police pushed back, and in the resulting conflict, six people died and seven hundred were injured. Governor Spiro Agnew called in the National Guard, which included Orioles relief pitcher Pete Richert. Shortstop Mark Belanger, also in the Guard, was assigned to a unit in D.C.

The Orioles delayed Opening Day to April 10. In the middle of riots, only 22,050 fans showed up at Memorial Stadium to watch the Orioles beat the Oakland Athletics, 3–1. Earl Weaver, wearing number 4 in honor of one of his heroes, 1940s Cardinals shortstop Marty Marion, coached first base uneventfully.

It wasn't only America that was changing. Major League Baseball was not the same operation Earl Weaver almost joined in 1952. There were now 20 teams, not 16, and St. Louis was no longer the southernmost or westernmost big-league city. There were Braves in Atlanta, Twins in Minnesota, and A's, Angels, Dodgers, and Giants in California. Teams traveled cross-country on jet airplanes. Instead of bidding on the best young players they could find on school and sandlot nines, big-league clubs since 1965 had picked them in annual amateur drafts.

Fans who headed to ballgames no longer hopped trolleys and stopped by the bar for a shot of Jack and a bet with the local bookie. They lived in car-centric neighborhoods and drove highways to games. In 1967, the first Super Bowl led the NFL's rush into Americans' living rooms. Baby-boomer ballplayers, born into a more prosperous land than Earl Weaver, were entering the big leagues with college educations and higher expectations.

Before the 1968 season, Marvin Miller, director of the Major League Baseball Players Association, secured baseball's first collective bargaining agreement, raising the minimum salary to $10,000 from $7,000. Miller had been chief economist for the United Steelworkers union in Pittsburgh before agreeing to direct the players' union in 1966. He faced an uphill climb persuading ballplayers, young, conservative, and skeptical of the labor movement, to embrace the union. He spent every spring training speaking to teams in clubhouses, making his case. In the end, Miller achieved one of the most extraordinary victories in the history of American labor. When he took over the union in 1966, the big-league minimum was $6,000 and the average salary $19,000. A decade later, he had secured free agency, and players were signing million-dollar deals. His work revolutionized American sports and inspired athletes in basketball, football, and other sports to fight for their own riches.

The Orioles' manager to start the 1968 season was forty-five-year-old Hank Bauer, a former Yankees outfielder who had skippered the O's since 1964 and won Manager of the Year awards in 1964 and 1966, and a World Series in 1966. Old Fistface had earned two Bronze Stars and two Purple Hearts as a Marine in World War II. He'd grown up in the 1920s to immigrant parents from Austria-Hungary in an even tougher part of St. Louis than Weaver, across the Mississippi in Illinois.

The 1967 season had been a disaster for the Orioles. After winning the World Series, the team finished in sixth place, with 76 wins and 85 losses. Harry Dalton had tried to get Bauer to resign during the offseason. He refused. Owner Jerold Hoffberger didn't want to fire Bauer and owe him $50,000 to do nothing, so he kept his manager. Still, Bauer knew that the Orioles would have to play well in 1968 or else he'd lose his job. He held a tricky hand. Frank Robinson was still the centerpiece of the team in 1968, but he was suffering from blurred vision after a tough slide on a double play in 1967. Star pitchers Jim Palmer, Wally Bunker, and Dave McNally were all sidelined with sore arms.

Weaver wasn't the only new face. Dalton had taken Weaver's suggestion and appointed as pitching coach George Bamberger, an unflappable maestro of hurlers from Staten Island who preached relentless strike-throwing. Bamberger remained on staff as the Orioles' pitching coach until the end of the 1977 season.

Baseball in 1968, the Year of the Pitcher, was dominated by hurlers mowing down hitters like bowling pins. Bob Gibson of the Cardinals set the modern ERA record with 1.12, and the Tigers' Denny McLain won 31 games, the last pitcher to win over 30.

In spring training, Weaver and his new boss, Hank Bauer, kept their distance. Bauer made it clear that Weaver was a second-class citizen, forcing him to pick up his own check when the staff went for dinner. Earl hit fungoes and flipped batting practice. The only thing Bauer asked Weaver to do was talk to Boog Powell about his hitting. Earl was happy with baseball's softest job, coaching first base, for a salary of $15,000 a year. "Best job I ever had," he said. "I was in the majors, getting in time toward my pension. It was nice."

Earl Weaver's new workplace was Memorial Stadium, a no-frills horseshoe-shaped park in northeast Baltimore.

The stadium, the only big-league yard without a roof over the upper deck, never lost its sweet minor-league feel and the aura of a garden where working-class Baltimoreans of all races could take their kids for a summer picnic. It felt *green*, because of the wide, beautifully manicured outfield and the cedars, cypress, and spruces behind the scoreboard. With a constant breeze, ballgames there felt dreamy and cool. Vendors grilled burgers, sausages, and crab cakes at their stalls, perfuming the stands with the smells of a family cookout.

The city erected the brick-and-concrete Memorial Stadium in 1949 on the site of an older field. The lobby contained dirt from every foreign country where an American soldier was buried. An art deco sign on the façade said: TIME WILL NOT DIM THE GLORY OF THEIR DEEDS. An urn in the lobby contained dirt from American cemeteries around the world. Inside, the clubhouses were cramped, and the stadium had city problems, like rats "big enough to stand flatfooted and screw a turkey," according to Boog Powell.

Like the Sportsman's Park of Weaver's childhood, Memorial Stadium was in spirit a public park. Sunk between its surroundings, you didn't see the façade until you turned a corner a few blocks away, and there it was, towering above, the church of baseball. It belonged to the neighborhood. There were no highways running alongside. Parking was tight. People who lived nearby sat on their porches listening to games on the radio. When they heard the roar of the crowd, they stopped talking and turned up the sound.

"The neighborhoods lapped up on three sides so that it always felt as if the Orioles were playing on the lawn of the biggest house on the block on a midsummer's night, after all the kids and dads are out throwing a few more balls around before it gets dark," wrote Peter Richmond in *Ballpark*. "Memorial's link to the gardens and the grass and the small wage-earner's streets was no small thing."

The 1968 Orioles started 43–37, 12 games behind the Tigers. It wasn't a terrible record, but by June, Dalton was persuaded that the ex-Marine Bauer had gotten too soft. At the All-Star break in Houston, Dalton made his move. He called Weaver at the Colony. He and Marianna were lying by the pool. They'd been relaxing, eating short ribs and noodles and playing gin rummy. The apartment manager told Weaver he had an important call. Could he call back immediately? "The person wants to talk to you right away," said the manager. "He said it was very, very important."

"Earl, we've made a decision," said Dalton. "I want you to become manager of the Baltimore baseball club. I want you and Marianna to check in to a motel. When the news breaks, there'll be a thousand calls."

Weaver was nervous. Dalton had picked him over more experienced candidates like third-base coach Billy Hunter and free agents like Yogi Berra, Gene Mauch, and Danny Murtaugh. Would the players respect him? Play hard for him? Win?

Dalton flew to Kansas City to fire Bauer, and then returned to Baltimore, where his wife cooked a late dinner and he and Weaver negotiated a salary.

Dalton offered $20,000, a $5,000 raise. Weaver said no, because he would have to give up his job making $7,500 managing in Puerto Rico.

Dalton agreed to pay Weaver $28,000. Bauer had been making $50,000.

"There is no happiness" in releasing Bauer, but the team had to change course to improve its play, Dalton said at the press conference the next day. "Today the Baltimore organization steps off on a new course. . . . We are appointing a major-league manager—signed into, developed, trained, and promoted through our own organization." Dalton added that Weaver had managed 15 of the 25 players presently on the club. "In short, Earl Weaver is a winner. He always has taken talent and made it into a winner or a strong contender."

How could he fix the hitting? reporters asked.

"I plan to scramble more with things like the bunt, the hit-and-run, and stolen bases in the early innings," said Weaver. One headline: "Weaver Won't Wait for Big Inning."

Of course, he would one day become famous for waiting for the big inning. But Earl Weaver, only thirty-seven years old, terrifyingly young for a big-league manager, was a man always open to transformation, unafraid of changing his mind, and gifted with the rare combination of ambition, knowledge, and a healthy beginner's mindset. He hung a sign in the clubhouse: "It's what you learn after you know it all that counts."

14

FRANK

Baltimore, 1968

I think it's a tragedy that baseball is still wallowing in the nineteenth century, saying Negroes can't manage white ballplayers.

—Jackie Robinson in 1968

In a city melting with racial conflict, Earl Weaver immediately promoted two Black players, Don Buford and Elrod Hendricks, over two white players, and started a third, Frank Robinson, on his course to becoming big-league baseball's first Black manager. These were not political moves: Weaver was interested in winning, not racial justice, but he navigated Baltimore's racial tensions while the city was still a powder keg, and his championing of Black players is part of his legacy, and his evolution a reflection of the complexity of race in America.

Weaver had been born into an all-white neighborhood in north St. Louis, and attended segregated ballgames at Sportsman's Park. As a young man, racial slurs like the N-word were part of his vocabulary, as they were for most white southerners. He had played most of his minor-league career in the Jim Crow South, where local governments and police forces enforced racial segregation into the 1960s.

But as he ascended baseball's ranks as a manager, Weaver evolved. "I came into baseball bearing all of the beliefs and prejudices of a kid from St. Louis," he recalled. "I had little experience with Black people and none with Hispanics, yet I had no problem discovering that some people were good people, whether they attended your church or voted for your candidate or dressed to your style or danced to your music. Baseball gave me the opportunity to open my mind."

The 1960s and 1970s were the high point of African American players. In 1968, 15 percent of big leaguers were Black, up from zero in 1946 and 9 percent in 1960. It would top out at around 18 percent from 1975 to 1986. (In the 1990s, however, the rise of the NBA and NFL, coupled with the migration of baseball culture to suburban Little Leagues and private travel clubs, diminished the participation of Black youth in baseball. In the 2020s, only around 7 percent of MLB players have been African American.)

The Orioles' Black stars loved Earl. And he loved them back. Players used to joke that Orioles star Eddie Murray was Earl's favorite son. Nineteen seventies Orioles outfielders Reggie Jackson, Don Baylor, and Ken Singleton all said Weaver was their favorite manager. Ken Dixon, a Black pitcher for the Orioles from 1984 to 1987, told me Weaver stood out from other white managers and coaches because he held players to a high standard without disrespecting them. "Once he called me in his office, and he told me I wasn't concentrating enough," said Dixon. "He looked at me and said, 'Now do your fucking job. I'm counting on you.'" By contrast, one Orioles coach called Dixon "boy" and spit at his feet. "You didn't get pats on the back from Earl, and he didn't pull any punches, but he was still able to tell me he was counting on *me*," said Dixon. "He was tough on me, but he talked to me like a man."

To have any shot at turning around the Orioles in 1968, the new manager needed to win over Frank Robinson. The Hall of Fame outfielder, nicknamed the Black Ty Cobb for his fierceness, was born in Oakland and educated at McClymonds High School, along with other superstar athletes like Bill Russell and Vada Pinson. The Cincinnati Reds signed Robinson when he was nineteen, and almost immediately he became one of the best players in the National League.

Peeved at being traded to Baltimore, because Reds owner Bill DeWitt thought he was "not a young thirty," Robinson had torched the American League in 1966, winning the American League Triple Crown with a .316 average, 49 home runs, and 122 RBI. In six years with the Orioles, he would lead the team to four World Series and two titles. He was the Orioles' first Black superstar and inaugurated an era of racial harmony on the team.

But racial prejudice in Baltimore lingered. Black residents, even Frank Robinson, struggled to find housing. Robinson's wife lost an apartment because she showed up at a place where the landlord had taken the meeting thinking she was the wife of *Brooks* Robinson. Frank threatened to quit the team. With the help of the Orioles front office, the Robinsons found a home to rent that was owned by a Black Baltimore Colts football player.

By the time Weaver got to the Orioles, Robinson had talked for years of becoming baseball's first Black manager. "The prejudice against Negroes in baseball is dying to a certain extent but it is still there," he said in 1967. "It is just a matter of time before some owner breaks the color line with a manager. . . . I'd love to be one."

Frustrated by injury and his poor performance, Robinson was in a funk, and refusing to sign baseballs for fans. Weaver put in a crucial call with his friends in Puerto Rico and helped Frank get his old job as manager of the Santurce Crabbers for the 1968–1969 winter-ball season. Frank promised to back Weaver in the clubhouse—and set an example for other players by signing baseballs.

Over the next few years, Earl made countless public statements that Robinson deserved to manage in the big leagues. When the Washington Senators in 1969 named Hall of Fame outfielder Ted Williams manager, Weaver said Robinson was just as qualified. "Williams' coming back is great for baseball," he said. "We all know that. On the other hand, Frank Robinson went down to the Puerto Rican league last winter and got the feel of managing and handling players. This I feel qualifies him to manage just as much as Ted, perhaps more." On April 8, 1975, Frank Robinson finally made his debut as manager of the Cleveland Indians. Jackie Robinson's widow, Rachel, threw out the first pitch during a ceremony before the game.

Robinson praised Weaver. "The man made it a complete club," the out-fielder said in 1970. "He has 25 players, and they all come out to the park knowing they may be used. You know—pinch-run, pinch-hit, pitch to one man, catch an inning, go in the outfield late in the game." Weaver and Robinson were not close friends, but they respected each other as baseball men; Weaver later hired Robinson as an Orioles coach. At the plate in 1968, Frank Robinson caught fire under Weaver. After hitting 4 home runs and slugging .398 in the first half of 1968, Robinson hit 11 long balls and slugged .476 for the rest of the season.

Weaver named another Black player, Don Buford, a little-known switch-hitter from Texas hitting .234, as his everyday leadoff hitter, because he drew walks. Weaver valued walks and on-base percentage years before other managers. He prodded Buford to take even more pitches. Over the next 14 seasons, the Orioles, under Weaver, would lead the major leagues in bases on balls.

In Weaver's first game as Orioles manager, on July 11, in front of only 6,499 people at Memorial Stadium, he started Buford in center field and batted him leadoff. Buford walked and scored in the first and then homered in the fifth as Dave McNally shut out the Washington Senators, 2–0. After the game, Weaver again promised that the Orioles would "scramble" for runs.

He said: "By scrambling more, maybe we can produce one or two more runs a game. You know, steal a base, bunt for a hit. It'll take the pressure off our pitchers." He added: "I would rather lose while making a move than just sit and watch us lose."

He'd have them playing small ball. This was, after all, 1968.

Whatever his methods, Earl Weaver, big-league manager, was 1-0.

Weaver made the Buford move permanent. Buford hit .298 with 11 home runs, 45 runs scored, and 45 walks in the last 82 games of the season. He finished the season with 15 home runs and a .367 on-base percentage, when the league average was .297.

Weaver also played the catcher he'd discovered in Puerto Rico, Elrod Hendricks. He didn't hit as well as Buford, but Weaver gave him 145 plate appearances in the second half, up from 50 under Bauer in the first half. In part-time roles, Hendricks notched 12 home runs in each of the following two seasons.

Meanwhile, Weaver settled into his new role. He played pinochle with his coaches before every game and drank with them afterward. Players could run around and drink and chase women, but they were prohibited from the hotel bar, which belonged to Weaver and his coaches. Weaver, always well prepared, posted the lineup on the clubhouse door before the players arrived. If he used a red pen to make the lineup and the Orioles won, he had to use the same pen the next day. During games, he hovered on the edge of the dugout and paced like a lion surveying the savanna, ducking into the hallway to the clubhouse or behind a pillar to smoke cigarettes between innings.

Weaver cautioned his players not to take needless risks; not to engage in beanball wars or slide too hard into second to break up double plays. He made his outfielders play deeper than the league average: he preferred to give up bloop hits than risk conceding extra-base hits. Singles kept double plays possible, a percentage-based strategic edge. Weaver preached mastering simple tasks, forgetting about yesterday, and playing hard. "The main thing is to keep the players enthusiastic," he said in 1970. "When I walk in the clubhouse, I holler, 'Today's the day we have to win. We have to win the ball game today. That's all we have to do. Whatever we did yesterday don't count.'"

The Orioles won 11 of Earl's first 15 games and went 48-34 to finish the season. National baseball writers noticed the new manager catching fire in Baltimore but struggled to describe him without making fun of his appearance. "Earl Weaver doesn't look like a magician," wrote Dick Young. "He doesn't look like a big league manager. He looks like a basket ball. Not a basket ball player, a basket ball. He is 5-foot-7, when he wears very high spikes, weighs 175 on the tail end of a diet, and when he speaks he sounds as though he has just swallowed a handful of sand. He is a most unheroic figure." One problem: "It is questionable that his minor league color would go on major league TV." If they ever make "The Earl Weaver Story," "Ronald Reagan won't play it," Young concluded. "Mickey Rooney, maybe, if they fatten him up a little."

Toward the end of the 1968 season, Earl paid $28,000 for a modest brick home in a new subdivision called Perry Hall, a northern Baltimore suburb. Marianna and Kim moved in with him before the start of the 1969 season. By buying a house, Weaver violated an axiom baseball managers like to share with fellow members of a job with a famously short shelf life: always rent.

For the 1969 season, the Orioles gave Weaver a one-year contract. After the season, Weaver called Bob Brown, an Orioles PR executive, and asked him if he could help with a project. He wanted printouts of how well each Orioles hitter had batted against every pitcher in the league, and vice versa.

15

THE MIRACLE WAY

Baltimore, 1969

The greatest feeling in the world is to win a major-league game. The second greatest feeling is to lose a major-league game.

—Chuck Tanner

Earl Weaver, manager of the Baltimore Orioles, was still the same nervous little man with a quick mind, dry wit, and dark streak. Still a cussing, smoking, hard-drinking busher, with big-league imposter syndrome. "Believe it or not, Earl Weaver is a worrier," his old buddy Al Mallette reported. "He may not impress people that way because of his flamboyant approach to all matters concerning his life—baseball. But deep down inside, where the pain sometimes stings so much the ex-Pioneer skipper turns to a stomach soother, Weaver is a worrier."

Most newspapers picked the Orioles to finish third. If that happened, Weaver wouldn't last long. The Orioles were in third place when they fired Bauer. The new Baltimore skipper spent January making extra cash by selling Chryslers in Elmira.

Major League Baseball had worries of its own. The 1968 season had been a disaster. With pitchers dominating hitters and putting fans to sleep, attendance had dropped for the third straight season. The National Football

Judge Frank Robinson and the Kangaroo Court.

League was ascendant. To juice things up in 1969, MLB lowered the pitching mound to create more offense. It also split each league into East and West divisions, and added four teams: the Seattle Pilots and Kansas City Royals in the American League, and the San Diego Padres and Montreal Expos in the National League. Meanwhile, players agitated for better pay and work conditions from the owners, a clubby bunch of businessmen who thought their charges should feel lucky to play a boy's game for money.

It didn't help Earl's stress level that his brash young second baseman, Davey Johnson, bragged about using a computer to outmanage him. "Programming the Orioles Makes Weaver Look Bad," said an Associated Press story about Johnson, who was taking computer classes at Johns Hopkins University in Baltimore. Johnson had programmed eight lineups and said the best had him batting second. "Now I know what a manager has to go through," said Johnson. "I don't know whether to tell Weaver, but the sixth worst lineup was the one we used most of the time last season." Johnson later managed 17 years and won 1,372 games for the Mets, Reds, Orioles, Dodgers, and Nationals, and joined the chorus celebrating Weaver's genius.

Weaver resolved his anxieties by bringing to spring training in Florida an intense practice schedule, manic intensity, and complete intolerance for losing meaningless exhibition games. He implemented a rigorous routine based on the structure he had helped develop in Thomasville. Weaver might walk and talk like a car salesman on speed, but he was also an ambitious baseball manager who took his craft seriously. He aggressively played stars like Boog Powell and Frank and Brooks Robinson in exhibition games. The Orioles went 19-5 in the March practice season. "I didn't think I'd get fired in the spring or anything like that," he said. "But I didn't want the folks back in Baltimore to think Weaver was an idiot."

Weaver brought back the Oriole Way. Harry Dalton ordered the Orioles' director of player development, Don Pries, to write up a revised version of the Orioles' instruction manual, *The Oriole Way to Play Baseball*. Intended for every player and team in the organization, it covered every facet of the game, from pitching (throw lots of changeups) to clubhouse rules. Big-league teams had circulated manuals and memos about the right way to play baseball throughout the 1950s and 1960s. What distinguished the Orioles' approach was its thoroughness and, after Weaver took over, the club's dedication to implementing and enforcing the philosophy.

"THIS MANUAL IS PREPARED FOR YOU—USE IT," Pries wrote. "Look upon it as another method of making both the manager and player a much better qualified person in his chosen profession." The Orioles spelled out their plan to find talented athletes, nurture their individual craftmanship, and push them to excel as a team at every level. For all his irascibility, Weaver was a company man who worked well with others and relished his employer's institutional commitment to excellence.

The rules for managers included:

We have committed ourselves for development . . . Let's develop.
Be the best baseball teacher in the world.
Knowledge will overcome fear and indecision.
Be aggressive and enthused.
Create an atmosphere in the individual for the will to win.

Every detail mattered. For example, here's how the Oriole Way described the importance of pitcher fielding: "When a pitcher releases the ball, he is no longer a pitcher but now another infielder and ready to make all the plays." When covering first base, "pitcher should not snatch at ball. Don't fight it. Be relaxed when fielding this tossed ball."

The Oriole Way manual offered fifty-six specific, individual teaching points for each infielder, including:

Foot spread depends upon most comfortable position for individual
    infielder. Not too wide.
Have relaxed hands. Do not jab or be stiff with glove, relax.
Infielders must establish in his mind his weak and strong side. He
    then must lean toward side he doesn't go well to until this is
    improved.
Don't just throw for the sake of warming up. Throw for improved
    accuracy.

The manual preached constant communication with players. When a player is transferred in the minor leagues, the manual said, his manager should never dismiss him without "telling him of weaknesses he may have to work on."

There were rules for player behavior too, including:

No gambling at any time.

No profane language.

No roughhousing in hotels on the road.

No yelling at fans.

No unkind remarks at girls at any time.

No excessive laying in bed in the morning.

No excessive drinking of any kind.

No eating of junky food—Proper diet is essential.

Weaver made each player read the guidelines for their position and attend a classroom session where they had to write down what the manual said.

Weaver thought Bauer had let discipline slide. "Hank was from the Yankee school," said Weaver. "Just get the talent, put the ball and some bats on the field, and let's go get 'em. There wasn't a hell of a lot of a program." He made new rules to tighten discipline and prevent injury, such as no card-playing in the clubhouse, a midnight curfew, and no swimming. Players had to wear sport coats or sweaters. "I don't want any players walking around in a T-shirt or plain sports shirt at any time," he said.

The young manager also came into spring training with a new approach to using statistics. He had asked Orioles public relations director Bob Brown to compile the results of matchups between every Orioles hitter and pitcher versus every pitcher and hitter in the American League. He had noted variation in the performance of players against specific adversaries. Boog Powell, for example, might be a mighty slugger but he was toast against Tigers lefty Mickey Lolich. By creating a system of information, Weaver could orchestrate a steady stream of favorable matchups for his pitchers and hitters. Contrary to popular mythology, this data was typed, and later printed, on sheets of paper, not index cards. Weaver kept those for other purposes, such as scouting reports on what kinds of pitches to throw opposing hitters.

None of his ideas were entirely new. Baseball had been obsessed with statistics since Henry Chadwick invented the box score in the 1850s. In 1947, Branch Rickey hired the first team statistician, Allan Roth, to compile data for the Dodgers. Earnshaw Cook published *Percentage Baseball*, a seminal book of statistical analysis, in 1964. Macmillan published the first *Baseball Encyclopedia* in 1969. And across America, major- and minor-league teams, and baseball managers and officials like Earl's old friends Hal Contini in West Frankfort and Jack Crandall in Elmira, had been experimenting with data-collection efforts to help their teams.

Alan Schwarz, in his authoritative 2005 history of statistics in baseball, *The Numbers Game*, credits Weaver for accelerating the use of data in the dugout. "Weaver saw and used more than any manager before him," wrote Schwarz. Every time a modern manager looks at an iPad to check on matchup data, a TV screen flashes stat charts, or a blogger makes an argument on X using matchup data, they're channeling Earl Weaver. "Probably more than any other manager in history, Weaver had carefully defined roles for every player on his roster—not because he cared about the players, but because he cared about the games," wrote Bill James in *The Bill James Guide to Baseball Managers*. "It was important to Weaver to have a player matched up in his mind with every possible game situation."

Weaver's matchup data was far less predictive than he believed, but it forced him and his players to pay closer attention to details within the game, offered a framework for making decisions with analysis, and pointed toward a future of Bill James, FanGraphs, and Ivy League–educated front-office analysts. Weaver never studied probability theory, but he had known about numbers since going to ballgames as a boy with Uncle Bud, and he was the one who foresaw that it belonged in baseball.

In addition, Weaver persuaded the Orioles to hire Pat Santarone, his groundskeeper buddy from Elmira. Belanger and the other infielders who had played there vouched for the quality of his work. The Sodfather carried out his boss's orders, watering down the basepaths against fast teams and letting the sun harden the dirt against weak defenses. With Brooks Robinson at third,

Mark Belanger at short, Davey Johnson at second, and Boog Powell at first, Weaver reckoned that the faster surface would help the Orioles offense more than it would hurt his superior defense. He was right. The Orioles' batting average in 1969 jumped to .265 from .225, while defensive efficiency, the percentage of batted balls turned into outs, increased to .743 from .740, as the league's average dropped to .714 from .724. For the next twenty-two years, Santarone planted blends of four or five bluegrasses to give Memorial Stadium one of the sweetest sods in baseball.

Earl Weaver needn't have worried about his job. The baseball gods gave him one of the great teams in the sport's history. The Orioles lost their first game to the Red Sox, 5–4, in 12 innings. And they lost their third game of the season to Ted Williams's Senators. After that, they pulverized the league. The Birds went 16-7 in April, 18-8 in May, 21-6 in June, 17-10 in July, 19-12 in August, and 17-10 in September. At the end of the regular season, the Orioles had won 109 games, a sparkling achievement for the organization, and the fruit of the labor that had started in Thomasville in the 1950s.

Reaching the majors did not soften Weaver's temper. On August 2, Bill Haller ejected Weaver for smoking a cigarette in the dugout. Weaver puffed away three packs of Raleighs per day, and tried to sneak in a lung dart between each inning. In this game, Haller told him to stop. Weaver gave Haller the finger. With each hand. Haller tossed him. The league fined him $200. "I got permission long ago from my parents to smoke, and from my eighteen-year-old son, too," said Weaver after the game. "They used to carry whiskey bottles into the dugouts, chew all kinds of dirty stuff, and I can't stand behind the bat rack and smoke."

The next game, Weaver walked out to home plate to greet Haller with a taffy cigarette dangling from his lips. Haller threw him out before the first pitch. Weaver peeled off the paper from the fake cig, showed it to the umpires, and then put it in his mouth and ate it. The Orioles equipment manager sewed a special pocket inside his uniform to hide his cigarettes.

Just like in the minors, the Baltimore crowds loved the act. Writers scolded Weaver but had to admit that the manager was bound to be popular *because* of his behavior. "Chances are some fans this week will buy tickets to (1) see for themselves what that crazy Weaver is going to do next or (2) boo him or (3) be at the ringside in the event Earl punches an umpire," wrote Doug Brown in the *Baltimore Evening Sun.* "Next to winning, nothing sells tickets like controversy."

With Weaver's encouragement, the Orioles rebooted the Kangaroo Court, a role-playing game they had employed in 1966, and then abandoned as the team slumped, that gave players a forum for admitting mistakes and being vulnerable. Acting as judge, Frank Robinson stuck a mop on his head, a scene imitated much more recently by the hit TV show *Ted Lasso.* After every win, Robinson presided over up to three cases. Players could bring charges against each other for failing to drive in a run from third with less than two outs, for forgetting how many outs there were, or for sending a runner to his death on the basepaths. There was a Chico Salmon No-Touch Award for bad fielding plays, or the Weak Swing Award, a broken-off bat handle, which players joked belonged up the winner's ass. The biggest baserunning blunder earned a beat-up shoe.

The court came after Weaver too. In one game, he put Belanger in for defense and the shortstop made two errors. Billy Hunter brought the charge. "Your Honor, I'd like to charge Earl Weaver with misguided managing. He sent in Belanger for defense, and Mark made two errors."

"Guilty!" everyone yelled.

Encouraging the Kangaroo Court was a genius move. It forced players to pay close attention to the game and gave young ballplayers a forum for naming mistakes that could then be corrected, and expressing their vulnerabilities. "Some of the guys made funny speeches," said pitcher Pete Richert, "and it got to be a way where you could point out a guy's faults without a lot of resentment. It was a good safety valve, but you could only do it when you're winning."

The court fined Charley Lau's four-year-old son a dollar for not wearing socks to the ballpark, and Weaver a buck for muffing a ground ball while he was coaching first base in the 1969 All-Star Game. By the end of the season, the team had collected over $500 for a postseason party.

Mike Cuellar (23-11, 2.38) and McNally (20-7, 3.22) won 20 games and anchored a pitching staff with a 2.83 ERA. Harry Dalton obtained Cuellar in a trade for Curt Blefary following the 1968 season. Cuellar had gone 8-11 but had a 2.74 ERA for the Houston Astros. Dalton deduced that with better defensive and offensive support, Cuellar would dominate the league with his left-handed screwball.

The happiest surprise on the mound was twenty-three-year-old Palmer. In 1968, he felt so frustrated by his sluggish recovery from injury that he got licensed by Towson State University as a life insurance salesman. He also thought about trying to make the big leagues as an outfielder. He'd hit a home run in his first major-league game. When he pitched in the Florida Winter Instructional League, he couldn't throw hard. The Orioles left him unprotected in the expansion draft. Things turned around when he took a new anti-inflammatory drug and pitched in the Puerto Rican winter league for the Santurce Crabbers, managed by Frank Robinson. Palmer felt like his old self, and again threw in the upper 90s. He also received a jolt from the hard-driven Weaver. "By the time I came back, in '69, Weaver was in charge," he recalled. "And I do mean in charge, charged up, and charging . . . like a rhino in cleats. I was young. He was my first experience with a maniac." The weird odd-couple, Palmer-Weaver alchemy worked immediately: Palmer went 16-4 with a 2.34 ERA.

The Orioles knocked 175 homers, up from 133, and scored 779 runs, up from 579. Frank Robinson recovered his vision and hit 32 homers with 100 RBI. With the help of batting coach Charley Lau, who later became famous for working with Hall of Famer George Brett, the pencil-thin Belanger hit .287. Belanger, Johnson, Robinson, and Paul Blair all won Gold Gloves. The Orioles clinched the division on September 14 by beating Cleveland, 10–5. "The Orioles, deep in pitching and strong up the middle, are throwbacks to the classic Yankees teams," said *Sports Illustrated*. Finally the Orioles were reaping the rewards of the groundwork Paul Richards and Harry Dalton had laid in the 1950s. The success would spread to other organizations. The 1960s–1970s Orioles dynasty incubated the careers of John Schuerholz, who built the 1990s Braves dynasty; Lou Gorman, who later ran the Red Sox; and Jim Frey, who managed the Kansas City Royals to the 1980 World Series. Coaches George Bamberger, Joe Altobelli, Cal Ripken Sr., and Billy Hunter all became big-league managers.

In the first-ever American League Championship Series in 1969, the Orioles would face the AL West champion Minnesota Twins. They had their own terrible-toddler genius manager, Billy Martin, a disciple of the Yankees Hall of Fame manager Casey Stengel. The Twins had hired Martin before the 1969 season; he and Weaver would battle one another for the next seventeen years. They had a history: they had played each other during Earl's lone big-league spring training invite with the Cardinals in 1952.

Like Weaver, Martin was a scrappy former infielder with a temper and a savant's understanding of baseball. Unlike Earl, he could never keep a job. The Yankees hired Martin five separate times between 1975 and 1988. Martin is one of two managers, along with Davey Johnson, to take four different teams to the postseason. In Minnesota, Detroit, New York, and Oakland, Martin turned around flailing teams. "Billy understands baseball," Weaver once said; "he just doesn't understand life."

In 1969, Martin led the Twins to an AL West title with a 97-65 record. "We're impressed by Baltimore's 109 wins," he said. "But that's history." Minnesota "is an explosive team," said Weaver. "If you get three, four, or five runs ahead, you try to get more before [Harmon] Killebrew hits the ball out."

In the first-ever American League Championship Series playoff game, the Orioles beat the Twins in a 12-inning thriller. Boog Powell hit a game-tying home run in the ninth inning and Paul Blair won it with a surprise two-out bunt to score Mark Belanger in the twelfth. Pat Santarone had grown the grass long to make bunts difficult to field. Weaver later disdained the sacrifice bunt, but he never stopped preaching the bunt for a base hit. In game 2, Dave Mc-Nally pitched an 11-inning complete-game shutout, and Curt Motton singled in Boog Powell to walk it off for the second straight day. In Minnesota for game 3, the Orioles blew out the Twins 11–2 to complete the sweep.

The Orioles moved on to the World Series against the New York Mets. What happened next has been well chronicled. Cuellar beat the Mets 4–1 in game 1. The Mets won the next four games and took the World Series. In game 4, umpire Shag Crawford ejected Weaver. He had been complaining about balls and strikes all game. "Shut your mouth," Crawford yelled. As soon as Weaver moved to leave the dugout, Crawford tossed him. Weaver was the first manager in thirty-four years to get booted from a World Series game. "It really bothered my parents to see it on national television," moaned Weaver.

In game 5, the Orioles took a 3–0 lead into the sixth inning and gave it up, losing 5–3. Orioles players wept. How had Baltimore managed to blow such a lead? "You can't run a few plays into the line and kill the clock," said Weaver, mustering wisdom still quoted in the twenty-first century. "You got to give the other man his chance at bat. This is why this is the greatest game of them all."

In 1970, former busher Earl Weaver was on top
of the baseball world, October 6, 1970.

16

BUS-LEAGUE NAPOLEONS

Baltimore, 1970

There was the sudden realization that winning is possible on earth.
—Jack Kerouac, after watching Bobby Thomson hit a home run to
win the 1951 National League pennant for the New York Giants

Even though Earl Weaver lost the 1969 World Series, it propelled him to national fame. Instead of an old busher, he was now a young genius. National
publications fawned over him. Clubs all over the country invited him to speak.
In St. Louis, Weaver collected the St. Louis Baseball Man of the Year award. In
his speech, he thanked Beaumont High coach Ray Elliott and his dad. "I had a
very, very happy childhood because my parents gave me every opportunity to
play baseball," Weaver said. For the next decade, Earl Sr. usually spent a month
per season in Baltimore with his big-league-manager son. He never stopped
calling him Sonny.

Back at spring training, Weaver sounded paranoid. "If we lose opening
day, we'll be in last place," he said. On a trip to Mexico City, he threw a tantrum
after the Orioles lost to the Mexico City Reds, 5–4. "Guys won't take a pitch,"
he said. "They're trying to win a pennant in the first week of the season." After
his outburst, the Orioles won the next game easily, 11–1.

He needn't have fretted. On Opening Day, McNally beat Cleveland, 8–2.

After two months, the Orioles were 33-15, in first place with a 7.5-game lead on the Yankees. In 1970, unlike the year before, the Orioles were favorites. "I'm not worried about this team letting down this year, because Earl Weaver gets into it a little more than most managers," said Brooks Robinson. "He gets upset if we lose. He'll shake you." In April, Earl had a cyst removed from his vocal cords. "The operation lowered Weaver's volume but didn't stop him from voicing an early complaint in the night game against the Washington Senators," the Associated Press reported.

In 1970, the Orioles played like an orchestra hitting every right note on the beat. The team crushed the American League and won 108 games. Powell hit 35 home runs, batted .297/.412/.549, and was named AL Most Valuable Player. Frank Robinson hit 25 dingers and batted .306/.398/.520. Three Orioles pitchers won 20 games: Palmer (20-10, 2.71), Cuellar (24-8, 3.48), and McNally (24-9, 3.22). Blair, Johnson, and Brooks again won Gold Gloves.

The Orioles clubhouse stayed loose and confident. Weaver called only three team meetings all year. He thought they distracted players from doing their jobs. When former Oriole Curt Blefary told his Yankee teammates they could beat Baltimore because they "did not have big red S's on the front of their shirts," Orioles players had shirts printed emblazoned with the Superman S and wore them to batting practice.

In the ALCS, the Orioles faced the Minnesota Twins, this time managed by Bill Rigney. The Twins had dumped the self-destructive Billy Martin after he punched one of his pitchers, Dave Boswell. And again Baltimore swept the series, 3–0. The Orioles handled 111 chances with no errors; the Twins fielded 106 and made 6 errors, leading to 8 unearned runs.

In the World Series, Weaver encountered future Hall of Fame manager Sparky Anderson and the Cincinnati Reds. Like Weaver, Anderson was a scrappy infielder with a chip on his shoulder, but unlike Earl, he had spent one season in the big leagues in 1959, when he hit .215 for the Phillies. Anderson combined shrewd baseball judgment and discipline. Although George Lee Anderson earned the nicknamed "Sparky" for his feistiness, he was ejected only 56 times in 26 seasons with the Reds and Tigers, compared to 96 in 17 seasons for Weaver. Anderson understood the limits of his profession. "I don't believe that a manager wins games," he said. "Personnel does."

Anderson's history "parallels amazingly that of Earl Weaver, a bus league Napoleon, who stepped out of the rear door and led Baltimore to two colossal seasons," wrote the *Sporting News*. "Managers don't put people in the park," said Anderson. "I believe the clubs are coming to realize this. They are now looking for organizers. Managing is nothing more than organizing."

In the 1970 World Series, the Orioles crushed the Reds, 4 games to 1. A dream come true. Delirious Orioles players dumped their little manager into the clubhouse whirlpool bath. The hero was Brooks Robinson, who batted .429 and caught everything in sight. His performance dominated the story of the 1970 World Series, yielding highlight plays at third base that would enthrall baseball fans into the next century. Robinson, the mild-mannered son of an Arkansas fire captain, was kind and generous, and possessed an aw-shucks charisma that melted cynics. He praised Earl Weaver for his sense of humor and baseball judgment. "He didn't overmanage," he said. "He knew we had talent and he didn't get in the way of it."

Only thirteen big-league teams have ever won 108 games or more in a regular season. The 1969–1970 Orioles are still the *only* team in baseball history to win 108 games or more in back-to-back seasons. In his first five seasons, Weaver (1969–1973, 495 wins, .620) recorded the third-best winning percentage of any manager's first five years, behind only Frank Chance (1906–1910 with the Cubs, 540 wins, .693) and Al Lopez (1951–1955 with the Indians, 482 wins, .626).

Did Weaver deserve credit for the Orioles' ascent to the top of the baseball world? He had led one of the greatest back-to-back performances of any team in baseball history. It was certainly unprecedented for a rookie manager. The question still cannot be answered. Managerial skill remains shrouded in mystery. "The manager is one of the last frontiers of understanding baseball," said MLB official historian John Thorn. "How do you quantify the unquantifiable?"

You can divide the history of the baseball manager into five phases: Captain (nineteenth century), Teacher (early twentieth), General (midtwentieth), Strategist (late twentieth), and CEO (twenty-first). The 1970s, the age of the Strategist—starring Earl Weaver, Billy Martin, Sparky Anderson, Dick Williams, and others—were a time of high managerial drama based on the premise that hiring a good manager might buy you the potion you needed to win a World Series.

In 1970, more managers were starting to look like Weaver, Anderson, and Martin, failed players who had turned their frustration into abilities for teaching and talent evaluation, and a fierce desire to win. They amplified the popular archetype of the manager as tobacco-chewing philosopher-king. Their success led front-office analysts, fans, journalists, and historians to assume that a great manager could lead any group of players to victory.

To be sure, throughout baseball history, managers have worked with all kinds of résumés. Eight, including Tony La Russa, Branch Rickey, and Miller Huggins, have had law degrees. Six, most famously Connie Mack, have worn civilian clothes in the dugout. Fourteen managers, including former Braves owner and CNN founder Ted Turner, have managed for only one game. The 1977 Braves had lost 16 straight games. Turner told his manager Dave Bristol to take off ten days so he could manage the team and analyze its weaknesses. In 1961 and 1962, the Chicago Cubs rotated nine different coaches through their dugout, giving one man at a time a chance of leading the team. It didn't work. The Cubs lost 90 games in 1961 and 103 games in 1962 and finished next-to-last both seasons.

Earl Weaver himself disavowed the notion of managerial genius. "The Orioles made me," Weaver said after winning the 1970 World Series. "I didn't make the Orioles." Weaver understood that the secret of managing, if there is one, was to pick good players, prepare them properly, set high standards, and set them free to play. As Yogi Berra said, "This ain't like football. There ain't no trick plays."

A baseball manager does six essential things: organize preparation, motivate players, choose starting lineups and pitching rotations, substitute players during games, make in-game decisions like bunting and stealing, and talk to the media before and after games. Some of these matter less than fans think. For example, there are 362,880 ways to arrange a nine-man lineup, but modern analysis has shown that order doesn't matter remotely as much as who is playing. Billy Martin was on to something in 1972 when, while managing the Tigers, he picked his lineup out of a hat. His Tigers beat the Indians, 3–2. Good managers know it really is all about the players.

The illusion that managers can win close games with their brains has amplified the perception of managerial genius. A decision to bunt that leads to the winning run scoring appears decisive to observers who forget the 75 other plays and 250 other pitches that might have had different outcomes.

Weaver's record in one-run games illustrates why the skill of managing baseball teams remains opaque. In 1970, the Orioles went 40-15 (.727) in one-run games, the fourth-best season record in baseball history. The 1981 Orioles went 21-7 (.750), the third-best all-time record, giving Weaver two of the top-five all-time records in one-run contests. It sounds impressive, as if Weaver were a chess master skilled at tight endgames. But close ballgames are more like dice rolls than chess. If winning them, *outmanaging* your opponent, were a replicable skill available only to geniuses like him, how to account for Weaver's five seasons with *losing* records in one-run games, including 26-32 (.448) in 1972, 23-24 (.489) in 1973, and 25-27 (.481) in 1975, all winning seasons for the Orioles? Weaver's career record in one-run games was 450-335 (.573), basically the same winning percentage as his overall record of 1,480-1,060 (.583). Bill James found possible advantages in one-run contests for teams that, like Weaver's Orioles, drew a lot of walks, issued few, and had low ERAs, but those factors didn't play nearly as big a role as chance. "One-run games involve a huge amount of luck," James concluded. "This may be the only safe statement that can be made about them."

Despite all the advances in analytics, there's still no consensus among analysts on how much difference a manager makes. Gene Mauch, who managed the Phillies, Expos, Twins, and Angels over twenty-seven seasons, had a losing record and never took a team to the World Series, but he kept getting jobs because he was considered a great manager. Mauch joked that he managed 486 games a year: 162 in preparation, 162 in real life, and 162 in postgame analysis.

Sitting in the corner of the clubhouse after the Orioles had won the 1970 World Series, Earl Weaver Sr., "a little round man in a pink shirt," according to one observer, sipped on a beer. "Funny game," he said. "You win, you're a hero. You lose, you're a bum."

The little boy he'd coached on the St. Louis sandlots was a hero. "You made all the right moves," said Elrod Hendricks. "You're beautiful."

"Nice going, little fella," said Jerold Hoffberger to his manager.

"Earl doesn't get nearly the credit he deserves," said Frank Robinson.

Anderson said, "It's time Earl got the credit he deserves. He's won 217 games in two years and he's won the World Series. I know people say he has a great team, but I've got a great team, too, and he beat us." Weaver deflected the praise. "Everything has been easy for me. Twenty-five ballplayers made it easy." He added: "It's the best feeling I've ever had in my life."

At the end of the season, the Tigers hired Billy Martin. "If I run second to Earl Weaver next season, I'll shoot myself," said Martin.

17

PITCHING

Baltimore, 1971

When I pick up the ball and it feels nice and light and small I know I'm
going to have a good day. But if I pick it up and it's big and heavy, I know
I'm liable to get into a little trouble.

—Bob Feller

When Orioles pitchers moaned about their boss, they often repeated Dave Mc-
Nally's joke: "All Earl knows about pitching is that he couldn't hit it." That can't
possibly have been true. Four of Weaver's pitchers—Mike Cuellar (1969), Jim
Palmer (1973, 1975, 1976), Mike Flanagan (1979), and Steve Stone (1980)—
won a total of six of the Cy Young Awards given every year to the league's best
pitcher. No Oriole won the award before Earl Weaver, and no Oriole has won
since. Overall, Weaver managed twenty-two different 20-win performances,
easily the most by any manager since 1920. Only *two* Orioles pitchers (Steve
Barber in 1963, and Mike Boddicker in 1984) have won 20 games with an Orioles manager other than Weaver. Palmer alone won 20 games eight times.

Nothing epitomized Weaver's excellence at managing pitchers as much
as 1971, when the Orioles became the second team in baseball history with
four 20-game winners, after the 1920 White Sox. Weaver got these premier
performances out of Palmer, Cuellar, McNally, and Pat Dobson.

An extraordinary quartet of 20-game winners: Jim Palmer, Dave McNally, Pat Dobson, Mike Cuellar; September 23, 1971.

Selecting and motivating pitchers is central to the baseball manager's job, because the position is central to the sport's mechanics. Baseball betting, old-time gamblers joked, should really be called pitcher betting. If the pitcher throws strikes and changes speeds with fast, moving, and well-placed pitches, opposing hitters will likely strike out, or tap grounders or soft flies for outs; regular out-making teamwork boosts spirits and after three outs sends the defense sprinting off the field eager to hit. A positive rhythm takes over the team.

If the pitcher walks batters or gets hit hard, infielders and outfielders lose their focus, runners pollute the basepaths, and morale sags. Weaver's Orioles preached relentless strike-throwing, changing speeds, working fast, and a strategy of throwing to a pitcher's strengths as much as to a hitter's weaknesses.

Weaver liked to simplify pitcher's assignments. Don't fool around, he'd say; pound the strike zone with your best two or three pitches, change speeds, and let the defense do the job. He picked good pitchers, gave them massive amounts of innings, and kept them healthy, or pushed them to pitch hurt.

It's tempting for pitchers to aim for the edges of the strike zone, because those pitches are harder to hit, but those pitches are also more likely to result in balls outside the zone, and walks, which are actually worse than batted balls because they can't be caught and converted into outs. Most pitchers, coaches, and managers are afraid to embrace a strategy of bluntly keeping pitches over the plate, because they're afraid of getting hit hard. Not Weaver, who preached changing speeds over precise location, and trusted his defense.

Weaver harassed and ruthlessly demoted pitchers who didn't throw strikes. As he put it: "If you don't get the ball over the plate, the batters will keep walking around and stepping on it." The 1971 Orioles finished second in the big leagues in ERA, but only twentieth out of twenty-four teams in strikeouts. Between 1969 and 1982, the Orioles finished first in the American League in ERA at 3.30, but tenth in the league in strikeouts per nine innings. That was possible because they had great defense, and finished second in fewest walks per nine innings.

From 1968 to 1980, the Orioles had at least one 20-game winner in every season. From 1969 to 1982, while leading the American League in ERA at 3.29, the Orioles pitched 783 complete games. No other AL squad had more than 634. The yeoman's work done by his starters allowed Weaver to carry fewer pitchers and freed up roster spots to use on platoon players, pinch hitters, and defensive specialists.

Weaver credited his pitching guru, a soft-spoken failed big-league hurler with a lifetime 9.42 ERA named George Bamberger, the Orioles' pitching coach from 1968 to 1977 before he left to manage the Brewers. Weaver was skilled at delegating oversight. "Earl gets coaches who are teachers, then he doesn't get in their way," Ray Miller, Bamberger's successor and a future MLB manager, told Tom Boswell. "He doesn't tell me, 'Why don't you teach Sammy Stewart the window-shade-release slip-pitch?' He says, 'Jesus Christ, I'm sick of lookin' at that horseshit changeup. Get him a new one.'"

Bamberger believed that pitchers got hurt by throwing too little, and made his pitchers play catch for fifteen minutes every day between starts, along with regular bullpen sessions throwing hard two days after every start. His pitchers ran every day, even on the road, thirty minutes or more of sprinting from foul pole to foul pole. Running later fell out of fashion as a training regimen for pitchers, but it was core to the Orioles' philosophy. "When you pitch, and your legs get tired from lifting them up on every windup, you can lose coordination," argued Bamberger.

The most important pitch, he added, "is a strike. But the trick is to change speeds. Trying to pinpoint a pitch is crazy. Throw the ball down the middle, but don't throw the same pitch twice. Change the speed."

The Orioles would not have had four 20-game winners without using a four-man instead of a five-man rotation. In 1971, Weaver gave 142 of 158 starts to his big four. Somehow, they never got hurt. "The most amazing thing about Earl Weaver's record is his phenomenal ability to keep his starting pitchers healthy, while pitching them 260 innings a year," wrote historian Bill James. Why this worked is another Earl Weaver mystery. Was it the running? The changeups? Luck?

At first glance, Weaver's pitching strategy seems reactionary, but some baseball analysts now believe that a four-man rotation would be more effective, as long as pitch counts are kept down, because you're giving a higher percentage of your starts to your best players. Managers switched from a plurality using the four-man rotation to a plurality using a five-man rotation in 1925, according to an article published by Frank Vaccaro in the fall 2011 edition of the *Baseball Research Journal*. In 1925, the five-man cycle was used in 38 percent of games, and the four-man cycle in 34 percent of games. From 1887 to 1897, the three-man rotation was in favor, and from 1898 to 1924, the four-man system prevailed.

At the heart of the Orioles' pitching in 1971, and for the next decade, was Palmer. Using a high leg kick that delivered a roaring fastball, Palmer developed a unique style that mixed different speeds and locations and forced contact for Orioles defenders to gobble up. His relationship with Weaver was so central to the team, and the story of baseball during that era, that it became part of American folklore. Palmer wrote an entire book about it, titled *Together We Were Eleven Foot Nine*.

At the heart of the relationship was a productive friction that always seemed to result in more wins for the Orioles. Weaver and Palmer fought and fought, and won and won. They drove each other crazy and had nothing in common except for fierce determination. After Palmer got roughed up one time, Weaver said: "Me and Palmer don't like to give up six runs nowhere at no time to nobody." On September 26, with three other starters having already won 20 games, Palmer, who had 19 wins, shut out Cleveland, 5–0. The Orioles had their fourth 20-game winner.

The Orioles acquired Pat Dobson before the 1971 season from San Diego. The right-hander from a small town near Buffalo, New York, had caught Earl's eye by once striking out twenty-one batters in a game in Puerto Rico. He slung a big curveball that the Orioles adroitly harnessed in 1971, the only season Dobson ever won 20 games.

McNally was a clever strike-throwing lefty from Montana with a devastating slider. The Orioles signed him to an $80,000 bonus in 1960 when he was eighteen years old. He came up through the Orioles system, playing for Weaver in Elmira in 1962 and making his big-league debut that year. He won 20 games four times, every year from 1968 to 1971, and won 181 games for the Orioles over thirteen seasons before they traded him to Montreal after the 1974 season.

The most colorful of the quartet was Cuellar, nicknamed Crazy Horse for his weird sense of humor and superstitions. Cuellar was from a sugar-worker family in Cuba and joined the Cuban army so he could play baseball. Scouts noticed him pitching for dictator Fulgencio Batista's army team in the winter of 1954–1955. He bounced around and ended up with the Houston Astros. In 1968, he was 8-11 with a 2.74 ERA. The win-loss record made him look like a mediocre pitcher. The Orioles pounced, acquiring him with Elijah Johnson and Enzo Hernandez for Curt Blefary and John Mason. Cuellar thrived in Baltimore, chucking screwball after screwball at confused hitters. He went 23-11 in 1969 with a 2.38 ERA and 18 complete games. "He was like an artist," Palmer said after Cuellar died. "He could paint a different picture every time he went out there. He could finesse you. He could curveball you to death or screwball you to death." Said Billy Martin: "His fastball couldn't black my eye, but he owns my hitters' minds."

Cuellar flew with lucky blue clothes, insisted on eating his pregame meal with his catcher, and smoked nine cigarettes during games, one per inning. He hung a sign over his locker that said: "Bring it sweetheart." He sat on the lucky end of his training table and made the same number of steps between the dugout and the water cooler every time. None of that bothered Earl, who was almost as superstitious as Crazy Horse. Weaver avoided looking at clocks if the Orioles were leading, changed pens after each loss, and preferred to rest his foot against the "good-luck" pole in the Memorial Stadium dugout.

In the spring of 1971, *Sports Illustrated* ran a cover story on the Orioles, titled "The Best Damn Team in Baseball." It predicted another romp. "The Orioles became truly inhuman in 1970. They wore spikes; everybody else wore sneakers. At least that is the way it must have felt all season long to the other teams in the American League. . . . Now Las Vegas has them favored 1 to 3 to win their division and start it all over again. Somehow the odds don't seem to fall terribly short."

In the middle of the 1971 season, Weaver managed what is widely considered the greatest All-Star Game ever played. For the first time, two Black pitchers, Vida Blue and Dock Ellis, started on the mound. Twenty Hall of Famers played in the game, including Hank Aaron, Willie Mays, Reggie Jackson, and Roberto Clemente, and two, Sparky Anderson and Weaver, managed. Aaron, Clemente, Jackson, Johnny Bench, Frank Robinson, and Harmon Killebrew all homered. Jackson hit one off a light tower on the roof. Juan Marichal and Jim Palmer each pitched two scoreless innings. The team was so good that

Pete Rose didn't get to hit, and Tom Seaver and Steve Carlton didn't pitch. The American League won, 6–4, the only win for the AL between 1963 and 1982.

The Orioles' offense slipped in 1971. Frank Robinson led the team with 99 RBI. Buford topped the American League with 99 runs scored. In the American League Championship Series, the Orioles swept the Oakland A's, making them 9-0 in three ALCS.

Weaver promptly picked a fight with the greatest dynasty in baseball history. The Orioles were so good, he said, that 1950s Yankee shortstop turned national broadcaster Phil Rizzuto "couldn't make this team." The 1949–1953 Yankees won a record five straight World Series, all with Rizzuto at shortstop.

"What does that man know about it?" said 1950s Yankees manager Casey Stengel, needling Weaver where it would hurt. "He never played in the major leagues."

"What could Weaver have known about me?" responded Rizzuto. "Weaver was 6 years old" when he made his debut in 1941, he added.

"That shows you what a smart guy Rizzuto is," said Weaver. "I wasn't 6. I was 11. I was born in 1930. Subtract 1930 from 1941 and you get 11. Any schoolboy could tell you that. But not Rizzuto."

"If Weaver's team is so good, why didn't they beat the Mets two years ago?" asked Stengel.

In the World Series, the Orioles faced an iconic team, the Pittsburgh Pirates, led by the thrilling Puerto Rican superstar Roberto Clemente. On September 1, 1971, the Pirates became the first major-league squad ever to field an all–Black and Latino starting nine.

The Orioles won the first two games in Baltimore. Back in Pittsburgh, the Pirates captured games 3, 4, and 5. The Orioles won game 6. And the Pirates won game 7 by a score of 2–1, behind pitcher Steve Blass. The series was the Clemente Show. The Great One hit .414 and ran the bases like a wild horse and made sliding catches and cannon throws. Clemente "has no weaknesses," said Weaver. "And you can bet we looked for one in our scouting report."

The Pirates also got phenomenal pitching. In game 4, the first night game in World Series history, the Orioles scored three runs in the first off Luke Walker. Then Bruce Kison relieved with 6.1 shutout innings. Dave Giusti pitched the last two innings for the save. "Without Blass, we might be popping corks," said Weaver. In game 7, Weaver tried to rattle Blass. He complained that the pitcher's foot was in contact with the rubber on the side instead of in front or on top. It didn't work.

Weaver misfired by playing Boog Powell after he had fractured his right wrist. Powell went 3-for-27. He also kept his right-handed hitters in the game against the sidearming Kison. In game 7, down 2–0, the Orioles put two runners on to start the bottom of the eighth inning. Weaver then ordered outfielder Tom Shopay to bunt. The sacrifice worked, putting runners on second and third with one out. The next two hitters grounded out, scoring only one run, leaving the Orioles down, 2–1. A manager who became famous for hating the bunt went by the book, bunted, and lost a World Series game 7. If Weaver had let Shopay swing, the rally would have had a higher chance of generating game-winning runs.

For the second time in three years, the Orioles had lost a World Series after a dominant regular season. Weaver kept the clubhouse closed for five minutes, so could he tell his players how proud he was of them. When he opened the doors, the reporters walked in on grown men crying. After taking questions, Weaver went into the showers and threw up.

Weaver took a phone call from President Richard Nixon. "The President said he thought he would call because he knows how it feels to lose," Weaver reported. "I don't think he could have picked a better time." On the way back to his office, he ran into Earl Sr., still a Republican Party member in St. Louis. "Hey Dad, I just talked to your boss," Earl Jr. said. "He said we conducted ourselves very well. So I'm going to have to register next year." (Earl Jr. was never interested in politics. He opposed the Vietnam War, and in later years, like any wealthy Floridian, he grumbled about taxes.)

He was philosophical, and defiant, about the tough 1971 World Series loss: "Ten years ago if someone had told me I'd be managing in the majors; if they told me I'd be the manager of three successive championship teams that won more than 100 games a season; if they told me that I'd carry on a phone conversation with the president, I would have laughed right in their face. I'd dream it, sure. But I'd never dream they would come true. Now it has."

After the World Series, General Manager Harry Dalton resigned from the Orioles to sign a five-year contract with the California Angels. Hoffberger named Frank Cashen as his replacement. Encouraged by Weaver, Cashen's first big move was to trade Frank Robinson. The Orioles had a surplus of young outfielders, including top prospect Don Baylor. Robinson was set to make $130,000, and the Orioles needed to save money. Despite posting the best record in baseball 1969–1971, they drew only around a million fans a year. Throughout the 1970s, there would be talk of moving the team to Washington, D.C., or somewhere else with a better economy than Baltimore's.

The Orioles went to Japan after the end of the season. It was an 18-game, 31-day trip. "I'm really looking forward to the trip," said Weaver. "I wish we could go as world champs. . . . But we can't. But we'll give them a good show."

Earl's garden relieved his stress during losing streaks, May 30, 1980.

18

STRIKE ONE

Baltimore, 1972

Even Napoleon had his Watergate.

—Danny Ozark

On April 1, 1972, for the first time in the 103-year history of professional base-ball, big-league players went on strike. In only six years, union boss Marvin Miller had fostered defiance and demand.

Weaver, a company man, opposed the strike even though one of its lead-ers was his star third baseman, Brooks Robinson. "Who'll follow me and get their year's salary?" he said. "I feel sorry for the owners, who are going to lose a lot of money."

It irked Weaver that the new generation of ballplayers wouldn't put up with the same hardships he had. The players complained there were no sand-wiches in the Orioles' clubhouse. Only apples, oranges, celery, soup, cot-tage cheese, and crackers. "What's the sense in us getting 'em fat in our own clubhouse?" asked Weaver. "Let them spend a nickel and buy themselves a hamburger away from the ballpark later on." Second baseman Davey Johnson hammered back. "If a couple of guys have a weight problem, get tough with them," he said. "Fine them. But don't take it out on everyone."

Weaver in the spring of 1972 was focused on becoming the first manager ever to win 100 games in four consecutive seasons. His star was rising. The national media was starting to pay attention to this little guy in the dugout. He was about to publish his first book, *Winning!*

Weaver's anti-union stance rankled Marvin Miller. In a union meeting at Brooks Robinson's house, Miller threatened legal action for coercion. "There's a fine point in labor laws, and he's going way overboard," said Miller. "His attempts to break the strike have been as a representative of management—which has nothing to do with being a field manager." Miller dropped the threat after Weaver walked back his comments. Weaver eventually came to support the players' union, and free agency after it arrived in 1976.

On April 13, the owners and players finally agreed to terms, including a new pension plan. Once teams started training again, Weaver predicted another championship. After sweeping a two-game series with the Yankees to open the season, the Tigers, managed by Billy Martin, arrived in Baltimore. Reporters loved to quote Martin, and he almost always delivered spicy copy. The Orioles are "dead without Frank Robinson," Billy said. "We are a better ball team. We know it, and the Orioles know it." Martin took issue with Weaver bragging that his 1969–1971 Orioles were the greatest team he'd ever seen. "What's the matter with him? Didn't they have television in the minors? Didn't he get to see those great Yankee teams back in the Fifties?"

Martin said he wanted to punch Weaver in the nose.

"Actually, I respect Billy for having the guts to say his team can beat ours," said Weaver. "The other guys say that I ought to win with all the talent the Orioles have."

"But doesn't Martin annoy you?" Weaver was asked.

"Why?" he said.

"Because he's so cocky?"

"Ain't I?" Earl asked.

Martin was right. The 1972 Orioles struggled, and for the first time in the big leagues, Weaver had problems.

Robinson's departure had left a huge hole. Weaver put on a brave front: "The fifteen games Robinson won with his bat, I'll win with my managing." Said Davey Johnson, "I knew that we were in deep trouble after that."

The team had enjoyed one last hurrah together, traveling to Japan as representatives of Major League Baseball for an 18-game, 31-day trip starting October 23. The Japanese baseball community had hoped the Orioles would beat the Pirates in the 1971 World Series, so that they could have a true World Series. The loss was disappointing, but the Orioles impressed their hosts with brilliant baseball.

Earl recalled a long plane trip via San Francisco and Honolulu, and the "wine and champagne, and after dinner the Drambuie, Irish Mist, and Cognac" and scotch, bourbon, and Jack Daniel's. "The Happy Hour was endless, as was the laughter, until darkness delivered a number of people into sleep." The Orioles played 18 games, going 13-2-3, in front of packed crowds. Waiters in tuxedos brought them raw fish, cakes, and tea in the dugout. Marianna and Earl got fancy massages in their hotel rooms. They drank sake and attended sumo. An English-speaking wrestler, Hawaiian-born Takamiyama Daigoro, palled around with the Orioles and helped translate. When he picked up Earl, players chanted: "Drop him! Drop him!"

Weaver let the players party, but he insisted they take the games seriously. According to Japanese press reports, when Dave McNally begged out of a start and other players tried to follow suit, Weaver issued a warning at a team meeting in Kyoto: "Whoever doesn't want to play speak up now. I'll call you a taxi for the airport. But don't expect to play next year for the O's either."

In Hiroshima, the Orioles posed for a picture in front of Peace Memorial Park, built to honor the pain and terror of the atomic bomb the U.S. military dropped on the city twenty-six years earlier. "The most interesting place we visited was Hiroshima," said Weaver, showing more soul than caricatures of him allow. "When we got there and saw that Peace Memorial Park it was most amazing sight I ever saw in my life. All they want over there is peace, and it sounded wonderful, and so sincere."

On the field, the visit highlighted Weaver's managerial style, and differences between American and Japanese baseball. In interviews with Japanese journalists, he said he fined players for being late, but never for poor performance. Baseball is a difficult game, he explained, and he assumed players were trying hard. He said Japanese hitters needed to lift weights and get stronger so they could hit more home runs, and Japanese pitchers needed to run more so they could go deeper into games. The Japanese press concluded that their version of the game needed to switch from a "baseball of defense" to a "baseball of power."

Back in America, the newspapers discussed the manager's strategic approach. "Weaver says 'statistics' dictate his moves," read one headline. "I use my players according to statistics I have gathered over the past few years," said Weaver. People were starting to criticize him for losing two World Series in 1969 and 1971. Why had he used Tom Shopay as a pinch hitter in the World Series? "My statistics were wrong there, but most of the past three years they have been correct," Weaver said.

In May, William Morrow in New York published Weaver's first book, *Winning!*, ghostwritten by John Sammis. Kirkus gave the book a winning review: "Grandstand managers will find it the greatest thing since the hot dog. . . . Weaver might look and sometimes act like a clown, but as managers go (and they usually do) he talks like an All-Star."

In the book, Weaver told the story of his minor-league purgatory, of buses and rusty stadiums and one-restaurant towns and honky-tonks. He addressed his growing reputation with umpires. Through the years, he wrote, "I've managed to develop some great moves—vicious head yanks, wild arm gestures, and sweeping kicks with either leg."

However, it could be a lot worse, he noted. "I've also had full-blown shouting matches and returned to the dugout to manage," he said. Andy Cohen, his manager in Denver, had taught him not to "swear directly at" arbiters. The tantrums served a purpose. "All I'm trying to do is say that I thought an umpire missed a call," he wrote. "Everybody makes mistakes, but an umpire might miss a call because he hasn't borne down hard enough. I'm there to remind him to bear down a little harder if possible. If I make a scene, maybe he'll remember it a little easier."

Managers are limited in what they can do to help their teams win, Weaver argued in the book. "Baseball, while it is called a team sport, is also a highly individual sport. If all nine men have a good day as individuals, then the team as a whole will look good." That foreshadowed an important finding of the analytics revolution that a baseball team is essentially the sum of its parts. In the twenty-first century, general managers would build algorithms where they could plug in values of each player to come up with a total win expectancy for the team. One key attribute for managers, Weaver added, was to accept his players' flaws: "If you've got a third baseman who hits with tremendous power, you can't yell at him for making errors if you decide to play him."

He called the hit-and-run the "worst play in baseball." On the sacrifice bunt, Weaver wrote that he would rather have a runner on first base with nobody out than a man on second with one out. Modern analysts affirm this is the right strategic decision, based on run expectancy tables that show the number of runs a team can expect to score in each of the 24 possible base and out situations. The sacrifice bunt is usually a losing strategy, except when the hitter is so bad that making an out and advancing the runner does more for the team than trying to get a hit. That's what Weaver concluded. "Really the only time to use a sacrifice is when the chances seem less in favor of the man at bat advancing the runner," he wrote. "The situation applies when you've got a .220 hitter up there, or a pitcher (whose average generally ranges from .050 to .150)." In the book, Weaver did not preach "pitching, defense, and three-run homers." That would come later. But he did advance his prophetic phrase about outs. "You only get three outs an inning. Why give away any of them?" The rest of the book consists of model practice plans and technical guides for executing plays like rundowns.

Practice plans couldn't save the Orioles in 1972. Belanger hit .186. Buford hit .206. Davey Johnson hit .221. They missed Frank Robinson. Don Baylor, a young slugger the club hoped would replace Robinson's production, hit .253 with 11 home runs. After a poor performance, Weaver and his coaches usually hit the bar, "in dire need of a couple of stiff drinks to cut the throbbing edge after a slovenly loss."

For the first time, Earl feuded openly with players. In June, he remarked that some of his players might be getting over-the-hill. Brooks Robinson, maybe the nicest man to ever play Major League Baseball, was infuriated. "I don't enjoy going places to hear people say I'm over the hill, or know that they're thinking it," he said. "If a guy feels that way about something, I'd rather he spoke to me man-to-man."

In August, the team was hitting .230. "There's no rhyme, reason, or cause for it," Weaver said. "It just happens. And it doesn't matter who's out there pitching for the other team. It doesn't matter whether he throws a spitter, a knuckler, or a curve ball. We're missing them all."

As the Orioles slid, Weaver tried to reassure people around him he could handle it. "I'm going to start managing now," he declared.

"But, Earl, what have you been doing up to now?" Palmer asked.

"I just wanted to show you guys you're not the whole show."

Nothing worked. The Orioles limped to a third-place finish, with 80 wins and 74 losses.

The strike. The losing. A fight with Brooks. It was a lot to handle.

Luckily, Earl had his vegetable garden. When he moved to Perry Hall after the 1968 season, he installed a twenty-by-thirty-foot vegetable garden, next to a swimming pool. A perfectionist craftsman, Weaver fed his vegetables a liquid fertilizer every two weeks and added compost every year. He filed complaints against neighbors who let dishwater run into his yard.

Weaver grew tomatoes, green peppers, zucchini, and eggplant, and installed two freezers, one for meat and one for vegetables. The tomatoes were the big thing. He always had over thirty plants. He'd challenge Boog Powell, Harry Dalton, and of course Pat Santarone to contests.

The Tomato Wars made headlines.

In 1970, Santarone started growing tomatoes in the left-field foul grounds. He planted at least ten plants a year in a combo mix of infield dirt and ground sod. And when it was time to pick, he compared his tomatoes to Weaver's.

Santarone and Weaver talked trash. The fans loved it. In a 1979 interview, Weaver said his pal's tomatoes were "nothing more than scrub tomatoes . . . all pulpy inside." Santarone replied: "He's never grown that big a tomato in his life. He wouldn't know how." Santarone bragged that he had fertilized his tomatoes with manure from Secretariat, the Triple Crown–winning racehorse. "That Weaver—from the looks of his tomatoes, I believe he's getting his from a horse that ran ninth in a nine-horse race." Maybe, Santarone said, Weaver watered his plants with buckets of chlorinated water from his swimming pool. A lie, said Earl. "The truth is that in my weak moments I imagine this guy is my friend and I invite him to dinner and when I'm not looking he gets a bucket and draws water out of the pool and dumps them on the plants." Santarone:

"I'll say this for him. He's a tenacious S.O.B. He hates to be beat, whether it's baseball, golf, cards, or growing tomatoes."

In the 1980s, Santarone and Weaver developed and sold a fertilizer called "Earl 'n Pat's Tomato Food." Santarone died in 2008 at age seventy-nine. In an interview in 1991, Earl admitted: "He beat me every year." In 2022, the Orioles planted tomatoes at Camden Yards near the Orioles' bullpen, as an homage to Weaver's and Santarone's gardens, and their rivalry.

But for Earl in the 1970s, the garden wasn't just a performance. It was food. The *Sun* printed his recipes. For example:

Canned tomatoes: Soak the tomatoes in hot water for a minute to make peeling easy. Cut them in hunks. Place hunks in jar and use a rubber spatula down the sides to remove any air in pockets. Add a teaspoon of salt. With lid on, place jar in canner with boiling water just over jar top and cook for 45 minutes (half hour for pint jars).

Italian sausage: Deboned pork shoulder, trimmed of fat, add red pepper, fennel seed, salt, pepper and water, all stuffed into casings of cow or pig intestines.

Weaver's freezer, the *Baltimore Sun* reported, was packed with "packages of diced peppers and onion for making chili, and strawberries, which they wash, decap and package after adding two tablespoons of sugar per quart." The stories about Earl's gardening prompted fans to send him recipes. He shopped around, buying asparagus and peaches from friends.

Gardening was also how Earl Weaver found relief from his constant anxieties. In an unpublished 1991 interview, Earl talked about his tomato plants and their role in his mental health: "In the morning, I could go out and scratch the ground to make sure the plants have water, and get down on [my] hands and knees and think about last night's game and who you were going to play that night, and still take care of [my] crop. I love to play golf, but you couldn't go out on a golf course and do that. Because if you want to play golf, you have to concentrate on golf." Earl's morning routine in Perry Hall was coffee and cigarettes while reading the paper, and then work in his garden. To cool down, he would hop into the pool, where he'd swim around in circles, staring at the bottom. "I'd see that snorkel going round and round in circles," said Kim

Benson, his stepdaughter. "I'm sure people who read about Earl think, 'Oh, that poor girl who's married to him.' But he leaves the baseball at the park," said Marianna. "He can be very considerate and very gentle. He sure is with those lettuce plants. He treats them like babies. He talks to them."

Earl needed all the help he could get in 1972. His darkness often erupted after losses, or if a writer questioned his strategic approach. In September, he spit, twice, on a baseball reporter who told him he would have won a game in Cleveland if he had bunted. He was hoping the reporter, Chan Keith of the *News-American,* would punch him, so Weaver could hit him back without getting an assault charge. Keith didn't retaliate, and there were no further incidents. Weaver later expressed regret: "To my everlasting shame, I lost control." But he added that the incident had "released the rage in me" and contributed to a more forgiving attitude toward reporters.

Weaver also went after umpire Bill Haller, whose brother Tom was a catcher for the Tigers. "I don't think the brother umpire should be umpiring games involving the Orioles," said Weaver. "I get a funny feeling inside." Challenging the integrity of the game's judges was a scandal. "The proper response would be to fine the manager a substantial sum not less than $5,000, and to tell him that any repetition of such remarks would lead to his expulsion from baseball," wrote Leonard Koppett in the *Sporting News.*

Nineteen seventy-two had seen some good individual performances. Palmer again won 20 games, going 21-10. Twenty-three-year-old rookie Bobby Grich batted .278/.358/.415, with 12 home runs. But Earl saw his team now had big holes to fill. "I just got to get some sock back in the catching department," he said. "We got about 20 homers out of catchers in 1971. This year, we got four." And at the end of December, Cashen pulled the trigger: Davey Johnson, Pat Dobson, Johnny Oates, and Roric Harrison to the Atlanta Braves for Earl Williams and Taylor Duncan.

Earl had his catcher. But could he keep his team?

19

CLAP FOR THE CLOWN

Baltimore, 1973

I never questioned the integrity of an umpire. Their eyesight, yes.

—Leo Durocher

For the first time since his minor-league purgatory, Earl Weaver was falling backward. For a season and a half after the 1971 World Series, the Orioles played mediocre baseball, finishing third in 1972 and starting off feebly in 1973. Weaver seemed like just another cranky manager. A hack. He drank too much, moaned about his misfortune, and, in the offseason, grew a tacky mustache. "Nobody recognized me and it was great," he said.

Managers are hired to be fired, and Weaver was never immune from the risk. His predecessor Bauer had been let go halfway through the 1968 season. During the 1991 season, *thirteen* big-league managers, in a league with twenty-six teams, were fired. In 1988, the Orioles fired Cal Ripken Sr. *six* games into the season. In the 1970s, the Orioles' division rival, the Yankees, employed six different skippers.

Amid his frustration, Weaver declared war on American League umpires. He had always been a ferocious bench jockey, whistling or shouting until he got the umpire's attention and then complaining about ball and strike calls. He had cultivated the art from his earliest days in a baseball uniform. In the minor leagues, he once faked a heart attack. "If you're alive, you're out of the game," the umpire said. One night, when he was managing in Venezuela, he got into an altercation so intense that he and the umpire didn't notice that fans were throwing beer mugs at them. Players pushed Weaver and the umpire into the middle of the infield to keep them safe.

But 1973 was the year Weaver kicked his act into high gear. Umpires tossed him out of 16 games from 1968 to 1972, an average of once every 45 games. From 1973 to 1979, they ejected him from 58 games, an average of once every 19 games. He was getting tossed more than once a month.

The one-man Gashouse Gang wrapped Orioles games in a circus atmosphere. "If you umpired the Yankees and Orioles with Weaver and Billy Martin, it was like a war," said Larry Barnett, an AL umpire from 1969 to 1999. "There was real passion." The league often sent letters to officials warning that tempers would flare in the dog days of August.

Weaver's outbursts offered players cathartic relief from their own frustration, signaled his concern for the team, and fired up fans. "It was like watching Hulk Hogan milking a crowd right before he rips his shirt off," said comedian Bill Burr. Like a demagogue, Weaver knew how to give his audience an outlet for their passion. "He lit up the night," said Mike Olesker, a *Baltimore Sun* columnist.

Weaver was also getting to know the umpires personally, and developing individual material he would use with each one. He liked to pantomime his frustration for the crowd. Once, protesting a foul call, he built an alternate foul line out of paper cups to show the umpires, and the crowd, how badly the call had been blown.

Like professional wrestlers, Weaver and umpires perfected their routines, live on the diamond stage 162 times a year. "Weaver played Memorial Stadium like Elvis played Vegas," wrote Peter Pascarelli. "The sight of Weaver racing from the Orioles' dugout to argue elicited the same sort of delighted screeches that greeted the first strains of 'Jailhouse Rock.'"

Ejections had been legal in professional baseball since 1889. Before that, the men in blue could only fine game participants. In the first half of the twentieth century, managers like John McGraw and Frankie Frisch believed getting tossed whipped up their supporters' emotions. A stadium spurred to passion by perceived injustice could then goad on their players to greater performance.

Umpires tossed Weaver out of 96 games, fourth all-time, but he managed in fewer games than everybody else in the top five. He is the only manager to get tossed from both games of a doubleheader twice. The only men in the top ten with a higher ejection rate are Frisch, whom Weaver saw play as a boy in St. Louis, and his old Orioles boss, Paul Richards.

Here's the top ten:

1. Bobby Cox: 162 (out of 4,508 games, 3.6%)
2. John McGraw: 121 (out of 4,769 games, 2.5%)
3. Leo Durocher: 100 (out of 3,739 games, 2.7%)
4. **Earl Weaver: 96 (out of 2,541 games, 3.8%)**
5. Tony La Russa: 93 (out of 5,387 games, 1.7%)
6. **Frankie Frisch: 88 (out of 2,246 games, 3.9%)**
7. Bruce Bochy: 86 (out of 4,356 games, 2%)
8. Ron Gardenhire: 84 (out of 2,480 games, 3.4%)
9. **Paul Richards: 82 (out of 1,837 games, 4.5%)**
10. Clark Griffith: 73 (out of 2,917 games, 2.5%) and Jim Leyland: 73 (out of 3,499 games, 2.1%)

A close play would go against the Birds. Sometimes, before marching out to the field, Earl liked to wink at one of his coaches or players, or say: "Watch this!" Then he would jam his hat firmly onto his head so he could "beak" umpires in the chest. After he got in trouble for jabbing them, he learned to flip the hat around. Sometimes, though, his arguments were less calculated. He simply got so mad he couldn't see straight.

And in the reported scenes and dialogues, fans got extra entertainment. "I'd like to read your rule book," Weaver screamed during one fight in 1967 with Triple-A umpire Paul Nicolai. "You can't read," Nicolai shot back. "Not your book," Weaver retorted. "It's in Braille."

In early September 1971, umpire Jim Evans got called up to the major leagues. In his first game, he watched nervously as Earl Weaver walked up to home plate for the pregame exchange of lineup cards.

Weaver was one of the managers, along with Billy Martin and Dick Williams, whom older umpires had warned him about. The umpires looked out for each other, and Evans was only twenty-three.

The night before, Weaver had protested a fair-or-foul call that had gone against the Orioles.

To Evans's surprise, the manager said he'd seen the replay and admitted he was wrong. He apologized to the crew chief, a former NFL player named Hank Soar.

"I'm sorry, Hank," said Weaver. "I watched the replay, and ya got that call right."

All Soar could say was: "I told ya last night, ya little cocksucker."

That was the start of an education for Evans. "That very first night, I learned that the language on a major-league field could be pretty tough," he said, "but it wasn't taken personally if you had earned the respect of the participants."

Evans once took a stopwatch out to time a Weaver tantrum. "If you don't get off the field in one minute, this game's over," said Evans. Weaver grabbed it and heaved it into the dugout. Evans walked over and fished it out from beneath a bench. It still worked. Evans yelled: "Hey, it took a licking, and it keeps on ticking."

Evans recalled his father taking him to the circus when he was a boy. "You cheered for the clowns," he said. "And that's what it was like with Earl. Sometimes, you had to put your hands together and clap for the clown." Evans said he once put his hands together for Earl. The league fined him a hundred dollars. "Money well spent," he said.

Weaver argued when he thought the umpire had legitimately missed a play, but just as often, he came out to protect his player and keep him in the game. "And while he was out there, he felt he might as well make it entertaining," said Evans. "Earl argued differently at home games than on the road. He knew he had a fawning audience at home."

Later, after he retired, Weaver told Evans that "if he had been an umpire, he would have thrown himself out of more games than he actually was." In 1977, Weaver, after getting the heave-ho for the second game in a row, pointed to umpire Don Denkinger and pretended to throw *him* out of the game, a scene captured in a classic photograph.

There was a cat-and-mouse game around catching Earl smoking. Umpire John Rice liked to troll Earl and greet him with a slap on his chest, right where his secret cigarette pocket was, crushing the smokes. When Weaver started kicking dirt on home plate during one squabble, umpire Dave Phillips joined him. As if in a Chaplin film, the two men swung their knees over and over again, building a little sand castle on the plate.

In Oakland, after an ejection, Weaver hid in the dugout toilet. Umpire Rich Garcia peeked through a crack. "What are you doing in there?" he asked. Weaver's reply: "I'm in here throwing up because you guys make me sick."

In 1972, Weaver's own players had made him sick. He was especially frustrated by his hitters, who had batted a pathetic .229. With Weaver's urging, the Orioles had made some moves to upgrade their offense. The big prize was Earl Williams, the twenty-four-year-old power-hitting catcher who'd banged 33 homers in 1971 and 28 in 1972.

If the Orioles secured power hitting from a position like catcher that ordinarily didn't generate any, they would have an advantage over other teams. The value of offensive production relative to players who play the same position was a concept that Weaver grasped decades before it became mainstream baseball thinking. Weaver figured if he got 20 home runs out of the catching slot in 1973, the Orioles would be back on top of the American League East.

There were distractions in spring training, including more labor strife and the new designated-hitter rule, which permitted a permanent pinch hitter for pitchers. Weaver wasn't sure the offense-oriented gimmick would last, and he made each of his pitchers practice fifteen hours of bunting. "I don't think that it will be dropped before the season starts, but you never can tell," he said. In any case, he added, batting practice was "better for a pitcher's coordination and reflexes than standing around in the outfield talking to one another, shifting from one foot to another."

The biggest story of spring training might have been a sociosexual drama on the Yankees that represented the 1970s counterculture's infiltration of big-league clubhouses: Two Yankees pitchers, Fritz Peterson and Mike Kekich, had traded wives and children in the offseason. (It's a lesson in human nature that the swap was Kekich's idea but that his new marriage soon broke up.

Peterson, the guy who went along with it, made it work and remained married to the former Ms. Kekich until his death in 2024.)

Beat reporters asked their teams if they would heckle.

The Orioles would not.

In a story headlined "O's Won't Rattle Yanks' Swappers," Weaver said it wouldn't work. "It would only make them mad, and they'd probably do better against us," he said. "Why wake them up? Besides, after what they've already been through, baring their souls to the public, nothing we can say from the bench will disturb them."

The funniest response came from Orioles coach Billy Hunter. "I'm not sure it would be effective against those two guys," he said. "Anybody crazy enough to make the move they did can't be upset by bench jockeys. Kekich and Peterson need shock treatment. They're already in another world."

Orioles players expressed solidarity for their fellow big leaguers. "They're my personal friends from when I was with the Yankees," said Tom Shopay, the Orioles' most ferocious bench jockey. "I'm just not that low. My approach is to try to make opposing players laugh to get their attention off the game or to make them mad enough to make a bad play."

After winning four straight games to open the season, the Orioles puttered along, playing .500 baseball during the first two months.

Williams, the new catcher, didn't run out ground balls, missed signs, and showed up late to games and practices, which drove Weaver crazy. He, his coaches, and Cashen set up countless meetings with Williams, trying to set him straight. Williams insisted he'd conform, then go back to playing the way he'd always played. The bad vibes spilled into the stadium. Williams got into shouting matches with racist Baltimore hecklers.

Weaver was losing control of his team, and himself. In April, police arrested him for drunk driving. He was given a slap on the wrist, fifteen days without a license. At the end of May, the Orioles were 20-21. Nobody was hitting. They missed Frank Robinson, and Davey Johnson, who in 1973 hit 43 home runs for Atlanta. But, buoyed by newfound team speed, the Birds warmed up with the weather. They won 14 straight games in August for a season total of 97, and captured their fourth AL East title in five years.

20

. . . AND DEFENSE

Baltimore, 1973

Baseball is the only sport I know that when you're on offense, the other team controls the ball.

—Ken Harrelson

The key to the Orioles' 1973 turnaround: otherworldly team defense.

Among the many claims you can make about Earl Weaver, there's a good argument that he was the greatest defensive manager of all time, and that his Orioles were the greatest defensive dynasty in baseball history.

Consider this:

1. The best defensive statistic that can be used going back to the 1970s counts how many runs defenders saved compared to a league average. By that metric, the 1969–1986 Orioles were so dominant compared to other good teams during that time period that I had to check twice.

   Here are the top five teams:

   Orioles 831
   A's 322

Twins 300

Expos 287

Yankees 252

2. Weaver managed *three of the top four* defensive players of all time as measured by defensive wins above replacement: Mark Belanger (39.5), Brooks Robinson (39.1), and Cal Ripken (35.7).

3. FanGraphs ranks the 1973 Orioles as the best defensive team *of all time* by runs saved, 116.

4. Four of the top twenty-five teams by runs saved are Weaver Orioles teams: 1973, 1969, 1972, and 1975.

5. The 1973 Orioles scored 754 runs and gave up 561 runs. According to FanGraphs, their defense saved 116 runs, winning them an additional 12 games.

6. Four of the top eight fielders in Major League Baseball in 1973 played for the Orioles: Bobby Grich (29 runs saved), Mark Belanger (26 runs saved), Paul Blair (19 runs saved), and Brooks Robinson (18 runs saved). All four won Gold Glove awards. Overall, Weaver's teams won an astonishing 34 Gold Gloves.

How could a team play such tight defense so consistently? What did Earl Weaver have to do with any of this?

The Orioles' extraordinary defense was a combination of talent, focus on fundamentals, and hard work. It didn't hurt that Pat Santarone, one of the best groundskeepers in baseball, kept the Memorial Stadium infield manicured like Augusta National, and that the park's deep alleys suited pitchers and their fielders.

Weaver grasped how these elements fit together, and imposed the rhythms of winning team baseball familiar at all levels: Throw strikes. Catch the ball. Sprint off the field to hit. Don't beat yourself. Every spring and throughout the season, he encouraged Belanger, Robinson, and other infielders to take hundreds of ground balls a day. "I never left spring training with a blister on my hand," said Blair. "We didn't hit a lot. We worked on defense all the time. We worked on our plays, cutoffs, and such. It became second nature."

During the regular season, Weaver organized practices on off-days, and was especially relentless in practicing double plays. Also, following the Oriole Way, he drilled his fielders to move laterally with the pitch, guessing left or right based on its speed and location, and the angle of the hitter's bat, instead of forward or backward. A decade later, when Weaver came up with his ten laws for his book *Weaver on Strategy*, the only rule on fundamentals that made the cut was this: **"The key step for an infielder is the first one—left or right—but *before* the ball is hit."**

The star infielders' work ethic was contagious and forged a special culture that infected younger players like Bobby Grich, Doug DeCinces, and, later, Cal Ripken Jr. The Orioles defenders developed impeccable timing and a sixth sense for where each batted ball was headed. Center fielder Paul Blair, who won eight Gold Gloves from 1967 to 1975, was so fast at anticipating fly balls that Weaver said he "never saw his first step." If anybody slipped below the standard, Weaver got rid of them. One of the reasons the Orioles traded Davey Johnson after the 1972 season was that Weaver thought he'd gotten too fat and slow.

One key to the defensive excellence of Weaver's teams: zero tolerance for walking batters. Strike-throwing pitching staffs sharpen defensive focus. Poor control throws fielders off their game. Without a steady diet of plays to make, they grow cold and inattentive. The Orioles finished second in the American League in fewest walks allowed in 1973. Orioles pitchers threw strike after strike, forcing contact the Orioles' ironclad defense turned into streams of outs. "Like trying to throw a hamburger through a brick wall," said Tigers manager Mayo Smith.

As Brooks Robinson aged, the captain of the Orioles defense during the 1970s became Mark Belanger, a skinny, chain-smoking neurotic shortstop from Pittsfield, Massachusetts, who played almost 2,000 games for Weaver despite a career batting average of .228 and only 20 lifetime home runs. But what Weaver could see and correctly discern was that Belanger was one of the top defensive shortstops to ever play in Major League Baseball: Belanger and Ozzie Smith are the only shortstops in big-league history to have fielding averages over .975 with more than five chances per game.

Nicknamed "The Blade," Belanger displayed his brilliance with an eccentric style. He wore a small glove and never dove. He was so confident that, unlike most players, he never wore a plastic cup to protect his testicles. Instead he used a fast first step, a wizardlike spatial intelligence, and a pair of magic hands to sprint for and catch everything. He possessed an inner computer that could instantly figure out the calculus of hop, speed, and spin of any ground ball. As he caught the ball, it seemed to transfer instantly from his tiny mitt to his throwing hand with a proper grip across the seams. With a quick, over-the-top motion, he planted and fired ball after ball to first to steal base hits. He studied pitch locations, batter habits, and pitchers' fatigue.

The Blade, a future union leader, was a brooding, serious man, who could be found after every game puffing on a Marlboro and sipping a National Bohemian. He questioned teammates, feuded with Weaver, and barked, "We don't do it that way" at rookies. "Belanger's got unbelievable range," Weaver said before the 1973 season. "It looks like the damn ball slows up and waits for him to get there." Weaver said he'd keep Belanger in the lineup if he hit .000. It's no wonder that Belanger holds the American League record for most times being pinch-hit for: 333.

As a boy in Pittsfield, Belanger "never threw a ball without imagining a game situation," he said. "Our backyard was on a slope, the grass was always kept pretty short, so the ball was always flying at me. I'd get it to come back at different angles—the height would be different, the look of it different, I'd throw it one way so I could backhand it, another way so I could extend for it, and all the while the whole thing would be 'runner on first, one out, two-two game,' or 'second and third, nobody out, we're up by one.'" The Orioles signed him after a scout reported that Belanger at shortstop looked "like he's playing on roller skates to the accompaniment of music."

As the 1973 season started, Belanger faced a peculiar dilemma. "My wife's really been getting on me about quitting smoking," he said. "But I've been smoking for seven years and I haven't gained a pound. I'm still 170. And I'm scared if I quit smoking, I'd gain 10 pounds." That might help his hitting, he reasoned. "But at the same time I might lose half-a-step of my fielding range," he said. "I know what I get paid for. Boog Powell gets paid for his bat. I get paid for my glove." He continued to smoke. (And, sadly, it killed him. Belanger died in 1998 of lung cancer at age fifty-four.)

When the Orioles were in the field, Weaver often paced the dugout, yelling at anybody who violated his orders to impose a defensive curtain. "Jesus Fucking Christ. Catch the fucking ball. That's all ya gotta fucking do." Anything else was unacceptable.

The Orioles' attention to defense impressed Bobby Grich, the young second baseman signed by the Orioles as a first-round draft pick out of high school in 1967. Grich was a star prospect, but because of the glut of talent in the Orioles infield, he didn't become an everyday player until he was twenty-five. That caused considerable friction with Weaver, including a fistfight right after he got called up in 1970. Grich was about to hit when Weaver whistled for him to come out of the game for a pinch hitter.

As he walked back to the dugout, he slammed his bat and helmet and hissed at Weaver: "How the hell do you expect me to learn how to hit in the big leagues if you don't leave me in?" Weaver yelled, "You red-assed mother-fucker!" and jumped up at Grich. The two men wrestled and stumbled down the stairs. A coach who had been smoking a cigarette pulled them apart. After the game, Frank Robinson consoled Grich. "Don't worry, man, he irritates a lot of guys." After the fight, Grich and Weaver didn't speak for years.

In the end, Grich put together a career that by modern metrics, including his defense, power, and walks, arguably merits induction into the Hall of Fame, although he hasn't gotten the call yet. In 1973, Grich played 162 games, and earned MVP votes thanks to spectacular defense and a .373 on-base percentage. When we talked, I was most taken by Grich's description of the Oriole defense. "The Orioles had their own way of teaching footwork before every pitch," he said. He learned from Brooks Robinson, "a gift from God." Brooks, said Grich, "had a way of keeping his feet a little closer together. Shoulder width, his hands were right in front of him, ready to go either way."

Here, Grich's description drifted into poetry: "As the ball is on its way to home plate, you jump up in the air, you get up on the balls of your feet. You come back down to a flat position with your feet when the ball's about halfway there. Just as the ball is getting to the hitting zone, you are on the rise and you are coming up to the balls of your feet, so that, as the ball hits the hitting zone, you are on the rise, your heels are coming up, and you are almost weightless." On every pitch, the Orioles had four infielders perching themselves like ballerinas about to fly through the air. With 100 percent of their weight on the balls of their feet, said Grich, infielders can cover eight feet in the less than the half second it takes a hot smash to get to their position.

The Orioles defense made the great pitching look even better. During Jim Palmer's career, the batting average against him on balls in play was only .251, far below the league average of .280 during that time. In 1973, Palmer went 22-9 with a 2.40 ERA over 296.1 innings pitched; Mike Cuellar went 18-13; Dave McNally 17-17; and Doyle Alexander 12-8. They didn't try to strike out every hitter, just made pitches and set the machinery in motion. Pitchers were expected to be expert defenders too. In spring training, Weaver made each of his pitchers practice fifteen hours of each important defensive skill, including bunt defense, covering first, and turning double plays. Palmer won four Gold Gloves.

Buoyed by their defense, and phenomenal team speed, the Orioles won their fourth AL East title in five years, going 97-65, eight games ahead of the second-place Red Sox. They led the league in stolen bases and walks, which helped them finish third in the league in runs scored. Al Bumbry won the AL Rookie of the Year award, batting .337/.398/.500 with 73 runs scored in 395 plate appearances. The Orioles finished eighth in the league in home runs, with 119. The best banger was Earl Williams, who finished with 22. Weaver stuck with him, and coped with his catching by playing him plenty at first base.

Alas, they lost 3 games to 2 in a tough American League Championship Series to the Oakland A's, in the middle of winning three straight World Series. After the season, Earl was given his first Manager of the Year award by the Associated Press, which called him "Patient Earl Weaver, who remodeled the Baltimore Orioles from a slow, slugging team into a fast, opportunistic club that recaptured" the 1973 American League Eastern Division pennant.

"I don't think it was my best managing job," said Weaver. "It was the same managing job I always do."

21

SUPERNATURAL MANAGER

Baltimore, 1974

She thought Earl Weaver was not fatherly enough to be a proper manager, and often, when he replaced some poor sad pitcher, who'd barely had a chance, she would speak severely into the radio, calling him "Merle Beaver" for spite and spitting out her words. "Just because he grows his own tomatoes," she said, "doesn't necessarily mean he has a heart."

—Anne Tyler, *Dinner at the Homesick Restaurant*

Earl Weaver's career is a paradox. He motivated his players, and their teams won, but Weaver rarely behaved in the way we think leaders should. Battling the demons that had bedeviled him since his bush-league days, Weaver sometimes got sloppy with his drinking. Players and writers gossiped about him. Weaver's alcohol habit never prevented him from preparing for, or managing, contests, but after games, Weaver usually imbibed at least four cocktails—he favored gin and tonics or whiskey sours—and multiple beers. He liked to order a second drink before the first was finished. On the road, he would sometimes end up passed out in bars, restaurants, hotel lobbies, hallways, or airport lounges, or on buses, trains, or airplanes.

How could this work for so long? How could the Orioles play so hard for a turbulent, messy boss? It's a fascinating question that gets to the heart of Earl Weaver's success, our complicated natures, and the nature of leadership.

Earl Weaver's drinking came paired with a work ethic and passion that made him care, almost violently, about every pitch, every game, every practice. That focus, on winning, on playing the game *right*, was intoxicating. He made his players better because "he took it all so seriously that he made you think the game was—important," said pitcher Mike Flanagan. He battled for his players. Don Baylor recalled getting drilled by Cleveland pitcher Dick Tidrow after hitting a home run. Weaver threw a long tantrum, screaming at Tidrow: "I hope you get hit by a truck this winter, I hope you get hit!" Toward the end of every season, Weaver tracked which players had incentive clauses in their contracts and tried to give them the playing time they needed to fulfill them.

He meticulously prepared his teams during spring training. He didn't make promises or lie, and he was funny. Players often hated him in the moment, but he never held a grudge, so his presence never weighed them down. They felt free to play their hearts out. "He didn't give a shit about what happened off the field," said outfielder Dan Ford, who played for Weaver in 1982. "But we get to the field and put that uniform on, *let's go*. You come to the clubhouse and he's marching through the clubhouse like a general, you're playing to win." Weaver never imposed strict curfews, or ripped players behind their backs like some managers, or punished players for speaking their minds. "He treated you like a man," said Ken Singleton. "And he was the best manager I ever had. He always had your back. But the drinking was a part of him."

Lest we be tempted to judge, hard drinking was a part of American pro sports culture in 1970s. Teams, including the Orioles, often supplied postgame beers to players and coaches. Boog Powell joked about drinking two six-packs after every game: one to quench his thirst, and one to savor. After road games, Weaver and his coaching staff usually held court in the hotel bar (players not allowed). "That whole coaching staff drank," said Terry Pluto, who authored the 1981 biography *The Earl of Baltimore*. "They had beer in the clubhouse. Guys threw beer in their sport coats. Beer didn't even count as drinking. It was just beer. It was like a Diet Pepsi. Then you went *drinking*. I learned with Earl to not go out with him. I'd meet him for breakfast."

Heavy is the head that makes the lineup. Bill James once estimated that eighteen of the twenty-five greatest managers were alcoholics. Drinking was in the Weaver DNA, part of his family's way of life. Earl had grown up with Uncle Bud in honky-tonks, pool halls, and hotel piano bars. Men of Weaver's generation drank in part as a response to a culture that didn't encourage men to talk about their problems, be vulnerable, or seek help for mental health.

There was often a comedic element to Weaver's drinking. In a Minneapolis restaurant one night after a loss to the Twins, he and his coaches were waiting for a table and dissecting the game, analyzing every "shitty pitch" and "goddamn hit." They got a table. After eating, Earl stood up and said: "Where's the fucking toilet?" Somebody in the room responded: "In your mouth." After visiting the men's room, Earl returned and said: "You lose a tough one and you can't get a table in the dining room and you have a few drinks and pretty soon the 'cocksuckers' and 'motherfuckers' just come out." It was his attempt at an apology.

Weaver liked to have a few drinks, and sing. He had a photographic memory for popular music, and could name thousands of tunes. "I got a good voice," he bragged. "I play the ukulele and can sing the hell out of 'Old Rugged Cross.'" But a fun round at the piano bar or a game of cards often soured. Once, to wake him up during a flight after he had passed out, players stuck a cigarette in his mouth and lit it. He choked on the smoke and woke up. One time, after Singleton flew to Las Vegas for a TV appearance with Earl, he had to wake up Earl after he'd fallen asleep on the floor of a rental car agency in Oakland.

On April 16, 1973, a Monday, Weaver was driving home to Perry Hall with Marianna when Maryland State Police trooper Jim Slocum pulled them over because the car was swerving. The officer arrested Earl, who reacted like the Orioles had lost a play at the plate. He called Slocum, who had acne, "crater face and a dirty word," and kicked the police car door. "Half the vehicle was up on the median strip," said Slocum. "There was a strong smell of alcohol on his breath. His eyes were bloodshot. His balance was swaying. His speech was slurred." In 1981, Weaver got a second DUI when he swerved his Cadillac and ran a red light. "If you're a teetotaler, I guess this looks pretty bad," he said. "On the other hand people in this business [the world of baseball] probably are not going to think it's too awful." He added: "That's my lifestyle. That'll probably never change. What should change—what will change—is that I shouldn't get behind the wheel." He never got any more DUIs.

In June 1974, *True* magazine reported that Weaver "has been warned by Orioles management to cease making a public spectacle of himself around gin mills when the team is on the road." It related how, at the Blue Ox restaurant in Minneapolis, he stood up and blurted: "I am a supernatural manager!" Orioles general manager Frank Cashen heard him and burst out laughing. "What are you laughing at?" barked Weaver, rising up from his padded chair and pointing his finger at Cashen. "That's going to cost you $10,000!" The punch line: Cashen gave Weaver a $10,000 raise in his next contract, because the Orioles were winning. Cashen once flew to California for damage control after Weaver was seen staggering through the Los Angeles airport. "I've never seen a human being that drunk," said one Oriole. "Walking through the airport, it was two steps forward, and one back." In the Anaheim visiting clubhouse one night, Weaver dumped his dinner into his lap, and then stumbled into the kitchen looking for the cigarette machine and the bathroom.

Orioles catcher Rick Dempsey confronted Weaver about his drinking. Dempsey's dad had been an alcoholic, and when Rick got to Baltimore in 1976, he saw the same tendency in his manager. "Earl, you gotta stop drinking, it's gonna kill ya, it killed my father at age sixty-four," Dempsey told Weaver. Weaver just stared back. After Weaver retired, when they were together at a banquet, Weaver said to Dempsey: "Jesus Christ, I appreciate when you told me to stop drinking. I didn't—but I appreciated it."

Around his family, Weaver only occasionally addressed his drinking. "He did tell us, about drinking, that everybody needs a crutch," said his daughter Terry. Weaver got to the park on time every day, performed his duties, and avoided a tragedy like the automobile crash that killed his pal Billy Martin in 1989. Other members of the Orioles generally didn't talk about it. Only occasionally, like a roast in 2000 where Jim Palmer made fun of his drunk driving, did the issue spill out in public.

Even in 1974, people were mystified by Earl's Jekyll-and-Hyde duality. His managing "is the exact opposite of his personal deportment," *True* wrote. "In the dugout, Weaver is a master of detail and organization, a shrewd judge of playing talent, and a decisive strategist who enjoys the professional respect of even those players who'd like to wring his neck."

Weaver himself defined leadership with one word: *honesty*. His golden rule: "No promises to anybody. And no lies. Those two go together, if you tell one lie to one player, it gets around instantly. You cease to exist."

In 1974, as his team struggled, he saw himself and his shortcomings honestly enough to lead by letting his players take over the team. After winning four of the first five AL East division titles, the Orioles again seemed to be fading. The highlights of 1974 were the Oakland A's, who were chasing their third straight World Series championship; Hank Aaron breaking Babe Ruth's home run record; and pitcher Tommy John undergoing the surgery to repair a torn elbow ligament that would bear his name. The Red Sox were dominating the AL East, with the Yankees in second place. It looked like a classic Boston vs. New York pennant race.

On August 28, with only a little over a month to go in the 1974 season, the Orioles were stuck at 63 wins and 65 losses, in fourth place, 8 games behind the Red Sox. The front office was panicking. Hoffberger and Cashen were unhappy with Earl. After a 5–4 loss to the White Sox on August 14, Hoffberger barged into Weaver's office and slammed the door shut to admonish him for the team's poor play.

On August 22, after losing to Texas to fall 8.5 games behind Boston, the Orioles' players convened a players-only meeting at Paul Blair's house. They agreed Weaver was in a managerial slump, and voted to set up a shadow government and call their own steal, hit-and-run, and bunt plays, and bear down on proper fundamentals like moving runners over and hitting the cutoff man. "The insurrection of 1974," outfielder Don Baylor called it later. Younger players were nervous. "Deep down inside, I was scared," said Baylor, who later managed nine years in the big leagues. "There I was, my third year in the big leagues and about to enter into rebellion against Weaver." Once, Billy Hunter flashed Baylor the bunt sign, but Brooks in the on-deck circle told him to hit away. Baylor hit a double off the wall. "You had better be glad you got a hit," Weaver told Baylor when he got back to the dugout.

How did Earl allow this subversive behavior? He never said. "Knowing Earl, he probably thought it was funny," said Baylor. "He loved defiance. He was probably saying under his breath, 'I don't know what they're doing, but they're winning.' That's the only thing that ever really mattered to Earl, anyway." The insurrection was only outwardly defiant to Earl. Its true purpose was players pushing each other to play better.

The loose, self-governing Orioles won 28 of their last 34 games, including a 10-game winning streak, and finally a stunning 11-of-12 streak, including three walk-off wins, to close the year. Weaver never addressed the Blair house mutiny, but several players described it to me and it was covered in local newspapers in 1974. That season's success also points to the subtlety of baseball team chemistry. Weaver loved winning more than being right. If that meant players going behind his back, so be it. He prepared his troops for battle and then backed off. The messy, volatile Weaver had once again figured out a way to lead. "If Earl had put his foot down and demanded we stop putting on our own signs, we would have obeyed," recalled Palmer. "But there was a trust between us that allowed for creativity."

Weaver often relished confrontation with players. If they learned to handle him, they would do better in the pressure cooker of big-league baseball games. "If you couldn't handle him, he didn't want you up with the bases loaded in the bottom of the ninth," said Orioles third baseman Doug DeCinces. In spring training of 1975, Weaver sent a pitcher named Dyar Miller down to Triple A. Miller, who had recently had a baby, asked for a raise from his $1,600-a-month salary. Weaver and the Orioles said no. An angry Miller ended his spring by telling Weaver to "go fuck yourself." Miller pitched well in Rochester, and in late May, the Orioles called him up. Weaver sent word to Miller that he wanted a word. The rookie nervously walked into a room with Weaver and Cashen. "Go fuck yourself," said Weaver, cracking up. "He never held a grudge," Miller told me. "I only appreciated him after I started coaching myself, and the biggest thing I learned was not to hold a grudge."

In 1974, the Orioles resumed their Kangaroo Court, which had fallen out of favor with the departure of Frank Robinson. The players appointed Elrod Hendricks as the judge. Leaving a runner stranded at third base cost 50 cents. Failure to run out a ground ball cost 50 cents. They raised $90 for charity. They got Tommy Davis for wearing a Cubs T-shirt, Paul Blair for jogging in the outfield with chocolate, and Earl Williams for pimping a home run against the Twins. Going 0-for-5 got you the Weakest Swing Award. Brooks once got the No Touch Fielding Award for two diving tries at third base.

After a 12–6 win against the Tigers on September 30, the court was in session.

MANAGER WEAVER: "Guilty! Fined for bundling up and wearing a ski cap."

BROOKS: "Skip, you look like [a] seaman first class."

WEAVER: "I've been first class my whole life."

They all laughed and fined him a dollar.

The Orioles again played the A's in the 1974 ALCS. The Orioles won game 1 behind Mike Cuellar, 6–3. Then the bats fell asleep. The Orioles scored one run in their final three games, eliminating the Orioles and sending the A's to the World Series. After the season, Weaver got another contract for 1975, and a $5,000 raise. He posed in a Hawaiian shirt that showed his chest hair. Even if Weaver drove the Orioles front office crazy, nobody could dispute that he was a winner.

Weaver, Cashen said in a final assessment, "was a manager for all seasons. Some guys are good when they're got a winning ball club, but when things start to go bad, they don't know what to do. Or they're a good manager with a good ball club, but a bad manager with a bad ball club. Or they look like a pretty good manager, but they've never been in a pennant race. Earl had everything. He drank his brains out. But he was a fucking genius."

22

SPRING OF THE GUN

Baltimore, 1975

We forgot about the Canadian exchange rate, so it's really only 82 mph.
—Mike Flanagan, about teammate Mike Boddicker's
fastball during a 1988 game in Toronto

Earl Weaver marched around spring training in Miami in 1975 armed with a machine pointing at baseball's looming scientific revolution. One morning, Weaver showed off the "radar gun" prototype to reporters as Cal Ripken Sr. threw batting practice.

"Sixty-three miles an hour he threw that pitch," Weaver said, studying his new toy.

Weaver felt he had to needle Ripken for his slow tosses. "Take a little off, Cal," he hollered.

Weaver looked down at the gun. It displayed 4.

"Paul Blair just walked by at four miles an hour," he joked.

Earl Weaver saw clearly that technology belonged in baseball. "Scouting was imprecise," he noted. If there was an innovation available to help his baseball team, he wanted it. He made the Orioles one of the first teams to provide film feedback for his hitters after he took over in 1968, and in 1975 the club was the first to have a radar gun. Weaver loved his data-generating toy. He carried it on the team bus around Miami, trying to catch cars speeding and pointing it at airplanes.

The radar gun came from Danny Litwhiler, a former St. Louis Cardinals outfielder and then Michigan State coach who invented over one hundred baseball gadgets, including weighted bats, the flat glove infielders use to practice catching ground balls, and a special dirt that absorbs water. Litwhiler was born in 1916 in Ringtown, a horse-and-buggy hamlet in eastern Pennsylvania, to parents who ran a small hotel that catered to mining and railroad workers. He enjoyed a successful major-league career. In 1942, he became the first player in baseball history to play every game of his team's season without making an error.

In a charming memoir, *Living the Baseball Dream,* Litwhiler described a lost world of muddy baseball fields, catching up on statistics in the *Sporting News* while smoking cigars, and packing black shirts known as "thousand-milers" because they could survive that long on train trips without washing. At Forbes Field in Pittsburgh, baseball legend Honus Wagner inquired if he had any chewing tobacco. "Hi, young feller," he said. "Got any sweetenin' on you?"

After Litwhiler quit playing, he coached college baseball and started inventing. He liked to show up at the start of the baseball season with a new toy that might improve his players and inspire them with the notion that they had a secret weapon.

Litwhiler invented the wildest stuff: a "bunting bat" that was basically a bat sawed in half, forcing the hitter to bunt with the bottom half of the bat; a five-man batting cage; and an unbreakable pitching mirror that a hurler could throw into while watching his motion. Litwhiler had Pittsburgh Plate Glass Company design that one after reading about the glass used for NASA's moon project. The pitching mirror was three-quarters of an inch thick, three feet wide, and five feet tall, and cost $300. For a while, the Cincinnati Reds actually used one, until video made it obsolete in the 1980s.

The baseball writer Robert Creamer profiled Litwhiler for *Sports Illustrated* in 1963. "If Litwhiler had lived a hundred years ago he would have invented the telephone, the telegraph and the Murphy bed," Creamer wrote. The piece described one of Litwhiler's wildest inventions, the five-man batting cage. He divided a traditional cage into five sections and cut a strike-zone-sized hole into each section. Five pitchers stood outside and pitched to five batters inside the cage. "From Ty Cobb on down, batters have been told that the best way to sharpen their timing is to try to hit the ball back to the pitcher," Creamer noted. "Litwhiler's batters get their kicks when they hit through the holes and out of the cage. Thus, with no nagging from their coaches, they automatically try to do the proper thing—hit line drives up the middle."

All the tinkering worked. At Michigan State, Litwhiler went 488-362 and won two Big Ten championships. He coached big-league stars Steve Garvey and Kirk Gibson.

In 1974, when Litwhiler was at Michigan State, he saw a photo in the student paper captioned "MSU Police Get Radar Gun." He called his neighbor, the commander of campus police. Could this gun, he asked, measure the speed of a baseball?

I don't know, said the commander, but I'd like to find out.

The commander drove to the field and parked his car behind the pitcher's mound. According to the gun, the MSU kids were throwing in the high 70s, which Litwhiler knew was within range of what his pitchers were probably throwing. This idea was going to work.

Litwhiler bought a used gun from his police friend and shipped it to the manufacturer, Colorado-based CMI, and asked them to retool the machine so that it could measure the speed of small objects, like baseballs, with more precision. Within two weeks, Litwhiler had the gun back and was measuring the velocity of all his pitchers. That prototype went to Cooperstown (where it joined Litwhiler's record-breaking fielder's glove from 1942).

Suspecting that his invention would upend baseball, Litwhiler called the commissioner, Bowie Kuhn, who promised he would notify all professional teams about it. Telegrams, telephone calls, and letters poured in requesting more information.

Meanwhile, Litwhiler called JUGS Sports, which makes pitching machines. One of the problems was that radar guns, because they were designed for police cars, were powered by cigarette lighters. JUGS designed a gun powered by batteries and came up with a portable prototype that could measure 99 out of 100 pitches within one mile per hour.

"In 1975, I took it to spring training in Miami, Florida," recounted Litwhiler. "Earl Weaver, manager of the Orioles, became the first professional baseball person to use the gun. Earl had fun with it, clocking birds or anything that was moving. Ultimately, the gun cannot clock a person running. He did clock an airplane that was flying low for a landing. I believe around 175 miles an hour. Earl really liked the machine."

Earl Weaver was the first manager to use a radar gun, and to talk about what it might mean for baseball. Before he accepted Litwhiler's invitation, every manager and coach had relied on their own eyesight to gauge the speed of pitches.

"We could get a lot of use out of this thing," said Weaver. "I'd like to have it for timing Jim Palmer's fastball of a few years ago and comparing it with now. It would be invaluable for scouting. You'd know exactly how fast a pitcher was." It would help teams dissect old-school baseball concepts like "sneaky fast," he added.

It could be used for training and pitch design, he correctly predicted. "It would help us to get pitchers to throw at exactly the right speed," he said. "Ross Grimsley has a good changeup. His fastball is 82 miles an hour. His change is 62. We could get all our pitchers to try to have a 20 mph difference between their fastballs and their changes." He had never known why Grimsley's changeup was so effective, he confessed. Now he knew, thanks to the radar gun. He also discovered that one of his outfielders, Larry Harlow, threw 92 mph, harder than any of his pitchers. He resolved to pitch Harlow in a game, which he did a few years later.

Weaver told reporters that the radar gun's best use was measuring not sheer velocity but the *difference* in speeds between pitches. "If the guy's fastball comes in at 88, and his slider comes in at 88, too, that's no good. You'd want the slider a little slower, maybe 82. That's what makes the batter hesitate and stick his butt out."

The *Baltimore Sun* concluded: "The Orioles are only looking at the radar gun, even though Weaver would like the club to buy it. The cost of one is $1,200, which is a lot of money to a club as cost-conscious as the Orioles. Weaver is trying to convince general manager Frank Cashen it would be worth it." Cashen said the team couldn't afford it, but he left at the end of the 1975 season and was replaced by Hank Peters, who took over in 1976 and authorized the purchase of radar guns for the Orioles' scouting staff.

The technology was another tool for Weaver to push his team with. When pitcher Mike Flanagan tried to recover from an ankle injury in 1978, Weaver stood behind him in the bullpen with a radar gun. Flanagan threw as hard as he could. "That's not good enough," Weaver growled. "It was humiliating," recalled Flanagan. "But you looked back at the end of the year and you'd say, 'Boy, I got the maximum out of my ability.' The biggest fear of any player is that you go home after a season and say, 'God, if only I'd worked a little bit harder.' And I don't think too many guys of my [Orioles] generation have that regret."

Weaver equipped a former minor leaguer named Charley Bree with a radar gun for every game and made him record pitchers' velocities. "Earl was the first guy to use the radar guns to make in-game decisions," said Dan Duquette, a general manager for the Expos, Red Sox, and Orioles who started his baseball career with the Brewers in 1980 and observed a scout with a radar gun giving Weaver hand signals to indicate velocity. He asked Weaver what he was doing. Weaver responded: "Danny, I'm trying to figure out if my pitcher is done for the day before the hitter tells me by hitting a three-run homer." By the mid-1980s, an arsenal of radar guns pointed at the pitcher signaled the presence of a phalanx of baseball scouts.

In 1975, the Orioles also purchased new JUGS pitching machines that spat baseballs to home plate with two spinning tires. Teams were phasing out the slingshot Iron Mike machines, which had been used since the 1890s. Because they could spin balls, the new JUGS, which cost between $1,500 and $2,500, were called "curveball machines." Cal Ripken Sr. told reporters the Orioles had three of them.

Weaver, who had used a corked bat in the minor leagues, also ordered his groundskeeper and right-hand man Pat Santarone to experiment with bats. It started in Elmira in the early 1960s, where Santarone would put balls on tees and then hit them with corked and uncorked bats. "I don't think any of the bat companies conducted as many experiments as I did," said Santarone. "I had an innate understanding of what makes things happen in terms of velocity." His conclusion: "The corked bat didn't do anything differently. It's all in a hitter's mind." He was right: studies have shown that corked bats are ineffective because hitters lose in mass what they gain in velocity.

In a crazy experiment, he once plugged a bat with mercury and gave it to Singleton for a batting practice round. He bashed balls 500 feet, but it made a slushing sound that made it detectable. I texted Singleton to ask him about the story. He confirmed it, but added: BP ONLY! The Orioles were never caught corking bats under Weaver.

Weaver loved tweaking baseball, bending and pushing it to see what new shape might arise. When right-handed relief pitcher Sammy Stewart started experimenting with throwing a left-handed curveball, Weaver was ecstatic about the possibility, even though Stewart never tried the pitch in a game. "That's why I still enjoy coming to the ballpark," said Weaver. "You never know what the hell you might see." Weaver loved Stewart's weird pickoff move, where he stepped off the pitching rubber and flicked the ball backhanded to second base.

When Weaver visited struggling pitcher Ross Grimsley on the mound and memorably suggested that "if you know how to cheat, start now," he was pushing his own players to join him in looking for an edge. In 1983, Weaver admitted to *Playboy* that the Orioles had used amphetamines, or "greenies" in baseball slang.

In the mid-1970s, Earl Weaver also messed with the game rules. In late 1975, he tried a strategy that might be called "reverse pinch-hitting." After the rosters were expanded to 30 from 25 players in September, Weaver found himself with extra bats on the bench. Six times, he started young left-handed outfielder Royce Stillman at shortstop. But Stillman never saw an inning at shortstop. Each time, the Orioles were on the road, so after Stillman hit, Belanger, the great defender with the terrible bat, entered the game in the bottom of the first to play shortstop.

Here's how those six reverse pinch-hits worked out:

September 11: Orioles beat Indians, 10–2. Stillman bats second and singles. Belanger replaces him and goes 2-for-3.
September 12: Orioles beat Tigers, 6–4. Stillman leads off and pops out to first. Belanger replaces him and goes 0-for-3.

September 14: Orioles beat Tigers, 9–3. Stillman bats second and singles. Belanger replaces him and goes 2-for-4 with a double.
September 16: Orioles lose to Red Sox, 2–0. Stillman bats second and singles. Belanger replaces him as a pinch runner and goes 2-for-3.
September 17: Orioles beat Red Sox, 5–2. Stillman leads off and strikes out. Belanger replaces him and goes 0-for-4.
September 27: Orioles lose to Yankees, 3–2. Stillman leads off and flies out to center. Belanger replaces him and goes 1-for-3.

The totals: Stillman went 3-for-6. The Orioles won 4 and lost 2. Belanger went 5-for-20. On September 10, Weaver started Stillman once in center field. He popped out to third. Paul Blair replaced him and went 2-for-3. The Orioles beat the Indians, 6–5.

Under the headline "A Shortstop Who Isn't," *Democrat and Chronicle* writer Larry Bump explained the move to his readers: "Orioles manager Earl Weaver hasn't lost his mind. He has developed a new strategic move." He got Weaver on the phone. "It's just logic," said the manager. "The only reason we can do it is having enough people on the roster [30] instead of the 25 allowed prior to Sept. 1. Otherwise, I wouldn't do it and waste a pinch hitter."

Weaver said of Stillman: "I'm sure he'd rather be sure of getting his at-bat early in the game than not at all. And it looked like he'd be the third or fourth in line to come off the bench and hit in the late innings."

Weaver wasn't satisfied that the scheme was worth the trouble, and never made regular use of it again.

In 1980, however, he did try something similar that forced baseball to change its rule book. He noted that the other team could obtain a platoon advantage if it changed pitchers before his designated hitter batted. And since the DH didn't have to play the field, Weaver could start a pitcher on his off-day at DH, and then pinch-hit for the pitcher with the DH he wanted when that slot in the order came up. After the 1980 season, Major League Baseball changed its rule book to force the starting DH to bat at least once before coming out of the game.

The Orioles weren't only pioneering new technology. They were also upgrading their team. In December 1974, the Orioles traded Dave McNally,

Rich Coggins, and Bill Kirkpatrick to the Montreal Expos for Ken Singleton and Mike Torrez. The prize was Singleton, a switch-hitting power-hitting out-fielder from New York City with a skill for drawing walks. In other words, the Platonic ideal of an Earl Weaver player.

On top of all this, a month before spring training, the Orioles shuffled off Boog Powell and Don Hood to the Cleveland Indians for Dave Duncan and a minor leaguer. "It's obvious that I didn't live up to their expectations," said a bitter Powell, who hit 12 home runs and knocked in 45 runs in 1974. "I think I was better than my stats, but I can't do anything as a part-timer. The trouble is, they judge the whole season on stats."

Weaver had his eye on Singleton's on-base skills. In 1973, he had an ex-traordinary on-base percentage of .425 and hit 23 home runs. In 1974, he had another good on-base percentage of .385. But he hit only 9 home runs, making him expendable in the eyes of the Expos. Unlike other teams, the Orioles and Weaver understood Singleton's true value.

So, when Singleton showed up at spring training, to his surprise Weaver told him that he would bat leadoff for the Orioles. "I don't steal bases," the twenty-seven-year-old Singleton told his new manager. "I don't care," said Weaver. "It's about getting on base."

In the first game of his Orioles career, on Opening Day in Detroit, Single-ton drew a walk and scored on a Lee May three-run homer. After Singleton rounded the bases and returned to the dugout, Weaver stuck his finger in Sin-gleton's chest. "That's what the fuck I'm talking about," he said.

"He was more intense than any manager I ever had in spring training," said Singleton when we met for lunch in Florida. "Lots of drills. Defense was of utmost importance." Weaver's instructions to Singleton and his other outfield-ers were to play conservative, careful defense. "He stressed always keeping the double play in order," said Singleton. "Don't make a risky throw home and let that runner get to second base."

Weaver loved Singleton, a quiet man who became a veteran anchor for the Orioles until 1984. Immediately, Singleton took to the Orioles' intense, fast-paced spring training schedule, rotating from batting cage to pepper drill to live hitting to baserunning. "So far he has been every place he was supposed to be," Weaver said. "If this keeps up, I may not say 10 words to him all spring."

In 1975, the Orioles couldn't catch the Red Sox, who went to the World Series and lost a seven-game classic to the Cincinnati Reds. The Birds won 90 games, but finished in second place. Singleton (.300/.415/.454) drew 118 walks and had a brilliant first season with the Orioles. Don Baylor (.282/.360/.489) hit 25 home runs. Jim Palmer (23-11, 2.09) and Mike Torrez (20-9, 3.06) led the pitching staff. Palmer won his second Cy Young Award.

There were big changes happening off the field. On December 15, 1975, Hank Peters replaced Frank Cashen as the Orioles' general manager. Orioles owner Hoffberger wanted Cashen to take a senior job with his beer business.

Players' union boss Marvin Miller was nearing his ultimate goal for the players: free agency. After the 1974 season, Miller had used a contract dispute between the A's and star pitcher Catfish Hunter to have the right-handed ace declared a free agent. The frenetic bidding war that ensued, landing Hunter a record five-year, $3.5 million deal with the Yankees, proved that free agency would upend the game and make players rich. Already, in 1973, the players had won the right to arbitration, forcing up the average player salary to nearly $50,000 in 1976 from $12,000 in 1972.

In December 1975, a three-judge panel ruled that pitchers Andy Messersmith and Dave McNally, the ex-Oriole who had just retired after pitching his final season for the Montreal Expos, had played out their contracts and were thus free agents. The panel advised that players and owners should collectively bargain a right to free agency. This was revolutionary. Since 1879, baseball players had been bound to their teams. They could refuse to play, but they could not shop their services around. After the 1976 season, they could. By 1980, the average salary would triple to almost $150,000. By 2020, it would be well over $4 million.

23

FREE REGGIE

Baltimore, 1976

Ballplayers should get all they can in the way of salary from their bosses, and there should be no ceiling on salaries.

—Babe Ruth

Free agency threatened to blow up the Orioles. Team stars Bobby Grich, Don Baylor, Wayne Garland, and Mike Torrez were all eligible after the 1976 season and were earning less with the O's than they thought they deserved. "Suddenly we were all underpaid," said Palmer.

The empowerment of players would upend the baseball manager's job. He could no longer threaten players with benching, banishment to the bushes, or punches. If a manager antagonized a player, an agent would be on the phone to complain, and call other clubs looking for a place where their client would play. Instead of acting like a dictator, the post-1976 manager would have to learn to flatter and cajole ballplayers like a realtor showing off a three-bedroom.

The prize in 1976 was Reggie Jackson, the thick-legged, bespectacled, outspoken Oakland slugger who had led the A's to three straight World Series triumphs from 1972 to 1974. The bombastic superstar wanted a massive raise. Charlie Finley, Oakland's frugal owner, had offered him $165,000, only 18 percent higher than his 1975 salary. Trade me, said Jackson. The Orioles bit, and swapped Don Baylor and Mike Torrez to the A's for Reggie and Ken Holtzman, a two-time All-Star. Reggie was pleased. The Orioles were a winning franchise, and his mom worked in Baltimore, at the Fallon Federal Building. The Orioles now owned the rights to Reggie, but he still hadn't signed a contract for 1976. For Reggie to play, they needed to pay.

It wasn't clear that would happen. The Orioles ran a shoestring operation. The Orioles had other problems, starting with age. At 29.5, the Orioles were the oldest team in the league. "We fit in very nicely with all the old age pensioners" at spring training, said one player. The poster pensioner was Brooks Robinson, who was turning thirty-nine in May, and probably should have retired the year before. In 1975, he had batted .201 in 144 games. In spring training, after losing 5 games in a row, Earl walked into his office and smashed a phone and toppled a chair. "I ain't ever been a (blanking) loser in my life," he yelled in remarks reported in the newspaper style of the time. "And I ain't about to start now."

Tough as he sounded, Earl Weaver couldn't bring himself to ask Brooks to retire. When he wanted to make the point that fans should come to Memorial Stadium, he said: "You still pay only 85 cents to watch Brooks Robinson play third base. But it costs you three and a half bucks to go to a movie and listen to people talk dirty." Weaver's backing of Brooks infuriated Doug DeCinces, the promising young third baseman slated to replace him. "Earl gave Brooks every opportunity, and it cost me," said DeCinces. In 1976, Weaver gave Robinson 232 PAs, and he batted .211/.240/.307.

At the end of April, the Orioles were 6-9. Reggie still hadn't shown up, yet he managed to make himself the story. Before Opening Day, he sent Weaver and the Orioles a telegram: "To Earl Weaver and team: Good luck this weekend against the Red Socks. Know you understand why I'm not there. Am pulling for you." That raised eyebrows in the clubhouse. Who did this guy think he was? "I was half-expecting him to parachute in," said Palmer. "Reggie not being here is psychologically destructive to the ball club. We gave up three quality players to get him. If we have to start the season without him, the first inclination is to ask, why did we make the trade?"

When Jackson finally signed a one-year deal for $190,000 in late April, a banner headline in the *Evening Sun* blared: "Reggie Jackson Agrees to Join

Orioles Tonight." Weaver was delighted. "I felt so good when I heard the news that I went out and played in the dirt for the first time this spring," he said. "Reggie gives me a hell of a name to write in the lineup." Jackson understood his teammates' anger. "If somebody didn't want to come to my city, I would resent it," he said.

In May, Paul Richards, the Orioles skipper from 1956 to 1961, and who had been named the manager of the White Sox, brought his team to town for a reunion with Weaver. They beat the Orioles, 3–1, and Richards took advantage of the opportunity to preach. "It's hard to win a game but easy to lose one," he said. "If you keep from giving a game away, they'll give it to you eventually." Weaver was mad: "We're not hitting. It's embarrassing to watch them go up to the plate. I feel we're going to get 5 or 6 runs every night—until the ball game is over."

In June, the Orioles lost 9 games in a row. Peters threatened to fire Weaver, the closest he ever came to suffering the fate of almost every other manager. Mike Cuellar went 4-13 with a 4.96 ERA that year. Peters wanted Weaver to stop pitching him. The season provoked one of Weaver's most famous lines: "I gave Mike Cuellar more chances than my first wife." When a fan in Kansas City heckled him, Weaver sent a note into the stands. "You have no idea how silly and stupid you look standing behind that screen and yelling, making a fool out of yourself," he wrote. "Regards, your old buddy, Earl Weaver."

Wary of getting shut out of the free agent market, on June 15 Peters made a massive trade, dealing five players to the Yankees for five players, including pitchers Tippy Martinez and Scott McGregor, and catcher Rick Dempsey. "We feel that all of the players will help us," said Peters of the so-called five-for-five trade. "We had an interest in Dempsey for some time and feel that he could become a sound everyday player."

Reggie, meanwhile, was loving playing for Earl. His assessment: "Earl Weaver smokes too much and drinks too much. He has a voice that sounds like broken glass. He is short, feisty, has a ferocious temper, especially with umpires, and doesn't know when to keep his mouth shut. He has never been accused of being a diplomat and has never set out to win any popularity contests with his players. He is also one of the few baseball geniuses I've ever met."

Weaver and Jackson clashed over Jackson's habit of talking to reporters during batting practice, and his aversion to neckties. Early in the season, Reggie Jackson boarded a flight to Milwaukee dressed as stylishly as he could. He was wearing a crewneck sweater, a white button-down shirt, designer jeans, new loafers, and a black leather jacket. *Mr. Slick*, he thought to himself.

"If you don't put on a tie, you don't fly with us."

Reggie turned around and walked off the airplane. He thought it was silly.

Reggie walked to the United counter and asked how much it cost to fly to Milwaukee. It would be $120. Brooks Robinson ran after him and offered him a tie he'd gotten from a United representative. "Hey, why don't you put this on and get back on the plane? Everything will be fine, Reggie. It's not a big deal. We know you're still feeling your way here, we know you're still upset about being traded. Just be part of the team. Earl has a certain way of doing things, and we're all pretty much used to them. Come on."

Reggie tied the tie around the outside of his sweater. A mock gesture. He got back on the plane. "This dress code is ridiculous," he said. "Are they saying I don't look good?" Earl didn't say a word. The team flew to Milwaukee and checked into the Pfister Hotel.

Reggie walked into the lobby. There was Earl.

"Look. I want you on my ball club," said the skipper. "I need you to win. It's very important to everybody that you get along with me and I get along with you. And I'm a big booster of yours, Reggie. I really am. But you've got to understand one thing."

He poked his index finger at Reggie. "I . . . can't . . . have . . . you . . . shitting . . . in . . . my . . . face!"

"If I thought wearing a tie was that important, I'd wear one to hit and I'd wear the sonofabitch out to right field."

Earl jabbed his finger at him again. "I'm not trying to turn you into a fucking cadet, but . . . do . . . not . . . shit . . . in . . . my . . . face."

"I know what you're saying, and I've always respected you when we've been on opposite sides of the field, and if it's that fuckin' important to you, I'll wear a fuckin' tie."

They shook hands.

When Earl cursed, said Reggie, "it was like poetry." Jackson also said Weaver was a "crazed munchkin" who was "funnier and more fun than anybody I've ever been around." More soberly, Jackson reflected: "I loved the little Weave. If you made a mental mistake, you saw him waiting for you on the top step of the dugout when you came back in. He'd just say one word, 'Why?' And you better have an answer. On his team, if you didn't 'think the game,' you had a problem." In July, Jackson got hot, knocking home runs in 6 straight games. He finished the 1976 season with 27 home runs in 498 at-bats and a .277/.351/.502 slash line.

In a game against the Yankees, Dock Ellis drilled Jackson in the face, breaking his glasses. Palmer then hit Mickey Rivers in the back. The Orioles rarely engaged in beanball wars under Weaver, who thought the practice was dangerous and counterproductive.

Weaver didn't lose his chance to bash Yankees manager Billy Martin. "He's the smartest guy who ever lost four jobs," he said. "He's the smartest guy alive. He knows that one pitcher didn't throw at a hitter and another pitcher did." Martin was happy to snap back, in the inimitable and refreshing style of the 1970s. "The next time one of our guys is deliberately thrown at, I'm going to deck Earl at home plate," he said.

At the All-Star break, the Orioles had a losing record, 40-42, and the clubhouse appeared to be falling apart. Bobby Grich, who batted .266/.373/.417 and won his fourth straight Gold Glove in 1976, said he wanted to go play elsewhere. "If I'm going to sit all year, I want to be paid for it," said DeCinces, who still had to share time with Brooks Robinson. "I feel my career can't be screwed around with much longer."

All of America tracked the Jackson story, the Decision of 1976. On the road, Jackson invented reasons for why he would never sign in whichever city he was in. In Cleveland: there aren't enough newspapers "here to carry my quotes." In Milwaukee: "Too much beer, and I don't drink beer." The Orioles weren't going to be players in the new free agent game. They didn't draw enough fans to pay players the way the Angels, Yankees, Dodgers, and other teams would. The players knew it. "When Reggie came here, there were no illusions he would stay," said Palmer.

The Orioles played well after the All-Star break and finished respectably in second place, with 88 wins, the only time from 1968 to 1982 that Earl Weaver didn't win 90 games in a non–strike year. Weaver mostly declined to comment on the arrival of free agency, partly because he wanted a multiyear deal for himself. He threatened to change teams if the Orioles persisted in its policy of only giving him one-year deals. If the players were doing better, why shouldn't he? "If the club persists in its policy, and there are some unsettled managerial positions elsewhere, then I'd listen to whatever offers I'd get," he said.

Nope, said Peters. Weaver was still unsigned going into the season's final month. "Weaver is completing his eighth full year as the Orioles' manager—and his twenty-second in the organization," said Peters. "He has always worked on a one-year contract and, for the most part, has had to wait until the conclusion of one season to learn his fate for the next."

The *Evening Sun* profiled Marianna Weaver halfway through the season. Earl had never had his job on the line before. What was it like? "It's just something you have to accept when you're the wife of a baseball manager," she said. "Sooner or later you know it's going to happen. Why spend your life worrying about it?" Did she argue baseball with her husband? "The less you say to him about baseball the better. There just aren't any right words to say. Earl doesn't like to hear those old cliches like 'You can't win them all.' So we avoid the subject."

The disappointing 1976 season was the first time in Weaver's tenure that his team had gone two seasons without winning a division championship. At the end of September, the Orioles rehired Weaver for a ninth one-year contract. It was for $100,000—and included a severance deal in case he wasn't rehired for 1978. "I made up my mind over the weekend after weighing all the pluses and minuses," said Peters. "When you evaluate all that Earl has accomplished in his years as manager, I thought he was deserving of the right to return."

It was going to take a lot more to keep Reggie Jackson. On November 29, the Yankees, who had just been swept in the World Series by the back-to-back champion Reds, signed Jackson to a five-year, $3.5 million contract.

24

FAVORITE SON

Baltimore, 1977

Learn to know every man under you, get under his skin, know his faults.
Then cater to him—with kindness or roughness as his case may demand.

—John McGraw

You can divide Earl Weaver's major-league career into four teams:

Super Team (1968–1971)
Pitching, Defense, and Speed (1972–1976)
Earl's Genius (1977–1982)
Sad Comeback (1985–1986)

Those early teams were good, but even by Earl's admission, they enjoyed an edge in talent. He could plug in Palmer and Powell and the Robinsons and let them play. Starting in 1977, the Orioles' biggest star wasn't a player. It was Earl Weaver. He reserved his greatest umpire battles, sharpest strategic innovations, best quotes, and two of his three Manager of the Year awards for this third act. Saddled with a team that wouldn't pay top dollar for free agents, Weaver embraced the gritty, underdog spirit of Baltimore more than ever.

Free agency battered the Orioles. During the winter, four of the top five priciest players—Reggie Jackson ($3.5 million, Yankees), Wayne Garland ($2 million, Indians), Bobby Grich ($1.7 million, Angels), and Don Baylor ($1.6 million, Angels)—were former Orioles the team could no longer afford to employ.

Nobody expected anything of the broken Birds, or Earl Weaver, in 1977. The team had cleared out some of the remnants of the 1960s era, releasing Mike Cuellar and trading Paul Blair. Brooks Robinson was allowed to stay for one final season as a player-coach.

For the first time since 1967, "Baltimore has no chance to win anything," declared *Sports Illustrated*. Even the hometown *Sun* predicted that the Orioles would finish "last or next to last in their American League East division, mathematically out of pennant contention by early August, a month [by which] Earl Weaver's rasp will be reduced to a whisper. His future—indeed that of the team here—may be as quavering as his voice."

What happened instead was possibly the greatest managerial season of Earl Weaver's career. It was the year, wrote baseball historian Bryan Soderholm-Difatte, "when Earl Weaver became Earl Weaver." It wasn't until 1977 that Earl Weaver truly turned away from bunting and mixed and matched parts like a mechanic building a champion race car out of a scrapyard.

There were three components to Earl's miraculous managing in 1977.

One was a clear pivot to his famous big-inning strategies. Weaver slashed team bunt attempts. From 1973 to 1976, the Orioles averaged 99 sac bunt attempts a year and were above league average in three of those four years. From 1977 to 1982, that figure dropped 34 percent to 65 attempts a year, and they were above league average only once.

More importantly, Weaver juggled his lineup aggressively to make sure the Orioles had a platoon advantage. Baseball managers have known for over a century that right-handed batters hit better against left-handed pitchers than against righties, and vice versa. It might appear incremental: in 1977, right-handed hitters enjoyed a 26-point edge, and left-handed hitters a 21-point edge. But every point matters. Platooning had been around since the 1880s, although manager George Stallings of the Boston Braves the 1910s, and Casey Stengel of the Yankees in the 1950s, had been the most famously aggressive practitioners. Weaver upgraded the concept with data, using charts and printouts provided by Bob Brown to set his lineups, and designed new sophisticated platoons, for example rotating hitters based on how well they hit curveballs or fly-ball pitchers. In 1977, the Orioles had a platoon advantage in 64 percent of all plate appearances, well above the league average of 57 percent.

From 1969 to 1971, the Orioles used fewer pinch hitters than any other team in the league. From 1977 to 1982, Earl used over 150 pinch hitters per year, 29 percent above the league average of 137. In 1977, Weaver made 387 substitutions, 52 percent more than in 1976, and more than double his average in 1969–1971. Weaver experimented with new strategies in 1977, for example starting a good-hitting shortstop like Kiko Garcia and then bringing in Belanger as a defensive closer. All the pieces had to fit for Weaver to do this, and it worked because the Orioles' hardworking pitching staff allowed the Orioles to carry eight to ten pitchers, freeing up space for position players.

The second part of the Weaver reboot that began in 1977 was superior talent evaluation, by both Weaver and the front office.

Most scouts who went to see a teenage infielder from Los Angeles named Eddie Murray ahead of the 1973 amateur draft described him as a power hitter with suspect motivation. Too cool. Lazy. Lackadaisical. The Orioles assessed things differently, interpreting a psychological test to mean "his drive was well above professional average, and his emotional control was well off the charts," said Dave Rittenpusch, the Orioles scout who saw him. "It hit me that the emotional control was really masking the drive, and that the scouts who talked about his laziness must have an unconscious ethnic bias."

The Orioles picked Murray in the third round. After four solid minor-league seasons, the switch-hitting slugger arrived in spring training in 1977. He turned the heads of a group of veterans during his first round of batting practice.

"Who's this kid?" Ken Singleton asked veteran first baseman Lee May.

"Murray."

"Is that his first name or his last name?"

Murray flipped to the other batter's box and kept on hitting dingers.

"What position does he play?"

"First base."

Pat Kelly said to Lee May: "You're in trouble."

At the end of spring training, Hank Peters believed Eddie needed more seasoning and prepared to send him back to Triple A. Earl Weaver refused to let Eddie go. "If he's not with the ball club, I'm not with the ball club," he told Peters.

Earl won and Eddie went to Baltimore. Earl broke in Murray gently, at designated hitter instead of first base. The position of DH was only four years old, and teams had given the job to slower, older players. Making a young prospect a DH was counterintuitive, but Weaver hoped it would relieve Murray's anxieties about fielding, and give him time to scrutinize pitchers between at-bats. Weaver realized that he couldn't yell at Eddie the way he did at other players. Or shouldn't yell at Eddie, because Eddie, one of nine children, was sensitive and couldn't handle it. The other players teased Eddie. Earl's favorite son, they called Murray. The rookie slugger batted .283/.333/.470 with 27 home runs, won the 1977 AL Rookie of the Year award, and then turned in a twenty-one-year career—among the greatest of all time. "This man fought for me," said a grateful Murray in 2003, the year he was elected to the Hall of Fame.

The third secret of the late 1970s Orioles was Weaver's shrewd leadership. He adapted to the players' growing power within baseball by fostering an even looser clubhouse. Most work environments turn stale after a few years with the same boss. Under Weaver, the Orioles instead seemed to get fresher and goofier. The players learned to direct their mockery or anger at Weaver instead of themselves or a teammate. The result was a wild, emotional, fiery group, not unlike the Gashouse Gang teams Earl grew up with in the 1930s. Weaver loved it. "Brooks and Frank and Boog had to get old, the new heroes had to come," he said amid the team's 1977 surge. "Anyway, that horrible feeling's gone and everybody's laughing when you come in the clubhouse."

The manager didn't communicate in conventional ways, but he knew what each player might need. Eddie Murray didn't need yelling. Rick Dempsey did. It was the catcher's first spring training as an Oriole after being traded to the team during the 1976 season. "Catch the fucking ball, that's all you gotta fucking do," he said, mimicking Weaver. "At first, it shocked me that a major-league manager would yell at a player like that, and then I realized I'm gonna benefit from listening to this asshole." And as Murray later told *Baltimore Sun* reporter John Eisenberg: "He had a knack for pushing people's buttons, and he would piss you off, but in a way where you were going to show him somehow."

Young left-handed pitcher Mike Flanagan struggled to start the season and was terrified of being demoted but too afraid of Earl to ask about his status. One day in the urinals at Fenway Park, Palmer suggested that Weaver talk to the twenty-four-year-old left-hander. Weaver didn't do that, but he did tell a reporter: 'I'll bet my paycheck by the end of the year he's a winning pitcher, I'm going to give him the ball every fourth day." That cured Flanagan's anxiety. "That relieved all the stress that I was going to Rochester," he said. "It was simple as that. I went 13-2 in the second half and ended up 15-10."

One key aspect of Weaver's leadership: he worried about complacency. That's why he loved to get blown out. Better a 15–2 wake-up call than a six-game losing streak of close games. He was also harder on men playing well. "You got more hits in your bat than that!" he'd bark at a hot hitter. "The guy who gets two doubles don't know how good he is," Weaver explained to longtime Orioles front-office staffer Charles Steinberg. "The cocksucker who strikes out three times, he ain't got no hits in his bat, I can't help him." Steinberg observed: "He didn't get on you for inability. He got on you if you *had* ability and wanted to maximize it."

In 1977, Earl finally benched Brooks, but in April, the third baseman delivered a final transcendent moment against the Cleveland Indians, managed by Frank Robinson. In the bottom of the tenth, Weaver sent Brooks up to pinch-hit against Dave LaRoche with one out, two runners on, and the Orioles trailing 5–3. The weather was miserable. Soaked and sozzled, a tiny crowd chanted: "Let's go, Brooks! Let's go, Brooks!" Robinson worked the count to three balls and two strikes, fouled off a bunch of pitches, and then popped a walk-off three-run homer. The Orioles poured out of the dugout. For once, Earl was with them. He grabbed Brooks as soon as he touched the plate and led him arm in arm into the dugout. "This was my biggest thrill in a long time," Robinson said. "It's a day-to-day thing for me. I was lucky to get a contract this year." His buddy Frank, Brooks said, "probably looked up and said, 'Here comes old Brooksie. It's a tailor-made double play.'"

Weaver prided himself on his mastery of the rule book, and sometimes it won games for the Orioles. On June 29, the Orioles were leading Cleveland 3–2 with two out and runners on first and second in the bottom of the ninth. Rich Dauer threw a ground ball into the dugout. Two runners scored. Cleveland celebrated its victory. Not so fast. The runner on first was not supposed to score. The rule states that runners get two bases from the base they were on when the ball was pitched. "I had two pieces of chicken and my pants off," said Brooks Robinson. After Weaver pointed out the rule, the umpires ordered the teams back on the field. The Orioles held Cleveland in the ninth inning and won 5–3 in the tenth.

The Orioles exploded in July, going 20-8 and taking over first place, then slipped back in August. They were still in the hunt on September 15, when they were losing 4–0 to the Blue Jays in Toronto in the fifth inning. It was pouring rain. Earl, whose nickname in Canadian francophone media was *Le Hérisson*, or the Hedgehog, asked third-base umpire Marty Springstead to get the grounds crew to remove a tarp that had been placed on the bullpen mound in left field. The tarp was pinned down by bricks and Orioles left fielder Andrés Mora might get hurt, Weaver complained.

Like a teacher calling his children off a playground, Weaver whistled, and waved the Orioles off the field. Get back on the field in fifteen minutes or you lose, said Springstead. The groundskeeper rolled up the tarp a little. Not enough to suit Earl. "I can't afford to tell my players not to go after a foul ball in that area," he said afterward. "Mora almost broke his leg on that damn thing yesterday. If that had not happened, I might not have thought of it. If a guy slips out there and hurts his leg, how am I gonna feel?" Weaver said he tried to offer his own compromise. "I suggested that we even make the ball dead in that area, but Springstead wouldn't do it. It's only common sense, but evidently Springstead doesn't have any."

Forfeits in Major League Baseball games are extremely rare, but Springstead didn't waste any time in waving the game to the Blue Jays, 9–0. "I'm willing to accept any criticism on this," said Weaver. "But just remember this. Somebody could ruin his career falling on that thing, and I don't want to chance that for one ballgame. I plan on bein' with my boys for another five years."

After Dempsey came off the disabled list on August 21, Brooks went on the voluntarily retired list. On September 18, it was "Thanks, Brooks Day" at Memorial Stadium. The Orioles wanted to express their appreciation to the man who'd played twenty-three years wearing the uniform. Mr. Oriole.

The crowd was announced at 51,798. Brooks circled the field in a vintage 1955 Cadillac, chosen because that year was his rookie season. One sign in the stands read, "Brooks, not retired, just called up to Cooperstown." Another: "Take Brooks to the Series."

Brooks, of course, delivered a polished oration. "Never in my wildest dreams did I think I would be standing here twenty-three years later saying goodbye to so many people," he said. "For a guy who never wanted to do anything but put on a major-league uniform, that goodbye comes tough. . . . I would never want to change one day of my years here. It's been fantastic."

Weaver couldn't figure out what to say. He walked out to the microphone behind the mound and winged it. He thanked Brooks for being kind to him when he took over the team, "when he was a superstar and I was a rookie manager with 20 years in the minor leagues."

Fighting back tears, his voice barely audible, he said he wondered if Brooks would obey his signs that first season. "I've wondered every time since." Weaver thanked Brooks for saving his job "several times over the years" and concluded: "Brooks, thank you one million times."

After he was finished, Weaver walked over to his team and crouched down. "I thought of so many things while Brooks was riding around," said Weaver. "What I had planned to say didn't seem like nothin' to me. It wasn't true and honest feeling. So I just did it impromptu. No, I don't guess many people knew what I was talkin' about." Weaver got somber. "I'd like to be like Brooks," he said. "The guys who never said no to nobody, the ones that everybody loves because they deserve to be loved . . . those are my heroes."

After dipping into first place all summer, the Orioles slipped and finished in second place, two games behind the Reggie Jackson–led Yankees, at 97-64. Singleton had a brilliant season, batting .328/.438/.507, with 24 home runs and 107 walks. Bumbry stole 19 bases and hit .317/.371/.411. Palmer went 20-11 with a 2.91 ERA and finished second in the league's Cy Young Award voting, and four other pitchers, Rudy May, Flanagan, Ross Grimsley, and Dennis Martinez, won at least 14 games. Dennis Martinez, a twenty-three-year-old from Nicaragua, started only 13 games, and won 8 as a reliever. Weaver liked to break in young prospects slowly. The idea worked beautifully in 1977, with Eddie DHing in 111 games and playing first base in only 42, and Martinez working out of the bullpen for most of the season.

In the World Series, the Yankees beat the Dodgers behind a titanic performance by ex-Oriole Jackson, but Orioles fans were thrilled with their team's turnaround, and credited Weaver, who was named American League Manager of the Year for the second time. After nine one-year deals, the Orioles finally rewarded Weaver with his first multiyear contract, signing him through the 1980 season.

25

SON OF SAM

Baltimore, 1978

I'm not buddy-buddy with the players. If they need a buddy, let them a buy a dog.

—Whitey Herzog

In 1978, with the departure of Brooks Robinson, the mantle of Orioles player superstardom passed to Jim Palmer, turning the Palmer-Weaver feuds into the centerpiece of the team's narrative. An air of tension spiced with comedy took over the team. The players, who were gaining more power every year in base-ball's perpetual labor war, shouted at Earl. He hollered back. "Earl took the abuse because he gave it back tenfold," said Rick Dempsey, Weaver's most constant adversary after Palmer. "We put up with his shit, because this guy stood out as the best manager in the game. I threw a baseball bat at him. Thank God it didn't hit him, but it came close." Despite the new contract, Weaver fought his bosses too. During winter meetings in December 1977, he lost his temper and quit his job over a trade he didn't like. Peters refused to accept the resignation. Weaver changed his mind. The daily collective primal scream therapy boggled the mind. How could this assemblage of men work together? But the Orioles kept winning.

One of the players' favorite moves was making a honking collective sound

Earl Weaver and Don "Full Pack" Stanhouse, October 4, 1979.

directed at Earl: *Wa-Wa-Wa*. They competed for who could imitate his raspy voice the best. John Lowenstein or Rick Dempsey would stand in the front of the team bus and rasp: "Can't somebody make the fucking ball hit the outfield grass! Catch the fucking ball!" Every week, they voted for "The Son of the Week," the player they perceived to have been Weaver's favorite. Weaver loved the mockery, because it defused tension and kept the players loose. "He saw guys pulling together in a certain way, maybe against him, but that's exactly what he wanted," said Flanagan. "We were very tight. We had a common bond in a certain way, and that was to handle this time bomb in the dugout."

Less amused at the time bomb, umpires were starting to air their grievances against Weaver, often with nicknames: Napoleon, Ayatollah, Son of Sam. "He's about 3-foot-1," said umpire Ron Luciano, a frequent antagonist. "I tell him to get his nose off my kneecap." Luciano coined the Weaver Doctrine, which was that umpires should wait until the enemy had departed before cleaning home plate, in case he returned to kick more dirt.

Umpires liked to troll Weaver by calling him "Rooney," after the Hollywood star Mickey Rooney, who was 5'2". Weaver *hated* it. The only nickname he disliked more was "Toulouse-Lautrec," the French painter who was even shorter. One night, while a woman was singing the national anthem, Weaver asked umpire Dale Ford, "Dale, how many calls you gonna screw up tonight?"

"Rooney, it don't matter, cuz when this fat lady's done, you are too."

"Are you serious?"

"As a heart attack, get out of here."

Umpire Bill Kunkel fought back against the hat trick by stepping on Weaver's feet. Weaver's hat was still in Kunkel's chest, but he couldn't pull his feet away, and he was howling in pain. "That's when Earl started turning his hat around," said umpire Larry Barnett, a student of Weaver's adversarial dark arts.

In 1979, during a game in Cleveland, Weaver ran onto the field with a rule book, claiming that a runner had interfered with Dempsey's fielding on a bunt. Weaver opened the book at the page dealing with interference. Larry Barnett tossed him. Weaver ripped the book into shreds of paper, littering the infield. He picked up pieces and handed them to another umpire. Players in both dugouts howled with laughter. The crowd of 34,333 went wild.

To a standing ovation, Weaver tipped his hat and left the field. The Orioles won, 8–7. "There ain't no rule that says you can't bring a rule book on the field," fumed Weaver. "I told them guys that they made the wrong call. I told them it was in black and white. They wouldn't look so I ripped it up and it was all over the field in black and white." Sounding like a repentant serial killer, he added that it was "the first time" he'd ever ripped up a rule book, "and I hope I don't ever do it again."

In some cases, the bitterness was real. Weaver publicly challenged the integrity of umpires, including Bill Haller, Ron Luciano, and Steve Palermo. "If I didn't respect the umpire's uniform, he might be dead," he said about Palermo. Most of the umpires hated him during their years in the league. "Weaver is a militant midget," said Palermo in 1981. "He just uses us umpires as props in his circus act. We're straight men for his comedy. But baseball is not a circus and the game is not Earl's show."

Weaver saw arguing with umpires as his vocation. "You got to do what you think is right," he said in 1982, while posing with Luciano for a photo shoot to promote his book *The Umpire Strikes Back*. "As Polonius said to Laertes, 'This above all, to thine own self be true.'" It was the misfortune of *Miami Herald* columnist Edwin Pope to change the quote to "as Horatio said to Hamlet." The next time Weaver saw Pope, he gave him an earful about his misunderstanding of Shakespeare: "It's Polonius! If Polonius don't say it, I've lived 35 years of my life wrong! Now you want the entire fucking quote? Here it is! 'Neither a borrower nor a lender be, for loan oft loses both itself and friend, and borrowing dulls the edge of husbandry. This above all, to thine own self be true, and it must follow, as the night the day, thou canst not then be false to any man.'" Never, concluded Pope, "argue with Weaver about *anything*." Weaver, who didn't attend college, constantly picked up bits of trivia, delighting more educated interlocutors. By contrast, another gritty river-town ballplayer turned manager, Pete Rose, once hollered at pitcher and *Ball Four* author Jim Bouton: "Fuck you, Shakespeare!"

Weaver's intensity was always geared toward winning. In 1978, the Orioles hired Ray Miller, only the third pitching coach the Orioles had ever had in their twenty-four years in Baltimore. Harry "The Cat" Breechen did the job between 1954 and 1968, and George Bamberger took over from 1968 to 1977 before the Brewers hired him to manage.

In Palmer's first start, he beat Bamberger and the Brewers, 7–0. "He's just the best," raved Weaver about his star pitcher. "He makes it look so easy, but that's the way it is. He's just that good."

Like a married couple who can't deal with happiness, they could never stay at peace. Palmer couldn't keep his mouth shut, and neither could Earl. They bickered, and then shared their version of the fights with reporters.

In 1978, Palmer and Weaver had an epic fight over Weaver's yelling at pitchers.

"Earl, I've been here twelve years," said Palmer when they met in Weaver's office. "We've been together a long time. You've done a good job managing, but I can't handle coming back to the bench and you're second-guessing everybody and you're negative and you're yelling and everybody's wrong but you."

"You're wrong, Palmer! Why don't you just quit?"

"I don't want to quit. I need the money. I need paychecks. I have kids and a divorce."

"So we can't talk about this?"

"No, there's nothing to talk about. I'll talk to Hank Peters when we get back. It's best that I get traded."

"You mean, you don't want to talk about it?"

"Earl, we've been talking . . . we've been yelling . . . for ten years. It's probably best for both of us. You can get somebody else for me."

"So we can't talk about this? Then get the fuck outta here."

Weaver grabbed the door and whipped it open. It slammed back shut. Weaver bowed to Palmer as he walked out.

"We're having a team meeting," Weaver hollered. "Everybody sit the fuck down."

Weaver looked at his team. "Okay, who wants to be traded?"

Nobody moved.

"C'mon, raise your hand if you want to be traded. Because this guy"—he pointed at Palmer—"this guy wants to be traded!"

Weaver then gave a speech about how the team had to be more intense, and pitch and play defense better.

Palmer then went to Earl's office, where he was eating his chicken.

"Earl, that was chickenshit, really chickenshit."

After the next game, Weaver called Palmer into his office.

"Jim, I want to thank you for handling it like you did."

It was a love-hate relationship with plenty of love. When Palmer slumped on the mound, Weaver stuck up for him. Then, of course, they'd get into another fight, their tension fueling focus, excellence, and the Orioles' baseball dynasty.

Dempsey, the scrappy catcher from California with a laser arm and weak bat, had played with the Twins and Yankees before the Orioles acquired him in 1976. "I'm the boss around here," Weaver rasped at Dempsey. "You're the boss, all right," said Dempsey. "BOSS spelled backwards. Double S, OB."

But the catcher loved Weaver's leadership. Weaver "molded everything we did with fundamentals," said Dempsey. "If we made a mistake and had an off-day on the road, we'd be working on fundamentals." The two men fought like feral cats, throwing shin guards and bats at each other. One year, Dempsey grew his hair long and showed up at spring training dressed like a Hells Angel. "Who the fuck is that and how'd he get in our clubhouse?" Weaver rasped. "He is your fucking catcher, Mr. Genius," Dempsey said. The next year, Dempsey arrived clean-shaven in white shorts. "Tennis, anyone?" he demanded.

Dempsey related to Weaver because his opera-singer father was also a screamer, who named his son after a character he played in *Song of Norway* named Ricardo. "My dad used to get up at six a.m. in the morning and play the organ and want me to sing," said Dempsey. "I was a tenor, no doubt." Weaver "never passed up an opportunity to really chew into somebody," said Dempsey. "He was a showman like my dad, but I wasn't scared of him, cuz my dad was a lot bigger." Dempsey was also a showman and, during rain delays, performed a pantomime of Babe Ruth hitting a home run. It always brought the house down.

Weaver kept tinkering in 1978. He experimented with playing Eddie Murray at third base. He made his team practice their special double-steal play: with runners on first and third and a left-hander pitching, the runner on first takes a big lead, then the runner on third gets a head start and, as the pitcher throws to first, breaks for home. The Orioles used it to win a handful of games from 1978 to 1982.

If the Orioles blew a bunt defense or another fundamental play, Weaver made the team practice it during off-days, often inserting himself as a runner and inviting more mockery from his players. "I didn't pick you off because I didn't see you," Mike Flanagan told his undersize manager when he failed to execute a pickoff with Weaver standing in as a baserunner on first.

The 1978 Orioles expected to match their surprise 1977 performance. It didn't work out. The Orioles were not serious contenders, but they again won 90 games, going 90-71, and finished in fourth place. Palmer won 21. The Yankees again won the AL East, and the World Series.

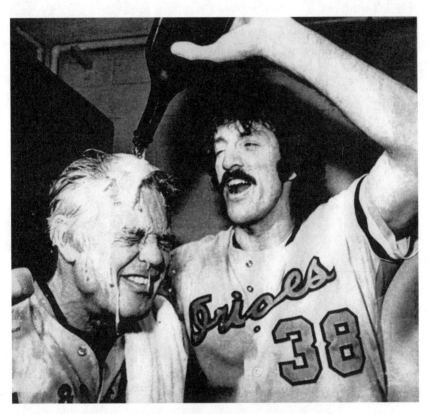

John Lowenstein encapsulated the zany spirit of
Earl Weaver's Orioles, October 6, 1979.

26

THREE-RUN HOMERS

Baltimore, 1979

The baseball mania has run its course. It has no future as a professional endeavor.

—*Cincinnati Gazette*, 1879

What made Earl Weaver famous was not just his cutting-edge baseball thinking and battles with the men in blue, but his classic wisecracks and philosophical musings. These usually came about in his daily briefings with notebook-toting newspaper reporters. Weaver had picked fights with the press in the past, but by 1979 he'd learned to charm and entertain writers.

Before and after every game in the late 1970s, a squad of beat reporters, including Terry Pluto, Tom Boswell, Dan Shaughnessy, Ken Nigro, and Peter Pascarelli, representing the *News-American, Baltimore Sun, Evening Sun, Washington Post,* and *Washington Star,* gathered around Weaver in the dugout or his drab beige office.

Weaver performed a routine that was part baseball seminar and part stand-up comedy. He dissected players, teams, and games, and mixed in stories, aphorisms, and old-fashioned one-liners. Before games, he addressed the media while watching batting practice with an eagle eye. "Is your daddy a glazer?" he'd admonish a reporter standing between him and the hitter at the plate. The journalists loved him, and could never get enough.

After games, Weaver sometimes held court in the nude, smoking Raleighs, drinking Schlitz (with salt), and munching on fried chicken. There was a urinal next to the manager's office, and Earl could continue his soliloquies while peeing. The daily Earl Weaver baseball lectures spiced newspaper stories and educated beat writers, while turning Earl Weaver into a widely quoted folk hero.

The postgame huddles were more relaxed and fun when the Orioles were winning, and in 1979, the Birds put together their most dominant season since 1971, winning 102 games and easily capturing Weaver's sixth American League East title.

Of course, Earl being Earl, he hazed writers. "Pluto, I always read your crap when I'm sitting on the toilet, helps loosen things up."

"That pad you're carrying is too big," he'd tell a rookie reporter. "Get one of those little pads that make you look like a professional."

He continued: "The next thing is that you're dressed like a jerk. Don't come around here dressed like a jerk. And the last thing is that you don't know shit, so don't ask me questions until you know what the hell is going on around here. Just stay out of my way because I ain't gonna answer dumb questions from a new guy who doesn't even know what kind of pad to use."

Orioles players and officials would find the reporter later and tell them not to worry. He does this to everybody. If the reporter could survive the initiation, Weaver would start giving them the good stuff.

As an eminent citizen of the game, Weaver educated writers about baseball. He walked them through his pitching and pinch-hitting decisions, as well as his latest tiff with Palmer. "Weaver took the time to teach us to see the game, how he managed the game," marveled Pluto. "He spoiled me for every manager after that I covered."

He did favors for the writers, like giving them "if" quotes to help them meet their deadlines: "If the thing goes long and we win, you can write that I said, 'It was a good one to win, it was a game we needed, Palmer gave us just the kind of pitching the staff needed tonight.' And if we lose, you can write, 'This is the kind of game we have to win if we're going to go all the way. Palmer just didn't have it again and you'll have to ask him what was wrong.'"

It was all worth it, because Earl Weaver delivered some of the best copy in baseball history this side of Yogi Berra.

"The Chinese tell time by the 'Year of the Dragon.' I tell time by the 'Year of the Back,' the 'Year of the Elbow.' Every year Palmer reads about a new ailment, he seems to get it. This year, it's the 'Year of the Ulnar Nerve.'"

"Don't worry, the fans don't start booing until July."

"We've crawled out of more coffins than Bela Lugosi."

"This ain't a football game. We do this every day." (This was to Boswell of the *Washington Post*, who was worried he'd overstayed his welcome during the pregame national anthem. Weaver then added: "Those horseshit cameras are always trying to catch me smoking during the anthem.")

"A baseball manager has no chance. If 30,000 people are in the stands, 15,000 will always think you're a moron."

"We're so bad right now that for us, back-to-back home runs means one today and another one tomorrow."

"The judge gave me custody of both of them," he said, pondering a feud between Palmer and DeCinces.

He called the injured list the "Dead List" because those players were dead to him.

"If baseball can germinate genius," wrote Boswell, "then Weaver is the bloom of America wit and savvy as revealed within our national pastime."

Boswell's favorite Weaverism was a philosophical aphorism that reflected the skipper's hidden depths: "Everything changes everything."

The writer, whose beat coverage of Weaver's Orioles ranks among the finest baseball journalism ever produced, explained his admiration for Weaver's philosophical depth in an email: "Few things are harder in decision making than changing your mind. It's inherently uncomfortable. . . . Can you accept constant change as inevitable, then almost welcome it and measure yourself by your ability to adapt? Earl was constantly open to new data, changing trends, new insights into his players or even how to play the game. In other words, though he'd never claim it, he was a genuinely original thinker."

Weaver's waggish repartee and fresh thinking are fun to read these days, with team PR monitors and media-trained players and managers, and when a lot of sports coverage is propaganda. The canned version of postgame bantering might be good for corporate profits, but the bland quotes are baseball's, and America's, loss.

It was during one of Weaver's postgame bull sessions with writers that he conjured up one of baseball's famous maxims.

For years, Weaver and Orioles team officials had a stock answer about their guiding organizational philosophy: "Pitching and defense." That had been the foundation of their success since the late 1950s. But it was repeated so often that it became a cliché, and a running joke. Pitching and defense, pitching and defense. Whatya got, Earl? Fucking pitching and fucking defense—hey, you got a cigarette?

After Pat Kelly hit a walk-off home run to beat the Red Sox 5–2 in the tenth inning on May 22, 1979, Earl was in the clubhouse doing his usual spiel. "Pitching, defense," he cackled. "And three-run homers." That started it. "Pitching, defense, and three-run homers" became Earl's mantra, spread like gospel by the baseball writers who adored him.

The manager and beat writers' cozy bond was disrupted in 1979, when, following a court order, female reporters arrived in baseball clubhouses. Weaver flunked the first test. He asked the first two who showed up if they had letters from their fathers, and, during a press scrum, publicly questioned the sexuality of *Baltimore Sun* journalist Susan Reimer. "It was devastating," she told me. "I was a young reporter, and this was an old boys' club, and they couldn't handle it being broken up." Weaver never apologized to Reimer, but as he usually did, he evolved, and spoke agreeably with other female reporters, giving them great copy and "if" quotes too.

Susan Fornoff, who reported on the Orioles for the *News-American* from 1979 to 1982, recalled that Weaver once questioned her judgment in reporting an article about an opposing pitcher shutting down Orioles hitters during a game. Off nights are part of baseball and not worth a story, Weaver insisted. After the story ran, Weaver told Fornoff: "Susan, I have to give you credit. That was a horseshit idea, but you made a pretty decent story out of it." He wasn't sexist, she thought, "but he didn't cut me any slack." Weaver also asked Fornoff exactly when she would visit the clubhouse, so he could make sure he was dressed. "He was nice to me," she concluded. "I thought he was a very decent person."

Nineteen seventy-nine was the summer of Bill Hagy, a beer-chugging, cowboy-hatted cabdriver who climbed atop the Orioles dugout to lead cheers. Hagy had been attending games at Memorial Stadium for years, but that summer he caught fire, presiding over a beer- and pot-fueled fiesta in section 34. He led the faithful in ritual chants, like "O!" at the top of the last stanza of the national anthem ("O, say does that star-spangled banner . . .") and personalized rhymes. For Singleton: "Come on, Ken! Put it in the bullpen!"

Weaver loved the spectacle, part of a show, starring him, that was finally drawing huge crowds to Memorial Stadium. The attendance slump in the 1970s was so bad that it seemed like the Orioles were always a losing streak away from moving to Washington, D.C.

On June 22, the Birds scored a dramatic comeback win that led to the coining of "Orioles Magic," a new advertising slogan that goosed attendance. Down 5–3 to the Tigers in the bottom of the ninth, Singleton hit a home run. Eddie Murray singled. Doug DeCinces came up. The section 34 maniacs chanted: "Come on, DeCinces: Over the fences." And that's what the third baseman did, hammering a two-run walk-off home run and driving the crowd of 35,000 into a frenzy.

After the 1979 season, the Orioles commissioned jingle writer Woody Woodward to write a tune called "Orioles Magic." Of course, it starred their manager.

When Weaver moves and we score the runs
Nothing could be more exciting
Nothing could be more fun!

Inside the clubhouse, Weaver and his players continued to have fun, and fight. Right-handed pitcher Steve Stone, the Orioles' first significant free agent, couldn't stand Weaver when he got to Baltimore in 1979. Shortly before the All-Star Game in July, Ray Miller approached Stone, who was 6-7 with a 4.40 ERA.

"I'm tired of hearing Earl complain about you and I'm tired of hearing you complain about Earl," said Miller. He set up a meeting in the coaches' room. The two men sat down, and Miller sat in between in case they fought.

STONE: "Earl, this is the way I feel: I find you one of the most disgusting
   human beings I've been around, either in baseball or outside of baseball.
   You sicken me, and I prefer that you trade me after the end of this year."

WEAVER: "Here's the thing. I got you as my fifth starter. And I'll trade you
   if I can find somebody better. But if I can't trade you, you're my fifth
   starter."

Earl pointed at his hand. "The book says you're a loser. I don't want you to
be a loser. But you're under .500."

STONE: "Earl, I've played for some bad teams."

WEAVER: "Yeah, but this ain't one of them, and you're 6-7 here. That tells
   me you're a loser. And like everybody else around here, I want you to be
   a winner."

He added that Stone would get only a couple of starts in the second half
unless he pitched like an ace.

During the All-Star break, Stone racked his brain about how to improve
his game. He developed a system of visualization and positive thinking, and
threw more curveballs.

In the second half of 1979, Stone was undefeated, going 5-0 with 8 no-
decisions during the second half. In 1980, he went 25-7, won the Cy Young
Award, and started for the American League in the All-Star Game. In the fifty
starts after he told Earl he never wanted to see him again, Stone went 30-7. "I
think Earl innately knew how to get the best out of every player," said Stone.
"And if he couldn't, he just moved you out."

Weaver, who bragged about the "deep depth" of his bench, platooned
like a Matisse choosing colors. Benny Ayala, Terry Crowley, Kiko Garcia, Pat
Kelly, John Lowenstein, Dave Skaggs, and Billy Smith all played part-time
roles. Singleton batted .295/.405/.533 with 35 home runs and finished second in the league's MVP voting to former Oriole Don Baylor. Flanagan went
23-9 and won the Cy Young Award. Palmer, McGregor, Stone, and Dennis
Martinez all won at least 10 games.

Executives around the league raved about the team's shrewd management.

"The Orioles are not prone to panic," said Blue Jays president Peter Bavasi. "They're imaginative and they're creative. They have had a certain management style with a certain sense of vision. They have been frugal, but they've been successful. An awful lot of clubs spend money to get to the position where the Orioles perennially find themselves."

Weaver downplayed his role to writers lionizing his managing. "We've got a much better club than people give us credit," he said. "I'm not working no fucking miracles."

In August 1979, Hoffberger, who had owned the Orioles since 1965, sold the team to Washington lawyer and power broker Edward Bennett Williams for $12 million. Like Hoffberger, Williams flirted with moving the Orioles to Washington but instead hired sales and public relations reps and invested in marketing the team.

The Orioles trumpeted themselves as the property not of Baltimore, but of "Birdland," a wide swath of the East Coast that included Washington, D.C., and parts of Pennsylvania, Delaware, Virginia, and West Virginia. One selling point: Weaver. Attendance boomed, rising 64 percent from 1.1 million in 1978 to 1.8 million in 1980. In 1983, the Orioles drew over 2 million fans for the first time. And except for the 1981 strike season, they drew over 1.5 million fans every season until 2019.

No matter how good things got, Palmer and Weaver still squabbled. Palmer skipped a few starts because his elbow was hurt. Weaver said: "I don't give a damn whether he ever pitches on this club. If he wanted to aggravate me, he did it. He got me very aggravated. Jim should act his age." In June, Weaver taped a note to Palmer's locker: "Happy Father's Day. Now Grow Up."

When the Orioles slumped through a 5-7 stretch in August, Weaver disrupted the slump with his theatrics. In a game against the Yankees, he approached the plate on three straight pitches to ask the umpire questions, freezing out pitcher Ron Davis, who then gave up a double and single and lost the game. Billy Martin tried to protest "Weaver's protest" with the league and was rebuffed.

In short order, Weaver got himself tossed three times. The turmoil around his antics cleared the air. The Orioles rebounded and on September 22 clinched Earl's sixth AL East title in eleven years. The heart of the club was its pitching staff: the Orioles led the league in ERA, and six pitchers won at least 10 games. Closer Don Stanhouse (7-3, 2.85, 21 saves) picked up the nickname "Full Pack" because that's how many cigarettes Weaver would smoke as he watched the walk-prone closer finish games.

In the American League Championship Series, the Orioles faced the California Angels, including former Orioles Don Baylor and Bobby Grich. In game 1, Palmer dueled Nolan Ryan into the tenth inning before Weaver sent John Lowenstein to pinch-hit for Mark Belanger in the tenth inning off John Montague. Lowenstein had hit a home run off Montague that season. The outfielder hit a walk-off *three-run homer* to win the game.

Lowenstein's stint with the Orioles from 1979 to 1985 was one of Earl Weaver's greatest managerial achievements. For nine seasons, the outfielder languished in Cleveland, never OPSing more than .749. With a degree in anthropology, Lowenstein was a clubhouse eccentric. Weaver played him perfectly, almost only against right-handed pitchers. In the next five seasons, his OPS was .833, .816, .710, 1.017, and .855. In 1979, the left-field platoon of Lowenstein, Gary Roenicke, and Ayala hit 36 home runs with 98 RBI. "The man's a genius at finding situations where an average player—like me—can look like a star because of subtle factors working in your favor," said Lowenstein.

For the second time in the 1970s the Orioles played the Pirates in the World Series. The Pirates were managed by Chuck Tanner, who led by making his players feel good. "Mr. Sunshine" versus "Mr. Computer" was how the Associated Press framed the matchup. Weaver "is baseball's Bobby Fischer," wrote the AP's Will Grimsley. "A mind like a steel trap, a plotter, a man of a thousand moves who leaves nothing to chance." The "printout pilot," one writer called him.

Mr. Sunshine beat Mr. Computer. The series was a sloppy business played in wet weather. The Orioles won three of the first four games, but, as in 1971, they couldn't close it out, and the Pirates won the series, 4–3.

For the third time, Earl Weaver was named Manager of the Year, but he was also for the third time a World Series loser. As always, there was plenty of second-guessing. In game 2, with the Orioles and Pirates tied 2–2 in the bottom of the eighth, he had let Lowenstein swing away with runners on first and second and nobody out. Lowenstein grounded into a rally-killing double play.

Weaver played hot-hitting Kiko Garcia over Belanger at shortstop, then watched Garcia make a crucial error in game 6. The final contest, Weaver's second game 7 against the Pirates, provided an extra dose of embarrassment for Weaver. In a 4–1 loss, he used a record five pitchers in one inning, the top of the ninth, shuffling out to the mound over and over again like an old man who forgot one more thing at the store, as the Pirates rallied for two insurance runs. "I feel bad," he said. "We won 102 ballgames in the regular season. We won 108 the whole year. We needed 109."

Much has been made of Weaver's record in the World Series. In four Fall Classics, his team won only one, in 1970. In World Series games, the Orioles' record under Weaver was 11 wins and 13 losses. However, the Orioles won four of their six American League Championship Series under Weaver, with 15 wins and 7 losses. That makes for a total postseason record of 26-20, a winning percentage of .565 that is not far from his regular-season winning percentage of .583. If a couple of games in the 1971 and 1979 World Series had broken differently, the conversation about Earl Weaver in the World Series would be very different.

As the following spring training was about to start, Earl Weaver Sr. was visiting Earl and Marianna at their winter home in Florida. On February 18, 1980, he collapsed in Earl's arms and died. His health had been failing and he'd recently suffered a stroke. Earl Sr. had been proud of the man he still called "Sonny" and had spent much of his previous dozen summers in Baltimore. Father and son liked to drink and play cards and squabble, and they always made up.

Earl Weaver and umpires performed like professional wrestlers, August 16, 1979.

27

YOU'RE HERE FOR ONE REASON

Baltimore, 1980

Billy Martin makes the game lean a little more toward professional wrestling. He might as well wear a hood and come to the park as the Masked Manager.

—Mike Downey

Somebody should have seen a hot-mic scandal coming. By 1980, Earl Weaver's verbal fireworks had captivated the baseball world with their combativeness, profanity, and clown showmanship. There had never been a manager who could electrify stadiums of 50,000 people the way he did, a little madman bouncing and barking between the baselines.

The world learned the deep depth of Earl Weaver's comic blue streak after a September 17, 1980, game against the Tigers at Memorial Stadium. The Orioles battled for another AL East title, and would end with the team winning 100 games for the fifth time in Weaver's tenure, but finishing second to the Yankees and their 103 wins.

On that night, first-base umpire Bill Haller agreed to wear a mic for WDVM-TV-9's *PM Magazine*, a local Washington, D.C., news show filming a segment on umpires' pregame routines.

"We spent three weeks preparing the story," said Murray Schweitzer, one of the producers on the show. "We mic'ed the umpires, and we spent an hour with them in their locker room, watching them put mud on the baseballs." They planned to record the umps for the game and capture an inside view of their profession.

Mike Flanagan, the Orioles' starting pitcher, plunked the leadoff batter, who trotted down to first base. Flanagan attempted a pickoff. Haller called a balk, saying the pitcher's right leg had illegally drifted "behind the rubber" before he threw to first.

Weaver stormed out of the dugout. Haller was still wearing the mic.

Weaver and Haller had a history. Haller's brother Tom was a catcher for the Tigers. In 1972, Weaver gave an interview saying that Haller had a conflict of interest and shouldn't be calling Orioles games. At the time, Bill Haller responded: "I've umpired games with Earl since we were both in the Georgia-Florida League. The little guy is a good manager. He is good for the American League and he is good for the game. But he couldn't be more wrong in what he said about me."

Weaver walked up to Haller and started barking.

WEAVER: That's bullshit!

HALLER: . . . behind the rubber.

WEAVER: Ah, bullshit!

HALLER: Bullshit yourself.

WEAVER: . . . You're here—you're here, and this crew is here, just to fuck us.

The TV crew, about to leave, got back into position. "We were trying to get off the field when the world blew up," said Schweitzer. Rick Amstrong, cameraman, was still lying on the warning track with an Ikegami HL77 camera on his shoulder. He was stunned. "The crowd was so loud, my earbud, I was hearing one percent of what they were saying," he said. "My soundman's telling me keep rolling, this is the best shit you've ever heard in your life."

HALLER: BOOM! [Throws Weaver out of the game.]

That ejection was one of six times Weaver was ejected for arguing a balk call. Here are the ten causes for which Weaver in his career was expelled more than once.

1. Balls and strikes—48
2. Check swing—10
3. Call at first base—7
4. Balk—6
5. Hit by pitch—4
6. Call at second base—4
7. Bench jockeying—3
8. Mound visit—3
9. Fair/foul—2
10. Call in previous game/pregame—2

Weaver was also thrown out once each for: Throwing hat; Smoking; Call at third base; Call in placement of runner after wild pitch; Throwing at batter; Trap/catch, Interference; Constant arguing. Of course, even though he had just been ejected, Weaver didn't leave the field immediately. He never did.

WEAVER: That's right. . . . You're here for one goddamn specific reason.

HALLER: What's that, Earl?

WEAVER: To fuck us!

HALLER: Ah, you're full of shit. Fuck you.

WEAVER: . . . this crew for years and goddamn years and years. And don't you ever put your finger on me again.

They went on and on, in an exchange that lasted over three minutes.

WEAVER: You watch, about five, ten fucking years from now, who's in the Hall of Fame.

HALLER: Oh, you're gonna be in the Hall of Fame?

WEAVER: You know it!

HALLER: Why?

WEAVER: You know it!

HALLER: For fucking up World Series? You gonna be in the Hall of Fame
  for fucking up World Series?

WEAVER: I've won more than I've lost, you know.

HALLER: Oh, no, you haven't, Earl.

WEAVER: Games! Count games, fucker! . . . You don't even know nothing
  about baseball!

My guess is that he meant his regular-season record, or total postseason games. If you add six league championship series to the mix, where the Orioles were 15-7, Weaver's postseason performance in games was 26-20.

HALLER: You better get going, Earl.

WEAVER: Oh, I better get going.

HALLER: Better get going.

WEAVER: What in the hell are you gonna do about it?

After Weaver was dispatched, Orioles officials waved the TV crew off the field. They walked up to the press box, hoping to film some of the game for B-roll.

Orioles assistant public relations director John Blake asked the crew for the tape. "We could see it was going to be a bad look for the Orioles," he told me.

The engineer, a large man who went by "Cheeseman," declined to hand it over. "Cheeseman said: 'No way you're taking this fucking tape,'" said Armstrong. (Attempts to track down Cheeseman were unsuccessful.)

Blake tried to get a police officer to arrest Schweitzer. The officer refused.

"They threw us out of the stadium," said Armstrong. "We drive back and our mouths are wide-open. It's the craziest thing you've ever seen. They cut that with beep after beep. He put on a hell of a show. Of course he knows he's being watched by thousands of people in the stands."

On the way home, Schweitzer called the WDVM sports department to tell them what we had just recorded so they could have it for the 11 p.m. newscast if they wanted. Once the sports department aired some of the confrontation, somebody leaked the tape. It went viral, 1980s-style. Every sportswriter worth their salt got a copy. At the 1980 baseball winter meetings in Dallas, delighted writers and executives listened to replay after replay. The Orioles threatened to sue the station but had no case because MLB had authorized the shoot.

After Weaver left the Orioles, pitcher Mike Flanagan liked to pop in the VHS tape of the fight to prove to new teammates that the stories he'd been telling about Weaver were true. When YouTube came along, somebody posted it. Haller was embarrassed. He told colleagues he regretted wearing a mic. Weaver complained it was "entrapment."

For Armstrong, it was a career-defining moment. "Dumb luck they called that balk five pitches into the game," he said. A few years later, Armstrong was filming a Weaver press conference. Earl grinned and wagged a finger at him.

One of the people who saw the tape was Ron Shelton, who in the 1980s was writing the great baseball movie *Bull Durham*. Shelton was mesmerized by the theatricality of Weaver and Haller. "Each guy is baiting each other, in very short dialogue, and they're kind of getting off on each other," he told me. "What they were doing was acknowledging and respecting the theater of it, and they knew what their parts were."

Shelton based the famous scene in *Bull Durham* where Kevin Costner beefs with the umpire on Earl Weaver's argument with Haller.

CRASH: It was a cocksucking call!

UMPIRE: Did you call me a cocksucker?

CRASH: No! I said it was a cocksucking call and you can't run me for that!

UMPIRE: You missed the tag!

CRASH: You spit on me!

UMPIRE: I didn't spit on you!

CRASH: You're in the wrong business, Jack—you're Sears, Roebuck material!

"I was inspired by the rhythms" of Haller and Weaver, said Shelton. "As they're baiting each other, and as soon as they start responding, that's when it becomes theater."

There was a purpose, said Shelton, to Weaver's manic madness. "I didn't see it as clowning, but it was performative in the way that a director also is performative," said Shelton. "Whether you're on Broadway or in movies, you're showing your players that you care. That's the big thing. Somebody can get kicked out of a game just so they know. Any guy who just sits on the bench calmly and philosophically generally loses respect. Earl Weaver's generation turned it into an art form, but I kind of respect that art form."

Shelton added that he modeled his directing style on Weaver. "I'm able to bark at somebody and then let it go. That's what Earl did. He wasn't a mean guy. Nobody ever called Earl mean. Billy Martin was mean."

Weaver claimed his outbursts were spontaneous, and insisted umpires had the right to say their piece, after he drove them crazy yelling at them on every pitch in his raspy, hissing voice, got in their faces, and scattered f-bombs on the field like infield dirt. "If they took that word out of his vocabulary, he'd a been a mute," said Larry Barnett, who umpired from 1969 to 1999.

Many umpires reconciled with Weaver after he retired, appearing with him at banquets to tell stories for some extra cash. Former American League umpire Dave Phillips had known Weaver since he was a young man, also growing up in St. Louis. His father was a minor-league umpire in the Western League. When Weaver was a player, "my dad ran him all the time," said Phillips. "And Earl was a fiery little bastard, so I kinda liked him."

Phillips ran into him when he joined the umpiring staff of the International League in 1967. Phillips was twenty-three. "I was doing quite well, and then I ran across that little bastard," said Phillips. His parents had come to watch him work a doubleheader in Rochester. In the first game, Phillips had the plate. Weaver, coaching third base, let him have it.

That was low!

That was high!

Bear down!

Open your fucking eyes!

You're fucking us!

"If you think he was bad in the major leagues, you should have heard him in the minor leagues," said Phillips. "He was always screaming. He took advantage of anything and everything he could."

At the end of the first game, Phillips's dad approached him in the locker room. "If this is how you're going to umpire, you need to pack your goddamn bags," he told his son. "Let's load the car up, let's just go home."

Phillips cried a bit, and then walked out to umpire third base in the second game. Early in the game, a Red Wings hitter banged a hit and slid into second. Phillips called him out. Weaver started running toward him. Phillips didn't let him say a word. He tossed Earl immediately.

"We had a very good understanding after that," said Phillips. "I didn't take any more of his bullshit from him the rest of my career."

In a game in the mid-1970s, Weaver ran out to argue.

"You've been fucking me" were his first words. "You've been fucking me because of Shag Crawford, you been fucking me because of that fucking Shag Crawford."

"Fuck you, Earl," Phillips responded.

Weaver waved his hat. "Earl, you touch me with that fucking hat, I'm going to knock you right on your ass," Phillips warned. "I was amazed at his reference to Shag Crawford, but realized Weaver was referring to an interview I had given a few years before in which I said that Crawford was one of my mentors as an umpire. And, guess what, Crawford had thrown Weaver out of game 4 of the 1969 World Series."

He added: "I used to hate Weaver, but I ended up liking the little son of a bitch. The bastard was a goddamn good manager."

The managers "like Earl, Billy Martin, and Leo Durocher were a big part of the pageantry of the game," said Phillips. "It's like fighting in hockey, people like that kind of action. Baseball is missing those fiery personalities which were a part of the game that is missing today." And whenever he speaks in public, said Phillips, "the first thing people ask about is Earl Weaver."

There were also, it must be said, a few civilized conversations.

In one spring training game in 1972, Jim Evans recalled, Weaver told him: "Ya know, Jim, this is a tough job you guys have here, sometime in the future, they're gonna have computers that call the balls and strikes." Evans said,

"Probably not in my lifetime, but if it does, it'll happen for managers too. One day they'll just put all the stats into a computer and it'll tell you whether to bunt and steal, and how to make your lineup."

How would Weaver have handled robo umps? "He and Billy Martin would have hammered the camera with a bat," said Larry Barnett. "I can't see them sitting there and saying, 'Wow that was a good replay.'"

The hot mic didn't dampen Weaver's fury. Six months later, in a 1981 *spring training* game against Kansas City in Florida, Weaver got into a dispute with umpire Vic Voltaggio because he hadn't properly registered the Royals' substitutions. Spring training games were more informal affairs, and Voltaggio hadn't thought it necessary. In front of disbelieving fans, an irate Weaver yanked the Orioles off the field, forfeiting the game to the Royals. "This counts to me," said Weaver. "There ain't nothing funny about it."

28

THE CHOSEN

Baltimore, 1981–1982

I found a delivery in my flaw.

—Dan Quisenberry

For decades, Earl Weaver had toured ballparks and bars across America with Cal Ripken Sr., wiry ex-catcher and high priest of the Oriole Way. In 1978, the Orioles drafted his oldest son, Cal Ripken Jr., a promising high school pitcher and shortstop. Earl had known the boy since his birth and had watched him shag fly balls in an Orioles uniform when he was eight years old.

Now he had to manage young Cal's ascension to the big leagues. It was a scary proposition. The Ripkens were like family, and in the worst-case scenario, Earl might have to tell Cal Jr. that he, like young Earl Weaver, had failed at his dream. In the new world of 1980s free agency, the Orioles needed an infusion of young talent to keep up with the Yankees, who, before the 1981 season, signed David Winfield to a ten-year, $20 million contract. Baltimore still didn't have that kind of money.

From the beginning, Weaver looked at Cal as a shortstop, even though at 6'4", 210 pounds, he outsized contemporaries at the position. Earl had followed Cal since high school, and knew he was a defensive wiz. As a freshman, Cal hit .065, but played shortstop and "sucked up everything that was hit to him," his coach said. By the time he was a senior, he hit .492 and pitched, winning 14 games and throwing a no-hitter.

Cal struggled at short during his early minor-league stints, so the team moved him to third. Poor Doug DeCinces. In the mid-1970s, he had waited his turn to play third base for the Orioles until Brooks Robinson retired. He'd played well, and now another phenom son of the Oriole Way was breathing down his neck. DeCinces had known Cal since he was a boy. He had once scooped him up in his arms to protect him from a kid with a gun shooting from beyond the right-field fence in Asheville, North Carolina. "If it ever did come to that point where young Rip took over the third-base job from me, well, that's baseball," said DeCinces.

On August 9, 1981, the day the MLB season resumed after a dramatic fifty-day strike, the Orioles called up Cal Jr. He'd been hitting .290 with 23 home runs and 74 RBI at Rochester. Peters asked Cal Sr. to call his son to tell him he was being brought up to the bigs.

Senior, a tight-lipped old-schooler, initially declined. He didn't want special treatment. He relented and drove Cal to Memorial Stadium on his first day. For father and son, it was a chance to get to know each other better. Like Earl and his children, they had often lived apart because of baseball. "I've always had a good rapport with Cal; I respect him and I know he respects me," said Cal Sr. In a 1981 interview, Cal Jr. said: "If I do well in baseball, everybody will say my Dad was chiefly responsible, but baseball took a lot of my Dad's time and most of the time my mother took me to Little League games."

On August 10, Cal, still only twenty years old, made his major-league debut: he pinch-ran and scored on John Lowenstein's single to right field to beat the Royals 3–2. Ripken played third and some shortstop for the Orioles in 1981 and acquitted himself respectfully on defense, although he batted a miserable .128/.150/.128 in 40 plate appearances. The Orioles finished 59-46 in 1981, only one game overall behind Milwaukee, but failed to qualify for the playoffs under a baroque split-season system.

As the Orioles planned their 1982 season, Weaver fought with Peters and the front office about the destiny of their young star. Weaver wanted him to play short. Peters said he was too big and should play third, with Bobby Bonner, a young prospect drafted the same year as Cal, getting a chance at short.

Peters won the debate. Before the 1982 season, he traded DeCinces to the Angels for outfielder Dan Ford. This accomplished three goals: it cleared the way for Ripken to play third, opened up a spot for Bonner at short, and punished DeCinces for union activism. When a second big players' strike, a fifty-day work stoppage, interrupted the 1981 season, DeCinces had acted as player rep.

As an older college draftee out of Arizona State, Bonner initially outplayed Ripken. In 1979, he hit a respectable .291/.322/.412 for Double-A Charlotte. In 1982, Topps published a baseball card with Ripken and Bonner appearing together as "Future Stars."

But Bonner was no Cal Ripken Jr. When Peters sent Bonner to the big leagues in 1980, Earl jumped on him like a wolf.

The first time they met, in the manager's office at Tiger Stadium, Bonner said he walked in and said: "Hi, skip, nice to meet you, I'm Bobby Bonner."

Earl responded: "Who the fuck do you think you are?"

"Well, coach, I'm Bobby Bonner, it's good to meet you."

"Who the fuck do you think you are?"

Bonner thought he was kidding and just stared at his new manager.

"I just got off the phone with the front office, and they said you're some hot-shot prospect and I need to play you," said Earl. "Well, I don't care what kind of pressure you're putting on the front office, I'm not going to put you in."

"Skip, I don't know what you're talking about. I've never put pressure on anybody. I'm just happy to be here."

"You just sit and learn, rookie."

Weaved played Bonner in only four games in 1980. He went 0-4 and, in Weaver's eyes, misplayed a ball in Toronto that cost the Orioles a game in which Eddie Murray hit three home runs. In a brief 1981 call-up, Bonner batted .296/.310/.370, good enough to earn him more playing time in 1982, if he just could escape the wrath of Weaver.

Part of the problem was a culture clash. Bonner had embraced evangelical Christianity after a wild youth of parties, cocaine, and LSD. On a road trip back from a speaking engagement, Bonner was stuck in a snowstorm with Cal Sr. When the crusty old coach expressed his desire for a drink, Bonner lectured him for an hour about how Jesus could save him from alcoholism. "Rip just stared ahead the whole time," said Bonner. "He never said a word."

Farm director Tom Giordano threatened to fine Bonner if he didn't stop leading team Bible studies, although when the Orioles had a prospect who seemed to be falling prey to the nightlife, they asked Bonner to counsel him.

On a flight to Seattle during the 1982 season, Earl and his coaches were drinking. Earl called Bobby over to ask him about his Christianity.

"Bonner, Bonner, come back here, we wanna talk to you."

Bobby walked over.

"Bonner, you think you're better than I am, don't ya."

"No, skip, I don't. As a matter of fact, I'm the chief of sinners. I'm the worst. And God saved me."

"No, you just think you're so good. You're so uppity-up."

Then the manager launched into a sermon of his own. "Lemme tell you about this Jesus thing," said Earl. "When Jesus was on the cross, and he was dying, and he said, 'Forgive them, Father, for they know not what they're doing,' and that means when I get drunk, God forgives me anyway, because *I don't know* what I'm doing. What do you think about that?"

Bonner then lectured his manager about Jesus Christ and, as he walked back to his seat, thought to himself: "Well, I'm never going to play again." He was right, but it was mostly his own fault. In 1982, Bonner batted .169/.198/.234 in 84 plate appearances.

Weaver enjoyed playing the Socratic gadfly. One of the most frequently cited Earl Weaver quotes is his reaction to outfielder Pat Kelly's admonition that his manager should "walk with the Lord." Earl's classic reply: "I'd rather you walk with the bases loaded."

Once, after Kelly hit a home run and returned to the dugout saying the Lord had been looking out for him, Weaver exclaimed: "What about that poor sonuvabitch on the mound who threw you the high slider? We better not be counting on God. I ain't got no stats on God. He always knows who's gonna win. We're just acting it out so 26 million people will pay to get through them gates."

Weaver said he did not go to church but was raised Lutheran, went to Sunday school for nine years, and prayed every day. He called himself a Christian. That, he said, was why he didn't carry grudges. "I can't live with hatred inside of me," he said. "That's what I learned. I ain't afraid of dying, either." He told

Playboy he believed in the Apostles' Creed and that Jesus was the son of God, but added that he didn't think Christianity clashed with reincarnation. "There are so many religions, and everybody interprets the Bible differently," he said.

Earl sometimes attended Kelly's chapel services. "Pat had been a reborn Christian for two or three years, and he wanted to get everybody on his side in ten minutes. I don't know why, but I always teased him."

One afternoon before a game, Weaver walked in on Kelly reading the Bible. Kelly was a terrible baserunner.

"Pat, can you find a chapter on baserunning in there?"

Kelly closed the Bible. "Earl, when was the last time you had this book open?"

Not since the start of the season, Weaver confessed.

"When was the last time you got down on your knees and prayed?"

"Last night—when I gave you the steal sign."

Kelly, not amused, told Weaver: "You're going to hell! You'll never get to heaven!"

They went at it, until somebody yelled, "Give it a rest!" and they quieted down.

Once, seeing Al Bumbry heading to chapel service, Weaver said: "Take your bat."

On the last day of 1983 spring training, manager Joe Altobelli called Bonner into the clubhouse.

"You're taking this Jesus thing too far," he told Bonner.

"Joe, He lives in my heart, so He goes where I go."

"Well, He ain't going to Baltimore."

After the 1983 season, another year in the minors, Bonner quit playing baseball to devote himself to missionary work in Africa. "Earl just destroyed that kid," said Hank Peters. Weaver later professed remorse about how he treated Bobby. He and Bonner didn't speak for twenty-four years, until they were both invited to a party to celebrate Cal Ripken Jr.'s election to the Hall of Fame in 2007. "I thought [Bobby] was a really good shortstop," said Ripken. "Things just didn't work out."

Bobby walked over to Earl.

"Hi, Earl, it's Bobby Bonner."

"Bobby, don't you hate me?"

"No, Earl, I love you." He gave Earl a hug. And Earl hugged him back.

"I don't have any bitterness," said Bonner. "I played with the best baseball players in the world." And he was never jealous of his famous rival, whom he respected as a superior ballplayer.

Starting the season at third base, Cal hit a home run on Opening Day. After that thrill, he notched just 4 hits in 55 at-bats, for a batting average of .117. To make things worse, in California, DeCinces played like an All-Star; trading him away likely cost the Orioles the 1982 American League East title.

Earl couldn't yell at Cal like he yelled at Dempsey and the others. Instead he sat next to Cal in the dugout and yelled at the field, as if thinking out loud, but in an Earl Weaver kind of way: "Take the fucking pitch down the middle, swing at the fucking pitch over his head or in the fucking dirt!" he'd say, to nobody in particular. "How's he ever going to hit that way?" It was confusing for Cal. "I didn't know if he was talking to me, or just muttering to himself," he told me.

Of all the players I talked to for this book, the one who emphasized Earl Weaver's human decency the most was Cal. "I find it stimulating to talk about Earl Weaver," he said. "People don't know about the empathetic side of Earl, and that's what I saw." A brand-name superstar, he has always been careful about how he talks about himself and his teammates, managers, and coaches. Earl was part of the big-league fraternity, which meant one layer of protection from prying writers like me, but he was also like family, an even higher grade. He had come from the same hardscrabble world of bush-league bus rides, dive bars, and dollar diners as Cal Sr.

Unlike the other players, whose attachment to Weaver wasn't as intimate, Cal declined to share stories about Earl's cussing, chain-smoking, or drinking. Cal allowed that his dad had spent "a lot of time in the bar" with Earl. Sometimes they'd fight, he said, and Earl would fire Cal, only to rehire him the next day. "Maybe drinking had something to do with it," Cal said.

Cal was equipped better than anybody else to accept Earl's limitations, to appreciate him for his devotion to baseball at the expense of a regular family life, because his dad had been the same breed of man.

Cal Ripken Sr. was born in Stepney, Maryland, in 1935. When he was nine, his dad, who owned a general store, was killed in a car accident. Baseball was one of the ways he and his brothers spent time together without adult supervision. Cal Sr. signed with Baltimore in 1956 and hit .253 in 583 games over seven minor-league seasons. After he quit playing, he became a devoted coach committed to preaching the Oriole Way, and played a key role in developing stars like Jim Palmer, Eddie Murray, and Mike Flanagan. "Practice doesn't make perfect," he said. "Perfect practice makes perfect."

Like Weaver, Senior embraced the itinerant baseball life. When I asked Cal Jr. why he never managed, he said it was because "my dad wasn't there for me a lot, and I chose to be there for my kids, who were eight and twelve when I retired." When Cal was a boy, the Ripkens lived part-time in fourteen towns in ten states over eighteen years: Phoenix, Arizona; Wilson, North Carolina; Pensacola, Florida; Amarillo, Texas; Appleton (Fox Cities), Wisconsin; Little Rock, Arkansas; Leesburg, Florida; Rochester, New York; Appleton again; Aberdeen, South Dakota; Tri Cities (Kennewick), Washington; Aberdeen, South Dakota, again; Miami, Florida; Elmira, New York; Rochester again; Dallas, Texas; Asheville, North Carolina; and, of course, Aberdeen, Maryland.

As young Cal rose through the ranks, Weaver and Ripken Sr. hovered like wolves protecting a puppy. During a spring training practice game, when Earl was managing a team with Cal Jr. on it and Cal Sr. was managing the opposition, Cal Jr. ripped a few balls, causing Earl to ask: Had Cal Sr. ordered his pitchers to throw meatballs to his son?

Not fucking likely, Cal Sr. hollered back.

When Cal Jr. didn't hit in 1982, it was no laughing matter. He would pop up or strike out, and walk back to the dugout. Almost every day, Earl invited Cal into his office. "He would reassure me that he wasn't sending me down," said Cal. "'You're playing really well at third. This is the next level. You tore up Double A and you tore up Triple A and you tore up winter ball. This is just the next step.'"

On the plane, in the clubhouse, and in the bar, Weaver and Senior schemed about how to get the kid going.

For a young man still getting his feet wet, it was overwhelming. Everybody was giving him advice. Fans. Bat boys. Only a few people seemed to help. Standing on third base, Reggie Jackson, now of the Angels, told him to just do things his way, which gave his confidence a boost. That, his dad's coaching, and Earl's patience helped him get back on his feet and start hitting.

One of the issues was that Cal Jr. stood with his heels practically in the back of the batter's box and lunged into the ball, often driving it the other way. That allowed him to hit both inside and outside pitches. To Weaver, this made no sense. Just crowd the plate and pull the ball. "You're standing too far from home plate," he told Cal. "Big-league pitchers can hit the outside corner." Cal disagreed. He could hit the outside pitches. During a pivotal batting practice session in Toronto, Cal Sr., a virtuoso batting practice pitcher, tossed nothing but outside pitches, giving Junior increasing confidence as he hit each ball harder than the last. It was a setup, conjured by Weaver to give Cal more confidence. "Huh, I guess you can cover the outsider corner," said Weaver as he walked away. The manager, Ripken emphasized, was not known as a "teacher," but he was a pitch-perfect talent evaluator, and wasn't afraid to admit he was wrong.

By the end of June, Cal was hitting .263. That solved one problem.

At the end of June, Weaver, tired of Lenn Sakata's average bat and bad defense, and of Bonner's abysmal hitting, moved Ripken to shortstop. When Weaver called Cal into his office on July 1 to tell him, he said: "When the ball's hit to you, I want you to catch it, I want you to get a really good grip on it, take your time, and throw the ball to first base. If you make a good throw to first base and he's safe, he's only on first." Later, Weaver, like a friendly uncle, added: "Play shortstop like you did in high school."

That was it. Ripken emerged as the league's best all-around shortstop, delivering big hits and eye-popping plays punctuated by his cannon arm. Ripken stuck at shortstop every day until 1997, cracking offensive and defensive records to become the Iron Man of baseball legend, a first-ballot Hall of Famer, and a pivotal character in baseball history.

Once again, Weaver had seen into baseball's future. The shortstops of the earlier generations were diminutive defense-first men like Phil Rizzuto, Bert Campaneris, and Luis Aparicio. Freddy Patek, who played short for the Kansas City Royals in the 1970s, was the shortest everyday player in baseball history, at 5'4". The best shortstop at the time of Cal's move to the position was Ozzie Smith, who hit 28 home runs in 19 seasons.

There was the occasional exception to inspire Earl. Marty Marion, a 6'2" shortstop, played for the Cardinals in the 1940s. He was one of Earl's favorite players, and Weaver wore number 4 in his honor. And Ron Hansen, a 6'3" shortstop, won a Rookie of the Year award for the Orioles in 1960.

Cal's ascension changed everything, opening the door for shortstops like Nomar Garciaparra, Derek Jeter, and Alex Rodriguez. By the 2020s, there would be a 6'7" shortstop, Oneil Cruz. Weaver consistently named moving to Cal to short as one of his proudest achievements.

In 1982, Ripken hit .264 with 28 home runs and 93 RBI to win the Rookie of the Year award. He also played 160 games, not missing any after a May 30 contest against the Blue Jays. He didn't miss another Orioles game until September 20, 1998, breaking Lou Gehrig's consecutive-game record in 1995. Cal also won two MVP awards, hit 431 home runs, and set a slew of defensive marks, including the shortstop record for fewest errors in a season.

Earl Weaver had been right all along.

The Orioles lost the 1982 pennant,
but fans stayed to thank Earl, October 3, 1982.

29

THANKS, EARL

Baltimore, 1982

Managing is like holding a dove in your hand. If you hold it too tightly, you kill it, but if you hold it too loosely, you lose it.

—Tommy Lasorda

For years, Earl Weaver had eyed 1982 as his final season. He was only fifty-one, but burned-out. Baseball was all he'd cared about since he was four. He'd failed at his dream of being a player, and his career as a manager, especially the parts where he had to crush other men's dreams, had felt like *work*. He was exhausted by the emotional bargain of his job. A manager leads with loyalty and wins by firing or relegating players. "It rips your heart, but it goes with the manager's office," he explained. "You can't help loving them, yet you can't afford to."

It was time for a break. "Just once, I want to see the sky turn to dusk without the stadium lights coming on," he said. He dreamed of dog races, afternoon cocktails with Marianna, and Florida golf courses. A frugal coupon clipper, especially with his beloved Raleigh cigarettes, Weaver was proud that he'd saved enough to retire.

As he contemplated his last baseball games, Earl Weaver was too thoughtful not to reflect on what he'd given up. Baseball, he said, had cost him "everything that people do on Saturdays and Sundays. . . . Everything that people do when they go home and kiss their wife right before dinner. The things that they do with their lives. What a husband does with his wife, during dinner, after dinner, before they go to bed. . . . Along with that, it kept me from being with my children when they were growing up."

With Weaver's head out of the game, the Orioles' 1982 campaign got off to a rocky start. On May 1, the Orioles were 6-13, 7 games behind the first-place Red Sox. The hitters weren't hitting. The pitchers couldn't get anybody out. Players complained to reporters that Weaver was unorganized and unmotivated. The Birds rallied to 44-38 at the All-Star break, 3.5 games behind the Brewers and Red Sox, who were tied for first place.

Of course, Earl as Hamlet was still Earl. On July 17, Weaver slapped umpire Terry Cooney in the face during a clash over a close call at first base. After American League president Lee MacPhail suspended him, he issued a lame apology: "If there was physical contact, and the films seem to indicate there was, I am truthfully sorry." Then, in a trolling statement, Weaver wrote: "Hi, newspeople. This is Earl Weaver just outside manager's corner!" MacPhail, he declared, "has again been kind enough to grant me seven days vacation during the regular season. The only thing unfair about this is that he gives his umpires two weeks during the year." Weaver called MacPhail "harmless," like "a little boy." By getting a week off and a $2,000 fine, Weaver wrote, he would be able to earn "five to ten" times that amount in appearance fees.

"You take the bad with the good," said General Manager Hank Peters. "In Earl's case, the good is far greater."

Around the country, fans cheered the man they had booed so often. In Toronto, the stadium announcer said: "The Toronto management would like to take this opportunity to wish Earl Weaver the best of luck in his retirement. Thanks for the memories." Writers bemoaned the imminent departure of their favorite manager. "He has fought with all the umpires, and studied his index cards and made all his moves and laughed a lot, and has been the best at his job by about five lengths," wrote Mike Lupica in the New York *Daily News*. "Even if he stays away for only one season as part of his retirement, he will cut out a huge piece of baseball's heart. In so many ways, he is the truest citizen of the game."

Players weren't sure what to think, although when cornered, most backed their manager. "We're gonna miss The Weave," said pitcher Sammy Stewart. "I don't know where they're gonna find another manager who'll take all the lumps that this club gives Earl." A new manager might be stricter. "There'll be a lot more rules," said Stewart, "'cause Earl ain't got any of 'em, except to show up at the park on time and wear a sport coat on the road."

The manager also had a book to promote. In 1982, Doubleday published *It's What You Learn After You Know It All That Counts*, a memoir ghostwritten by Berry Stainback. It was the fullest account of Weaver's life, detailing his upbringing with Uncle Bud, his painful minor-league purgatory, his springs in southern Georgia, and his battles with Palmer and Dempsey. His only regret, he told Lupica, "was that I never got to play in the big leagues, which every kid dreams about. Other than that, I've been the luckiest man in the world. I've been able to make a living and send my kids through college doing the only thing I ever loved."

What would he do in retirement? "Go to Vegas. Take a cruise. Go to Europe. Go to Gulfstream. Go to Hialeah. Play golf. Stuff my sausage and pepperoni. Cook dinner for my wife if I wanted to. Play more golf. I'll watch a ballgame if I don't fall asleep, 'cause I'm tired of pitching duels. That life doesn't sound so bad, does it? The only difference will be that instead of betting $10 when I go to the track, I'll bet $5, and I won't try to box any of them fucking exactas anymore. In fact, if I don't win money at golf one day, I ain't going to the track the next."

Writers speculated about who Weaver's successor might be. Would it be Senior, or another Baltimore baseball veteran like Joe Altobelli or Jim Frey? Or a bigger name from outside, like Tony La Russa or Frank Robinson?

Slowly but surely, the Orioles got their act together. In August, Palmer and Weaver met behind closed doors for, in Palmer's words, "the best talk we've ever had." When asked about the feud, Weaver snapped: "See what he says now. Don't drag up the old stuff." Still, on August 27, the Orioles were 7 games behind the Brewers with 34 games to play. It didn't feel like Weaver would be going out with a postseason run.

But Weaver still had a few tricks up his sleeve.

DeCinces's departure had left a hole at third base. Ripken was great, but he couldn't play short *and* third. Enter Glenn Gulliver. The Orioles picked him up before the 1982 season. With Evansville in 1981, he had hit .265 but recorded a mighty .405 on-base percentage.

In June, the Orioles brought him up and gave him 185 plate appearances. "Earl told me I was going to bat second and take the first pitch," said Gulliver. "He said you're not going to hit for a high average, but with your high on-base percentage you'll get on base in front of the big guys." And that's what happened: in 185 plate appearances, Gulliver hit .200 but recorded a .363 on-base percentage, 22 points higher than the team's overall .341, helping to turn around the Orioles' season.

The Tigers had drafted the Detroit native out of Eastern Michigan University in 1976, but he'd gotten stuck behind Alan Trammell and Lou Whitaker. Gulliver loved Earl because he believed in him, and because he was so passionate. "I fit into his mold," said Gulliver. "He was into every pitch. During the games, he cared so much, it was good. And nowadays, people manage with computers, and Earl did it all without computers." The following season, under Joe Altobelli, Gulliver's on-base skills were not as appreciated. Even though he batted .309/.464/.472 at Rochester, he earned only 57 plate appearances in Baltimore and never played in the major leagues after that.

In July, on a road trip to Seattle, Earl gave the baseball world another hilarious gift that has lasted into the twenty-first century. It's so outrageous and foul that it sounds like it must be a fake, while in fact it was intended as a prank and not to be aired. Before a game, Baltimore radio host Tom Marr and Weaver recorded a spoof version of his pregame "Manager's Corner" segment and sent it back to the station as a joke.

The introduction—"and now, for 'Manager's Corner,' with Earl Weaver"— sounds on-key, but a mischievous glee builds in Weaver's voice: "Hi, everybody, this is Earl Weaver with 'Manager's Corner.' Today I have Tom Marr, Orioles broadcaster, back on the show. And I understand Tom's been getting some mail with questions that supposedly I can answer. Now what the fuck are some of these goddamn questions, Tom?"

Then it gets crazy. Marr reads a question from a listener wanting to know if the Orioles miss Don Stanhouse. Earl: "Don Stanhouse was an asshole. He had us in trouble, had the fucking bases loaded goddamnit almost every fucking time he went out there. He liked to ruin my health smoking cigarettes and thank God we got Timmy Stoddard coming in out the bullpen now sticking a bat up their asses."

On team speed: "Team speed, for crissakes, you get fucking goddamn little fleas on the fucking bases, getting picked off trying to steal, getting thrown out, taking runs away from you. You get dem big cocksuckers who can hit the fucking ball out the ballpark and you can't make any goddamn mistakes."

Tom: "Well, certainly this show is going to go down in history, Earl. Terry Elliott of Washington, D.C., wants to know why you don't use Terry Crowley as a designated hitter all the time?"

EARL: Well, Terry Crowley's lucky he's in fucking baseball for Chrissake . . .

TOM: Well, certainly you've made your opinions known on the fans' questions about baseball, Earl, but let's get to something else. Alice Sweet from Norfolk wants to know the best time to put in a tomato plant.

EARL: Alice Sweet ought to be worried about where the fuck her next lay is coming from, rather than where her next goddamned tomato plant's coming from. If she'd get her ass out of the fucking bars at night and go hustling around the goddamned streets she might get a prick stuck into her once in a while. I don't understand where these questions are coming from, Tom. That's about it for "Manager's Corner." Go fuck yourself and to fuck with your show coming up next on the Baltimore Orioles Baseball Fucking Network.

Like the Haller tape, this was Weaver content too good to squirrel away on a cassette tape, and it eventually made its way to YouTube for a new generation of baseball fans to wonder at. Saying "Alice Sweet from Norfolk" in Baltimore still gets you a wink and a smile.

On September 19, the Orioles held "Thanks, Earl" day at Memorial Stadium. President Ronald Reagan sent a telegram. The Orioles retired Earl's number 4. They gave him a customized van, a set of golf clubs, a Caribbean cruise, a golf cart, and a diamond-studded number-4 tie rack. "Little did I know fifteen years ago how deeply attached I'd become to this city," Earl said in a speech. "I came here in 1968 when urban areas were being demolished by riots and fires . . . but, after the turmoil subsided, it didn't take me long to find out I was in a baseball town."

Weaver thanked Marianna and his children for "putting up with a mind completely dominated by my job for some thirty-five years" and the Orioles for coping with a "moody, irrational, and sometimes rude individual." He lapped the field in a 1954 Pontiac convertible, blowing kisses to the crowd.

Before the game, he signed a two-year contract with the Orioles as a consultant. "As far as I'm concerned, that's a lifetime contract," said Edward Bennett Williams. "It's at your option. As long as you wish, there's a place for you with the Baltimore Orioles." Rich Dauer, the scrappy big-league second baseman Earl dreamed of becoming, hit a game-winning home run to win 4–2 in ten innings.

The team closed strong, propelled by excellent pitching. They finished with the best team ERA in the American League. A resurgent Palmer went 15-5 with a 3.13 ERA. Twenty-year-old Storm Davis came up and went 8-4 with a 3.49 ERA. Cy Clone, Flanagan called him. Everything seemed to work out in the end. The Orioles finished fifth in the league in runs scored and third in the league in home runs. Eddie Murray hit .316 with 32 home runs and 110 RBI. John Lowenstein hit .320 with 24 home runs. There was the Earl Weaver defense too. The Orioles committed the fewest errors in the American League, 101, and recorded the league's second-best defensive efficiency, .719.

The season-ending 28-5 hot streak was classic Earl Weaver. He managed playing time and pitching strategy so well that his teams were fresh down the stretch and usually outplayed their opponents in the final months. In fifteen full seasons, the Orioles won over 60 percent of their games in the second half ten times. Overall, Weaver recorded a .603 winning percentage (693-457) in the second half, compared to .567 (725-554) in the first half.

In the last weekend of the 1982 season, Baltimore, 3 games behind Milwaukee with 4 to play, beat the Brewers twice on Friday and once on Saturday, to set up a winner-take-all game on national television for the 1982 American League East division championship. On the mound Sunday it was Jim Palmer against Don Sutton, two future Hall of Famers. It seemed like a fairy-tale ending to Earl Weaver's career. "Who knows. I may be back in baseball some day," he said. "But there will never be another day like this in my life."

The night before the game, Weaver watched *The Dirty Dozen*, ate a tomato-and-cheese sandwich, and went to bed at ten after two.

In the morning, the sky was pure blue. Fans packed Memorial Stadium, and brought signs.

WIN IT FOR THE DUCK

WE'VE GOT WEAVER FEVER 4

GOODBYE EARL!

It felt like the World Series. The last time two teams tied for first place had met on the last day of the regular season to contest a division or league championship was the Dodgers and Phillies in 1950. "I was laying on the floor of my sister's house listening to reports of that game, probably by Harry Caray," said Weaver. "That was my third year as a player in professional baseball."

Before the game, Weaver thanked the players for their effort.

Dauer said: "Whew, we thought you were going to tell us you weren't going to retire."

Palmer struggled, Robin Yount hit two home runs, and the Brewers built a 5–2 lead before putting the game away with five runs in the top of the ninth.

In the sixth inning, Earl Weaver walked out to the mound to take Palmer out of the game for one last time. "Earl told me how we've done a lot of things together and how I've had a great career," Palmer said, "and I told him, 'I know, but all that really doesn't matter today.'"

Even though the Orioles were losing, the crowd maintained their intensity throughout the game. "It was probably the most dramatic game I ever pitched—even more than any World Series game," said Palmer.

After the game ended, Orioles fans gave Earl Weaver the gift of gifts. For the first time in his life, he would be cheered after a loss.

Not just cheered. *Loved.*

"WE WANT EARL! WE WANT EARL! WE WANT EARL!"

Earl walked out into the arena. He waved and clapped. He hugged Harvey Kuenn, the Brewers' manager. The stadium thundered and chanted: O-R-I-O-L-E-S. They let Hagy, the team's unofficial mascot, walk out to the pitcher's mound.

Keith Jackson, doing the game for ABC with Howard Cosell, said: "In twelve of the fifteen seasons as manager here, he won 90 games. It is indeed a stirring tribute that 51,000 people, even though their team was losing, they stayed to cheer."

Weaver retreated to the clubhouse. Yeah, he said, he'd miss going north with the team in 1983. The nostalgia of being left behind in Florida "will only remind me of my playing days, when I didn't make the club. I remember Lynchburg. I had my suitcase in my hand, and was ready to get on the bus. Our manager came up and told me they got a second baseman and I was going to West Frankfort. So I stood there watching the bus leave, with my suitcase in hand." Then Weaver, as if he were learning to be a human again, said: "But you know, the guy I feel sorry for was the second baseman at West Frankfort." Finally, tough-guy Weaver could shed his armor. "I don't think I can be mean enough anymore," he said. "I was mean enough this year because I knew this was it, but I don't think I could be mean enough next year; that's why I'm stopping."

What would he have done, a writer asked, if he hadn't been a manager. "That's hypothetical," he said. "I have no idea, no idea at all. I've thought only about baseball since I was four years old."

Somebody mentioned people were still cheering for him. "They're still out there?" he asked. Weaver walked out and stood between two police horses. He imitated the bird mascot and, like a little boy, spelled out the team's name.

O-R-I-O-L-E-S.

Then he walked out of Memorial Stadium and drove to the Orchard Inn for dinner with Marianna and some friends.

30

DE-WEAVERIZATION

Baltimore, 1983–1984

Baseball and malaria keep coming back.

—Gene Mauch

The 1983 season concluded with Cal Ripken Jr. catching a soft liner to win the World Series for the Baltimore Orioles over the Philadelphia Phillies. ABC-TV commentator Earl Weaver, helmeted with a bouffant of curly permed hair, watched from the broadcast booth. The champs were his, and not his. For the first time since he was a boy, in 1983 he hadn't suited up as a member of a baseball team.

Orioles spring training camp in 1983 felt like Rome after the death of an emperor. The new boss was the soft-spoken Joe Altobelli, the inspiration for the character of Crash Davis in *Bull Durham*. Immediately, the skipper broke the mold by talking at length to every Orioles player. "The first time Joe said hello to some guys, he broke Earl's career record," Palmer cracked. Altobelli had paid his dues, working fourteen years as a coach in the Orioles organization and managing the San Francisco Giants, where he was Manager of the Year in 1978.

Orioles officials joking about De-Weaverization were only half kidding. For the first time since the Eisenhower administration, the Orioles started the season without the little dictator in uniform. He was still on their payroll as a consultant and scout. He kept his parking spot. For General Manager Hank Peters, it was a relief. Earl was great. Earl was a lot. "I'm always asked, 'Will Earl come back?'" he said. "If he were to come out of retirement, I expect he could probably do a better job with another club."

Altobelli fielded endless questions about Earl. "What's wrong with being compared to Earl? I kind of like it," says Altobelli. "If I have to live with it the rest of my life, I've lived with worse things."

When Earl appeared at practice, the players teased him.

"You've grown," said Lee May, making note of Earl's new hairdo.

"Got the stopwatch on me?" asked Al Bumbry.

"Nope," said Weaver. "I'll just write down 'fast.'"

Earl hit the road in Florida during the Grapefruit League. He scouted a couple dozen games. "I'm doin' it 'cause I'm gettin' paid," he said. "And I get 18 cents a mile, too."

Earl made himself at home at the Country Club of Miami, where annual dues were only $600. He owned a house on the seventh hole of the West Course. The clubhouse had burned down and they still hadn't rebuilt it. "Hope it stays just like it is," he said. "It drives away all the phonies." He roamed the course with a "No. 4" black and orange golf cart the team had given him with radio, electric fan, sunroof, and two beer coolers. Weaver joked to a visiting reporter that the only things that might bring him back to managing were inflation and bad golf. Earl loved to gamble on golf, and usually won. "If Earl has ever lost any money on this golf course, then it must have fallen out of his pocket," said a friend.

The 1983 Orioles didn't miss Earl. Not yet. It was too soon. "People were thinking we would go downhill, but because of what we did in '82, that enabled us to do what we did in '83," said Dennis Martinez. "The team was already together and ready."

In 1982, Earl had teamed up with Jim Palmer to broadcast the American League Championship Series, and done well enough that ABC Sports hired him in 1983 to broadcast eighteen *Monday Night Baseball* games and the World Series. It was an exciting opportunity, and a chance for the frugal and money-anxious Weaver to make some more money. Al Michaels recalled

Weaver writing numbers in a book on a ride to the airport. Michaels thought he was analyzing baseball statistics, but he was computing his fee for the broadcast. "I'm trying to figure out if I have enough money to live on for the rest of my life," Weaver explained.

Palmer made jokes about how Earl would be the first broadcaster thrown out of the booth, but behind the mic, Earl sounded stilted. His voice faltered. He didn't always look straight at the viewer. Anxious about his grammar and cussing on the air, Weaver was excessively formal, for example calling Cal Ripken Jr. "Calvin." Earl admitted that he was too restrained. "I should have jumped up and yelled, 'God damn, what a great throw. That's the turning point,'" he said.

ABC assigned Weaver to cover the 1983 Little League World Series, which Marietta, Georgia, won, beating the Dominican Republic in the final. The foulmouthed skipper kept his analysis clean and tight: "For a little fella, at 82 pounds, this [pitcher] is throwing the ball pretty good." Watching the Dominican Little League team walk off the field "with heads held high" meant "the losses the Orioles suffered in the seventh games of the 1971 and 1979 World Series didn't weigh as heavy in my memory as they once did," he said.

In June, *Playboy* published Lawrence Linderman's interview of Earl. The magazine joked that it considered outfitting him with kneepads, a face mask, and earplugs, but that Weaver was gracious. "He's got a sense of humor about himself that's wonderful," Linderman reported. He related a golf course conversation between Weaver and his buddies. "Now we'll finally get to hear all about Weaver's hot sex life," a friend said as they teed off. "I ain't shit," said Weaver. "Just ask my wife."

In the interview, Weaver said he was "100 percent for free agency" and noted that money had motivated players to prepare better. "The attitudes in spring training are 1,000 percent better than they used to be," he said. "When players had to sign for what the general manager and the owner wanted to pay them, they'd come into spring training and say things like, 'Screw this; I worked my butt off last year and got nothing for it.'"

Before the 1983 World Series, Weaver resigned as a special consultant for the Orioles. ABC policy prohibited team employees in the booth during the series. Giving up his Orioles gig opened up Weaver to offers from other teams. In 1983, any offer—and there were many, including from the Yankees, Expos, and Cubs—had to be routed through the Orioles front office. Earl wasn't interested. "I wouldn't swap my lifestyle now for $1 million," he said.

Weaver picked up a column from the *Baltimore Evening Sun*, titled "Earl Weaver's Inside Baseball." Via a *Sun* ghostwriter, he penned earnest columns praising the DH rule and advocating banning beanball pitchers for life, all doused with plenty of baseball clichés, like: "The cream will come to the top and when the leaves turn brown, only the best will still be around."

The delights of home made up for missing out on baseball, he told his readers. "Being able to come home and cook a pot roast, stuffed peppers, ham hock and beans or barbeque ribs in the evening has been very soul satisfying—as well as fattening," he wrote. "I do miss seeing Cal Ripken make that easy throw across the infield from shortstop, Rich Dauer execute the hit-and-run, Eddie Murray hit one of those home runs that is as high as it is far, or Rick Dempsey making a perfect throw to second to get a potential base stealer."

On August 26, 1983, after getting inducted into the Orioles Hall of Fame, Weaver wrote: "The results of those 14.5 years I spent as manager of the Orioles are history and are recorded for everyone to see. If I had not been there, it's possible that the record might be better. It's also possible it might be worse, no one will ever know. Sometimes I wish the hand could be replayed, as in duplicate bridge, but in the game of life you only get one chance."

Earl also got a book deal in 1983. Terry Pluto, a Cleveland-based author who'd written the first biography of Weaver, *The Earl of Baltimore*, published in 1981, proposed to ghostwrite a book about how to play baseball. The idea landed on the desk of Jeff Neuman, an editor for Macmillan in New York City. "When it came to me, the proposal was a book on how to play baseball, how to field a ground ball, how to pitch, how to field," said Neuman. "I said that's not what we want to hear from Earl Weaver." Neuman's idea was to have Weaver and Pluto write a guide to Weaver's strategic thinking. "The book market for sports was more aimed at the spectator than the participant, with golf being the exception," said Neuman. "After college age, who's playing hardball?" And, he added, "this was also the time when Bill James was starting to get popular, so it was for armchair managers and general managers."

Pluto flew down to Hialeah, Florida, and spent three days with Earl and Marianna. They talked every morning. In the afternoon, Weaver played golf. They'd have an early dinner, and then Weaver would go out drinking. "His ability to focus was remarkable," Pluto said. "He was very smart, and he was wonderful to me." The result was *Weaver on Strategy: A Guide for Armchair Managers by Baseball's Master Tactician*. Named by *Esquire* as one of the one hundred best baseball books ever written, it's a rich, shrewd, and witty baseball testament. Weaver makes fun of managers' own use of clichés. For example, if you lose a game in spring training, Weaver recommends using what he calls the "Loss in Daytona Beach theory": "You can substitute any city, but this excuse is to be used when you get bombed on the road in the spring. So you lose to Montreal, 20–3, on March 22 in Daytona Beach. Who cares?"

Pluto centered the book on Weaver's ten laws:

1. No one is going to give a damn in July if you lost a game in March.
2. If you don't make any promises to your players, you won't have to break them.
3. The easiest way around the bases is with one swing of the bat.
4. Your most precious possessions on offense are your twenty-seven outs.
5. If you play for one run, that's all you'll get.
6. Don't play for one run unless you know that run will win a ball-game.
7. It's easier to find four good starters than five.
8. The best place for a rookie pitcher is long relief.
9. The key step for an infielder is the first one—left or right—but *before* the ball is hit.
10. The job of arguing with the umpire belongs to the manager, be-cause it won't hurt the team if he gets thrown out of the game.

Weaver on Strategy put the reader in the dugout and like *Winning!* is full of insights that modern baseball analysis has proven true. For example, Weaver writes that "a good clutch player is usually a good player to begin with." He repeats some of his familiar mantras: "I've got nothing against the bunt—in its place. But most of the time, that place is the bottom of a long-forgotten closet."

It is also psychologically revealing. Weaver explained why he never got close to his players. "If you haven't slapped a guy on the back and told him what a great person and player he is, then it's much easier when the day comes and you have to call him into the office and tell him he screwed up," he wrote. "I'm not going to make any promises. That was one of my methods of dealing with players. No promises. None. If you don't make any promises, then you won't break any. Don't back yourself into a corner."

In 1983, nobody put the Orioles in a corner. Cal Ripken was the American League Most Valuable Player, batting .318/.371/.517 and playing all 162 games at shortstop. Eddie Murray hit .306/.393/.538 with 33 home runs, and finished second in the MVP voting. And there was plenty of Earl Weaver–style magic. On August 24, the Orioles went into extra innings against the Blue Jays. A series of convoluted moves led to infielder Lenn Sakata catching. The Blue Jays, eager to steal on Sakata, took massive leads off first. Tippy Martinez picked off the first baserunner. Then the second. And then, unbelievably, the third. Sakata hit a three-run homer to win the game 7–4. "Altobelli let the engine run," said Ripken.

The Orioles beat the White Sox in the ALCS and the Phillies in the World Series. "Are you satisfied now?" Hank Peters asked owner Edward Bennett Williams during the championship celebrations. "I'm worried about next year," said Williams.

The 1984 season was a letdown. The Birds started 5-13 and never recovered. And Altobelli didn't go berserk. Didn't fight umpires. Didn't yell at players for missing the cutoff man. That's when the front office and players started missing Earl. They needed a jumpstart. Not that it mattered, because the Tigers started the season 17-1 and 35-5, and ran away with the AL East. On May 17, the club released Palmer, who wept openly at his goodbye press conference.

At the end of the season, ABC hadn't renewed Weaver's contract. It wasn't clear he would be asked back. He decided he wouldn't do TV in 1985. Although he and Williams kept in touch, he turned down offers to manage from six teams. "I couldn't make myself do the things that would have to be done in order to become a winner," Weaver said. "And if I ever put on a baseball uniform again, I want to be a winner, get thrown out of some games, have some conflicts with some ballplayers. Right now, I couldn't see myself doing that."

The 1985 season, he declared, "would be my first full year of retirement."

31

THINGS FALL APART

Baltimore, 1985–1986

I managed a team that was so bad we considered a 2-and-0 count on the batter a rally.

—Rich Donnelly

The Orioles' fifth-place finish in 1984 shocked Birdland. The only time Earl Weaver finished as low as fourth, in 1978, he still won 90 games. The 1984 Orioles won 85 games on fumes.

A kind, judicious man, Altobelli was the perfect pilot for the 1983 championship team, but he lacked the fire the Orioles needed when they slipped in 1984. Clubhouse chemistry is complex. The same group of ballplayers can play hard and win with a manager one year and sour on him the next. Long runs of success like Weaver's from 1969 to 1982 are rare.

The Orioles organization was in a funk. The pipeline of young talent had run dry. Key scouts had defected to other teams. The Orioles drafted miserably in the early 1980s, picking flops Joe Kucharski, Wayne Wilson, and John Hoover in the first round from 1982 to 1984. Cal Ripken Sr. was coaching big leaguers instead of developing minor leaguers. Pitching guru Ray Miller left after the 1984 season to manage the Twins.

Before the 1985 season, owner Edward Bennett Williams bolstered the offense and bullpen in the free agent market. The 1984 team finished second in the league in ERA but scored 118 fewer runs than in 1983. The Orioles ponied up for outfielder Fred Lynn ($6.8 million for five years) and closer Don Aase ($2.4 million for four years) from the Angels, and outfielder Lee Lacy ($2.2 million for four years) from the Dodgers. The Orioles released franchise stalwart Ken Singleton.

The Orioles, wrote *Sports Illustrated*, were playing with "swallowed pride": "In the past, when the Orioles required, say a centerfielder, they would trot down to one of their farms and pluck a home-grown product. They were, as most farm-system folks tend to be, even a little preachy about never spending big money for what you can grow yourself. So what happened this winter? Why, the gentlemen farmers not only entered the player free-agent market, they fairly burst into it with a loud and unseemly rattling of coin."

The Orioles' new strategy: three-run homers, three-run homers, and three-run homers. The 1985 team banged, topping the league with 214 roundtrippers, and finished second in the big leagues in runs scored. But for the first time since the 1950s, their pitching and defense stunk.

On June 13, 1985, Williams fired Altobelli and brought back Earl Weaver. Earl had given his word that, if needed, he would come back to save the franchise. The way it happened was slapstick. Earl and Marianna had been visiting the grandkids in Atlanta and St. Louis over a two-week trip in their 1983 Chevy van, and had driven back to Baltimore to visit Kim. Williams grabbed Weaver off his vacation and made him an offer he couldn't refuse. He'd be the highest-paid manager in baseball, at $500,000 a year. "Earl just can't stand it that I'm back and he isn't," said longtime rival Billy Martin, back for another tour with the Yankees. "He'll come back so he can try to beat me."

The front office fumbled the transition. "Does anybody know if I've been fired?" Altobelli asked when he got to the ballpark on June 13. It was 10:35 a.m. "I don't know the answer," said the loyal baseball soldier. "I've been here since nine a.m. and I don't know what's going on. I can't tell you anything. I don't know anything." Somebody asked him how he was doing. "How the hell should I be?" Prowling around, a dismayed Altobelli muttered: "I thought this was a world-class operation but I guess I was sadly mistaken."

Weaver's reinstatement thrilled many fans. "I'm ecstatic; I've got tickets tonight," Shelley Atlas told the *Baltimore Sun*. "It's baseball, apple pie, hot dogs . . . and Earl Weaver." Some had gotten tired of Weaver. "His act has gotten stale," said Larry Allen. "Weaver becomes the star. Watching him is like watching pro wrestling. His first ten years were okay, but then he went bananas. It was a carnival." The players said Weaver would help them win. "We needed a kick in the butt," said Storm Davis.

Weaver was in no position to kick anybody's behind. He had not been following the team, and hadn't even planned to see a game while in town. As preparation, he asked the Orioles to make Cal Ripken Sr. manage one game as an interim, so he could listen to the game on the radio with the team media guide in one hand, taking notes. "I haven't seen a big-league pitch up that close for two and a half years. Maybe anybody would look strong to me," he said. "You had to figure, 'This guy's throwin' good.' Or is he?"

Even friends played the comeback for laughs. Groundskeeper Pat Santarone gave Weaver the four smallest tomato vines in the left-field corner. "He says he might sing to them at night," said Santarone. "Earl's got a lousy voice for singing, though. A great voice for umpires, but a lousy voice for singing."

From the beginning, the comeback looked like a mistake. "I'm putting a reputation on the line here," said Weaver. "There's a chance that things could go sour and that everything I accomplished here might take on a different color. That might be hard to live with." The Orioles were 30-26 when Weaver took over and went 53-52 under him to finish 83-79, in fourth place. The magic was gone.

Eager for one more big paycheck, and loyal to Williams, Weaver agreed to return. For four months in 1986, the Orioles played solid baseball. After beating the Texas Rangers 9–2 on August 5, the Birds were only 2.5 games behind the first-place Red Sox. Their record was 59-47, 12 games over .500. On pace for another 90-win season under Earl Weaver. A strong finish would give the Birds another division title. On August 6, the Orioles lost a gross ballgame, 13–11, to the Rangers. Weaver used five pitchers, who surrendered the 13 runs on 19 hits and 5 walks. The next night, they lost another slugfest, 9–8. Then they lost again. And again. For the rest of the season, the Orioles won only 14 games, while losing 42.

For the first time in his life, Earl Weaver quit on his team. When he stopped trying, his team stopped trying. That had always been part of Earl's secret. That he cared. In September, Weaver approached Peters. "We're not going anywhere, and I'm not coming back next year," he told his boss. "I'd like to go home now if it's all right with you."

Peters replied: "It's fine with me, Earl, but I'll have to check with Williams."

He called the owner.

"Tell that little son of a bitch he can go home, but he won't get paid," said Williams.

Peters called Earl. "Earl, quoting Mr. Williams, 'Tell that little son of a bitch he can go home, but he won't get paid,'" he said. "It's up to you, whatever you want to do."

Earl wanted the money. He stayed and went through the motions as the Orioles limped to the finish line.

Final tally: 73 wins and 89 losses and the first last-place finish in the history of the franchise since moving to Baltimore in 1954.

After a final dispiriting 6–3 loss to the Tigers to close out the season, there was no stirring farewell like in 1982. In the eighth inning, the scoreboard flashed: "Thanks, Earl, and Good Luck." That was it. "Unless the stock market goes through the floor, this is the last day I ever have to work in my life," said a beaten-down Weaver. "Anybody who says that isn't nice is lying." Even burned-out, he cared about his legacy. "I'm 420 games over .500," he added. "That's 10 years of 100-60 and then some. . . . On my tombstone, just write: 'The sorest loser that ever lived.'"

What happened during that season and a half in Baltimore, when Earl Weaver went 126-142, and slipped from second to fifth place all-time in managerial winning percentage?

It was clear that Earl didn't have the same fire. "Earl should have never come back," said Peters. "The only reason he came back was for the money." For Flanagan, the problem was team culture. "The new guys were nonbelievers," he said. "They didn't want to hear about the Oriole Way or Oriole Magic. Now there were different stories being told on the bus. All of a sudden, there were Pittsburgh stories and Boston stories." When Earl came back, "he was a little more tame," said Lynn. "As an opposing player I'd loved watching him.

When he came back, he was pretty much under control as far as his emotions. I don't know that he had the same fire."

The problem, too, was the players. "He didn't have the weapons he had before," said Ripken. "Normally, you rely on that strong pitching staff. Dad used to say normally our pitchers would give us three or four really good starts. If they all had three or four good starts in a row, that's when you run off 20 wins in 25 games. This time, we didn't have the horses."

Weaver observed that the manager in 1986 mattered less. "Things couldn't be the same anymore because of free agency," he said. "You have to buy the right free agents, those who adjust to wherever they go and don't do things the way they'd done them elsewhere." Weaver concluded: "Financially, it turned out very well for me because the salaries had escalated really high, but if I had to do it over again, I don't think I would have come back. I'm sorry I went back, I didn't enjoy it."

For Earl Weaver the man, there was a silver lining to souring on his vocation. His children, Mike, Rhonda, and Terry, and his grandchildren grew closer to Earl in retirement, especially after his first wife, Jane, died in 1994. Baseball had always limited their time together, and the children were starved for parental attention. After the divorce, Jane often left the children with their grandparents. "My dad and my mom were sort of the same in not being around," said Terry. "Grandpa and Granma Weaver were so nice, they were nice to kids at a time when people weren't nice to kids."

For the last three decades of his life, Earl and Marianna took his children and grandchildren on cruises, visited them in St. Louis, Houston, Atlanta, and Florida, and invited them on adventures, like lunch with Howard Cosell. Instead of sneaking in a few minutes between pregame meetings and batting practice, his family could now spend meaningful time with him.

Kim Benson, Earl's stepdaughter who lived with him and Marianna in Perry Hall, said she learned to appreciate what Earl had given her when she got older. "I remember when I was a teenager thinking I'm never going to be like him," he said. "Then one day when I was fortysomething, I realized Earl has taught me more about life without ever saying, 'Kim, you need to do this.'" The big lessons Earl taught her were how to work hard and "look out for number one."

The postretirement time was particularly important to Mike Weaver. As a teenager, he would have liked to rebel against his dad—"but he wasn't there to rebel against," he said. "There was never much of a relationship with him as a teenager." When Jane and Earl divorced in 1963, Mike stayed with his mom. He could no longer spend summers attending minor-league games and playing catch with ballplayers.

Like his dad, Mike was a good ballplayer and got drafted out of high school by the Seattle Pilots. The Pilots, an expansion team in 1969, lasted only one year and then moved to Milwaukee and became the Brewers. That made Mike one of only fifty players who ever got drafted by the Pilots. Instead of trying his luck in minor-league baseball, Mike attended William Jewell College in Missouri, where he graduated, he told me, "summa cum lucky." Like his dad, Mike Weaver is full of jokes and one-liners. In his twenties, he moved to Atlanta and got into loansharking. Mike's life fell apart. He was arrested for dealing drugs. For years, he and Earl seldom spoke.

After Earl moved to Florida full-time in the 1980s, Mike visited more. Earl took him to watch the two racehorses he owned, Promised Moment and Praises On I. "He'd have a couple million in the bank, and he wouldn't bet more than six dollars a race," said Mike. They won a few races, but Earl couldn't believe how much it cost to feed a horse—$1,000 a month per animal. So he got rid of them.

The improving relationship persuaded Mike to move to Florida in 1991 and forge a friendship with his dad. Earl helped Mike settle his debts and get a job at a golf course. They played golf together every Monday. On Sundays, Earl cooked hot roasts for Mike, with turkey and mashed potatoes. He would boss Marianna and Mike around the kitchen. "'Do it this way,' he'd say, just as if he was coaching a team," remembered Mike. "'You gotta have diced onions.' He was pretty precise, and that's why he was a good manager. He'd make these guys do what he wanted them to."

Part 5

FAME

Earl Weaver Baseball was the first great baseball videogame simulation.

32

VIDEOGAME

Redwood City, California, 1986–1987

> The dice sat there, three ivory cubes, heedless of history yet makers of it, still proclaiming Abernathy's strike-out. Damon Rutherford waited there. Henry held his breath, walked straight to the table, picked up the dice and tossed them down.
>
> —Robert Coover, *The Universal Baseball Association, Inc., J. Henry Waugh, Prop.*

In what sounds like the setup of a joke (Earl Weaver walks into a corporate boardroom . . .), Weaver flew to California in early 1986 to do some work in tech. The job: help Electronic Arts invent a revolutionary baseball videogame.

William "Trip" Hawkins, who had been an early Apple employee, founded Electronic Arts in 1982 and dreamed of making a videogame team sports simulation, with realistic graphics and statistics. His first love was football and so he recruited retired coach John Madden, but twenty-two players running around an open field was too complicated. *NFL Madden Football*, the revolutionary billion-dollar hit of the 1990s, would have to wait.

First, EA would do baseball, which was more linear. The "John Madden of baseball," Hawkins and his engineers decided, was Earl Weaver. The manager had never used personal computers, but the deal promised $50,000 up front, plus royalties that would eventually be worth hundreds of thousands of dollars.

The market was ripe for an intelligent baseball videogame. In the 1980s, Bill James's *Baseball Abstracts* were becoming bestsellers, and Americans were falling in love with fantasy baseball. Baseball had long invited simulations that allowed fans to indulge in their dreams of being baseball managers. A fantasy about a fantasy.

In the early twentieth century, game companies produced dice and spinning games that simulated ballgames with random outcomes. Earl Weaver fondly recalled rudimentary dice baseball games he'd played in St. Louis as a boy in the 1930s and 1940s. APBA (1951) and Strat-O-Matic (1961) were more sophisticated dice- and card-based games that let fans manage big-league teams. Jack Kerouac, the Beat writer, invented his own tabletop dice game. In 1961, John Burgeson invented a baseball simulation using punch cards on the IBM 1620. Other rudimentary computer simulations followed. Hawkins, the founder of EA, loved the board games. "I learned how Bayesian probability theory worked by studying Strat-O-Matic," he said.

The games revealed baseball's unique appeal as a plaything of the human imagination, an imaginary world of heroes that invites us to play God. In *The Universal Baseball Association, Inc.* (1968), novelist Robert Coover invented the character of J. Henry Waugh (a pun on "Yahweh," or God), a middle-aged man so obsessed with a dice-based tabletop baseball game that he makes up a fantasy world inhabited by his players that dominates his consciousness far more than his actual life. For Waugh, there was nothing like baseball, "the records, the statistics, the peculiar balances between individual and team, power and intelligence." We all have a little bit of J. Henry Waugh in us.

To make *Earl Weaver Baseball*, Hawkins leaned on a brilliant software developer named Don Daglow, who had designed text-based baseball simulations in the 1970s. For Intellivision's *World Series Baseball* for Mattel Electronics, which came out in 1983, Daglow developed a new algorithm for matching pitchers against hitters. The problem was that he had no idea how to make baseball come alive on a computer screen. He didn't know it, but he needed a ballet dancer.

In the early 1960s, Eddie Dombrower, a high school baseball player and rabid fan, read a *Life* magazine story about a ballet dancer named Edward Villella. Dombrower had been majoring in chemistry, but after a girlfriend took him to ballet class, he ended up taking lessons. He also realized that ballet was just as athletic as football. "Pretty soon I was doing a lot of ballet and not a lot of chemistry," he said.

After a ballet career, Dombrower studied math in college, and won a Watson fellowship to study the use of computers to notate ballet choreography. Dombrower learned to code on an Apple II, and designed a program that could animate humans. "I started with a hand because there are as many bits and pieces in your hand as there are in all the rest of your body," he said. "I then extrapolated it out to the rest of the human. I could pose it and animate it to about five or six frames a second." It was a breakthrough. Daglow hired him.

Dombrower grew up on the Dodgers and Vin Scully on the radio, and never stopped loving baseball. His first television memory was watching Sandy Koufax pitch to Mickey Mantle in the World Series. And now he was going to work with Earl Weaver.

In early 1986, Hawkins walked Weaver, dressed in a sport coat and tie, into Electronic Arts' gleaming new building in Redwood City. The Orioles manager declined a tour of the building. "I came here to work," he said. "Let's do this." After learning baseball in the tobacco- and alcohol-drenched stands of Sportsman's Park, Weaver was now going to help teach the game to sedentary baseball nuts on the other side of computer screens.

The engineers had prepared worksheets with lists of questions about baseball strategy and tactics, from cutoffs and pickoff plays to lineups and pitch counts. Weaver hadn't realized how seriously the men were taking the game. He asked for a blackboard, and for two days lectured them as if he were teaching a class, breaking to smoke Raleighs on the balcony, in the same way he caught puffs between innings.

What do the middle infielders do on a double in the gap? Weaver demonstrated how the shortstop or second baseman would get in position between the ball and third base and raise his arms to offer a target for the outfielder. He moved Dombrower and Daglow around the room, as if he were coaching. Weaver taught them how to set up a defense and make a lineup. He advocated a speedy runner in the seventh hole in front of single hitters in the eight and nine spots in the lineup.

Earl's self-presentation "was I may not be the sharpest tool in the box," said Daglow, "but I understand baseball better than just about anybody, and I'm going to leverage that understanding in a way that's going to produce wins, and I can make a difference as a manager doing that. He gave himself credit for narrow intelligence." When he met Earl, Hawkins said, he did not bring up math. "He didn't sound like an intellectual, he's coarse, but you could tell Earl was really smart."

Impressed, the programmers added an "Ask Earl" button for players to summon an artificially intelligent simulation of Weaver's strategic judgment. Daglow asked Earl if he would permit them to write another feature into the game, one where he marches out and kicks dirt on an umpire's shoes after a close play, a classic Earl Weaver move. He protested a bit, but then relented. "He said I don't like it, but what the hell, they deserve it," said Daglow. At 4:30 p.m., somebody suggested they take a break. They had early dinner reservations. "No, we're not done," he said. "Let's finish this job."

After Weaver's two-day visit, the engineers spent months working deep into the night to give their game magic touches. Previous videogames had been formulaic. Every double in the gap looked the same. "We wanted the doubles to look different," said Dombrower. The engineers wanted to make all twenty-eight stadiums play differently. They created a baseball field editor, the first in videogame history. "There would be wind in Chicago and nothing in the Astrodome in Houston. Everything would play realistically, the way the physics play out in real life," said Daglow. They built a replay system. "Don came to me with this algorithm, and I thought, yes, this can simulate baseball as well as anything," said Dombrower. "You have the Green Monster in left field. I layered on top of that a physics simulator so his algorithm could predict the outcome of a matchup between any one batter and any other pitcher."

Dealing with Earl Weaver could be stressful, even if disputes had comic endings. Once, Weaver yelled at a female Electronic Arts office manager because he couldn't reach Daglow or Dombrower. The manager hung up on him. Weaver called Don to say he was quitting the project and keeping the money.

Don walked over to Hawkins's desk. "Thank God you're here. Earl's threatening to terminate the contract," he said.

"Don't worry, I'll call Earl and calm him down," said Hawkins.

When Hawkins called, Earl yelled, "Get that bitch on the phone."

Hawkins looked at Don and deadpanned: "Get that bitch on the phone."

Hawkins said he'd look into it and call Earl back. He asked the office manager what had happened. She said Earl had shouted and sworn at her, so she'd hung up. Hawkins told her he supported her decision, and they were trying to decide how to pacify Earl.

"He wants to talk to you," Hawkins told her. "Would that be okay with you? You don't have to do it."

"Can I be honest with him?" she asked. Yes, said Hawkins.

When she called Weaver, she told him: "I hung up on you because you were yelling at me and using foul language and you wouldn't listen when I tried to help you." Weaver apologized and invited the office manager to dinner with the rest of the EA Sports crew, and to that evening's game.

In late August 1986, Daglow brought a computer with him to visit Earl when the Orioles were playing the A's at Oakland Coliseum. They let Weaver play a prototype version of the game in the visiting manager's office. They showed him the lineup designed by the AI model. It used the previous season's statistics. He complained that it didn't include this season's stats. "We had to educate him about the realities of data sets and how long it took to update them." Overall, said Daglow, "the videogame mystified him. He was from a different generation."

They could never get him to play. "During events, there was always a desire to have him play the game," said Dombrower. "He never, ever really did like sitting at the computer. We'd put his hand on the mouse. That was kind of the extent of him playing."

When the game was released in 1987, it was a groundbreaking hit. The political analyst and baseball writer Nate Silver has called it "the best computer game of all time." *EWB* revolutionized videogames because it was the first where you could make trades and simulate seasons, which made baseball fans of brainy kids who would grow up to take over Major League Baseball front offices in the twenty-first century.

"*Earl Weaver Baseball* was the first game where you could play an entire season," said videogame historian John Delia. "And you could use statistics and even plug in statistics to stimulate teams and seasons. And you could do defensive shifts, which was way ahead of its time." Delia praised the graphics too. "If you see the way the bodies are moving, and springing for balls and turning and pivoting, it was remarkably fluid for such an early game." And it was a template for all the great baseball videogame franchises that followed: *MVP Baseball, VR Baseball, MLB The Show,* and (my favorite) *Super Mega Baseball.*

EWB inspired young baseball fans to think strategically. Bryan Stroh, a former pitcher for Princeton and future senior executive for the Pittsburgh Pirates, schooled himself on baseball by playing *EWB*. It was the only game his dad encouraged him to play. "My dad knew exactly who Earl Weaver was and he figured the game was making me smarter," said Stroh. "It was the first game that made me think about managing as well as playing." The second version of *EWB* included Negro League teams, and that's how Stroh learned about the history of Black American baseball.

In 1987, EA ran a public simulation of the MLB All-Star Game, held that year at Oakland Coliseum. The software engineers secured box seats for Earl Weaver and his wife, Marianna. On the way to the ballpark, Earl said, "I don't feel like going. If I go, people are just going to want to talk to me. Let's go to dinner." They skipped the game and found a small restaurant in Sausalito.

33

COOPERSTOWN

Cooperstown, New York, 1996

> Earl is baseball.
>
> —Frank Deford

Earl Weaver was playing golf in March 1996 when Marianna ran out to interrupt his game to tell him the news. The Veterans' Committee of writers and former players had elected him, 1890s Orioles manager Ned Hanlon, and pitchers Bill Foster and Jim Bunning to the National Baseball Hall of Fame in Cooperstown, New York. His knees wobbled as he bogeyed the next hole. A Hall of Famer. It was a call he'd been waiting for since he quit after the 1986 season. He'd spent the decade since then golfing, traveling, and making celebrity appearances. In 1989–1990, he'd managed a forgettable season in the short-lived Senior Professional Baseball Association for retired ballplayers.

Once before, in 1992, the Veterans' Committee, which selects managers, had declined to induct Weaver. The spirit of the Veterans' Committee, made up of retired players, officials, and media members, was to wait a decade or more before inducting players who'd been passed over in voting, and managers, coaches, executives, and umpires. In 1992, they'd picked pitcher Hal Newhouser and umpire Bill McGowan instead.

In 1996, for the first time since 1971, the Baseball Writers' Association of

Earl Weaver was remembered for his passion, 1970s.

America declined to vote in any of the players they were considering, including Phil Niekro, Tony Perez, and Don Sutton. In March, when the Veterans' Committee, which selects entrants separately from the BBWAA, met to discuss whether to elect Weaver or other managers, he said he was ready to accept their verdict. "When they sit down at the table with all my numbers in front of them, the votes will either be there or they won't," he said. "Either way, my lifestyle won't change."

When Earl Weaver became a big-league manager in 1968, only seven managers had ever been enshrined in Cooperstown: Connie Mack (1937), John McGraw (1937), Wilbert Robinson (1948), Joe McCarthy (1957), Bill McKechnie (1962), Miller Huggins (1964), and Casey Stengel (1966). After 1968, Bucky Harris (1975), Al Lopez (1977), Rube Foster (1981), Walt Alston (1983), and Leo Durocher (1994) joined them.

Also going in with Weaver in 1996 was Ned Hanlon, manager of the go-go 1890s Orioles teams and the inventor of aggressive in-game managing. "He was always pulling something fast—anything he could get away with to win a game, kind of like Earl Weaver," said Albert Thompson, Hanlon's grandson.

Jim Palmer led the applause from Weaver's players. "Earl was the best manager of his era," he said. "He was scrappy, loyal, and never held a grudge." Reaching the Hall is "like a USDA meat approval," he added. "He's just gone from 'choice' to 'prime.'" Weaver credited his star players like Palmer and Frank Robinson and Brooks Robinson. "Those boys are the ones that put me in," he said. The new Hall of Famer sounded repentant. "Those incidents are still kind of embarrassing," he said. "When I see the clips, I say, how could I do that?"

The selection of Weaver as Cooperstown's thirteenth manager appears even more justified in hindsight. As of this writing, Weaver still has the highest winning percentage, .583, of any manager with over 1,000 wins since division play started in 1969.

Before his induction speech on August 4, a nervous Weaver reminded reporters that he had never wanted to manage. "If I could play now, I'd play," he said. "I wouldn't manage. You play baseball. You work at managing. The stress, it's going to get you." He said he'd thought about his speech every day since receiving the good news in March.

Then it was time. Weaver climbed the podium to stand in front of his childhood heroes, Cardinals Hall of Famers Stan Musial and Enos Slaughter. "How could any baseball fan not be humbled to be included in this group of gentlemen?" he said, neglecting to mention he'd played on the same team as his two heroes, during that long-ago 1952 spring training with the Cardinals. Weaver choked up. "Don't make me cry now," he said. "I don't wanna cry. I'm gonna cry. It's hot out there, people. We want to get back and get a beer or something."

Weaver started with a joke about how "all of those computer things that came back from Davey Johnson, all his lineups had him hitting fourth," but with "Frank, Brooks, and Boog on that team, I didn't think they were right, so I started my own." He then gave a fine speech, expressing his gratitude for his "special people," including "every Baltimore player who ever put on a uniform." He praised his mother and father, "who had me at the ballpark regularly before I was old enough for kindergarten," and "for encouraging me to stay in baseball throughout a twenty-year minor-league career." He did not mention Bud Bochert, his "favorite uncle," the bookie who'd taken him to hundreds of ballgames.

Earl thanked Marianna, "who listened to me rant and rave when things didn't seem right," and added, "I want to tell her I love her in front of everybody." He asked Kim, Mike, Rhonda, and Terry to stand up. "They understood why their dad was not there on graduation day, prom night, or all the other important days of their lives because I was on the road at some ballpark," he said. He also thanked Palmer, "the gentleman I had more arguments with than my wife, Marianna."

Tongue in cheek, Weaver thanked the umpires of the American League. "Counting balls and strikes and close plays on the bases, they must have made a million calls when I was managing and except for those 91 or 92 times I disagreed, they got the other ones right," he said. "Thanks for your patience, understanding, and keep up the good work, because the game can't be played without umpires."

Weaver also thanked his Hall of Fame players—Frank Robinson, Brooks Robinson, Jim Palmer, and Reggie Jackson, and future members Eddie Murray and Cal Ripken Jr.—and credited his coaches, especially his pitching guru

George Bamberger. He wondered how a guy who spent twenty years trying to make the big leagues ever made it and said it "took a lot of guts" for General Manager Harry Dalton, President Frank Cashen, and owner Jerold Hoffberger in 1968 "to turn a major-league club over to me, and if they knew how nervous I was, they might have had second thoughts." Finally, he thanked the "wonderful fans of Baltimore [for] letting me stay." Thousands of supporters, many decked out in Orioles orange and black, rose to their feet and applauded.

More managers followed Weaver: Tommy Lasorda (1997), Frank Selee (1999), Sparky Anderson (2000), Billy Southworth (2008), Dick Williams (2008), Whitey Herzog (2010), Bobby Cox (2014), Tony La Russa (2014), Joe Torre (2014), and Jim Leyland (2024). In total, there are now twenty-four managers in the Hall of Fame.

Weaver's plaque, lodged between Ned Hanlon and Phil Niekro and under Negro League pitcher and manager Rube Foster, reads:

MANAGED ORIOLES WITH INTENSITY, FLAIR AND ACERBIC WIT FOR 17 SEASONS .583 WINNING PERCENTAGE (1,480-1,060) RANKS 5TH ALL-TIME AMONG 20TH CENTURY MANAGERS WITH 10 OR MORE YEARS SERVICE. 94.3 WINS PER SEASON RANKS FIRST. FIVE 100-WIN SEASONS SECOND ON ALL-TIME LIST. WON SIX A.L. EAST TITLES, FOUR PENNANTS AND 1970 WORLD SERIES.

"No manager belongs there more," concluded Tom Boswell in the *Washington Post*. "As much as any one person in a generation, Weaver encapsulates the fire, the humor, the brains, the childishness, the wisdom, and the goofy fun of baseball."

34

THE EARL OF BALTIMORE

Davie, Florida, 2013

> If you don't think baseball is a big deal,
> don't do it. But if you do it, do it right.
>
> —Tom Seaver

In January 2013, Earl Weaver sailed aboard the *Celebrity Silhouette* cruise ship for the Original Baltimore Baseball Cruise. It had left Fort Lauderdale, Florida, on its way to Cozumel, Grand Cayman, Jamaica, and Haiti and was nearing the end of its tour. On the celebrity cruises, fans paid to socialize with Weaver and other ex-Orioles. It was a chance to reminisce about the old days, and make extra cash. Earl also loved the intensively competitive Ping-Pong games.

During the previous year's season, in 2012, the Orioles had enjoyed a miraculous comeback, breaking a streak of fourteen straight losing seasons with 92 wins and a playoff run. The team had unveiled statues of their six franchise icons—Brooks and Frank Robinson, Cal Ripken, Eddie Murray, Jim Palmer, and Earl. The statues are situated in the picnic area beyond the left-field fence at Camden Yards.

Earl's statue faces the five Hall of Famers, with hands in his pocket, peering up, chin out, ready to chew out a player or umpire. "I paid attention to how he stood," sculptor Toby Mendez told me. "There was a performative aspect to his stance when he argued with umpires." One extra touch: there's an outline of a cigarette packet in the inside pocket, and two buttons undone so he can reach for them, a detail Weaver loved when he saw the statue.

On January 18, at dinner aboard the ship with Scott McGregor, one of his pitchers, Earl said he didn't feel well and got up to go to bed. "Tell the boys I love 'em," he told McGregor. He started choking just before midnight and died that night.

In a stirring coincidence, Stan Musial, Earl's childhood hero, teammate on the 1952 Cardinals spring training roster, and fellow Hall of Famer, passed away the same day.

The popularization of analytics and probability theory in twenty-first-century baseball had raised Earl Weaver's profile. "Weaver was the Copernicus of baseball," Tom Verducci had written in *Sports Illustrated* in 2009. "Just as Copernicus understood heliocentric cosmology a full century before the invention of the telescope, Weaver understood smart baseball a generation before it was empirically demonstrated."

Now baseball managers, players, and writers joined the chorus.

"People talk about Moneyball, but long before that you had Earl Weaver doing it," said Dan Duquette, general manager of the Orioles at the time. "The simplicity and clarity of his leadership and his passion for baseball is unmatched. He's a treasure, and I'm so grateful I had the opportunity to work with him this year." No one managed a ball club or pitching staff "better than Earl," said ex-Oriole Davey Johnson, who was then managing the Nationals. "He was decades ahead of his time. Not a game goes by that I don't draw on something Earl did or said."

In the *New York Times*, Bruce Weber wrote that Weaver "marshaled a scholar's familiarity with the rule book, a statistician's data, a psychologist's motivational skills and a heckler's needle into a relentless advocacy for the Orioles." The headline called Weaver a "Volatile, Visionary Manager."

In the *New Yorker*, Roger Angell called him "the best naked talker I ever heard" and "an intellectual at heart." Angell also related a conversation he'd had after Weaver's retirement, in which he suggested Earl might want to coach a high school or college team: "'I *hate* kids and I hate fucking kid baseball,' he growled, cracking the conversation into laughter."

Weaver, wrote Bart Barnes and Matt Schudel in the *Washington Post,* "was in many ways the team's brightest star from the late 1960s to the early 1980s. He seemed to embody the spirit of working-class Baltimore. . . . For more than a decade, Mr. Weaver was the face of baseball in the Mid-Atlantic."

Some of Weaver's descendants remembered him by getting an orange number 4 tattooed somewhere on their body. Weaver's grandson, Mike Leahy, the musician who goes by Clownvis (half-Clown, half-Elvis), wrote about getting kicked off *America's Got Talent* in 2010: "He wasn't too happy with Clownvis on *America's Got Talent,* one of his favorite shows. But when I talked to him about it, I explained that when I was up there arguing with those judges, I was evoking HIM! I could tell he got it, although I also realized old people don't necessarily understand a punk rock attitude." Clownvis's tattoo of the orange 4 took up his entire back.

Washington Post columnist Tom Boswell cautioned people to look beyond the clichés: "Whatever you think he was, you're right. But he was probably also, to some degree, the opposite as well. Whenever you assumed he was a man of his time, defined and limited by immersion in his sport, he often showed he was ahead of the times and also, frequently, ahead of his sport. In death, we will see images of his tirades at umpires, be reminded of his funny wisecracks and of his sense of strategy that predated several 'Moneyball' theories by a generation. We'll see a hard, smart man with a Chesapeake crab's shell, little social polish, and a need to overcompensate for his lack of size and ability as a minor league ballplayer. We all saw that. But in nine years of covering the Orioles beat, I saw another Weaver, one that doesn't contradict the first, but rather broadens him. He didn't open up often, but when he did, you were floored. He knew himself— why he was who he was and why he managed the way he did—as well as anyone I ever covered. We knew he had examined baseball and hadn't missed much. But he'd also examined himself and analyzed in detail everyone around him, too."

Agent Dick Gordon led Weaver's memorial service. The players attending included Brooks Robinson, Frank Robinson, Jim Palmer, Eddie Murray, Rick Dempsey, Bill Swaggerty, Scott McGregor, Dennis Martinez, Tom Shopay, Boog Powell, Ken Singleton, and Don Buford. Jim Bunning, the Hall of Fame pitcher inducted in 1996 along with Earl, was there. So was Naomi Silver, owner of the Red Wings.

The 2013 Orioles were represented by Executive Vice President Dan Duquette, ownership representative Louis Angelos, Doug Duennes, the club's executive vice president of business, communications director Greg Bader, team radio announcer Fred Manfra, and batting practice pitcher Rudy Arias.

Terry Cashman appeared in person to sing his 1982 song "The Earl of Baltimore."

> *Brooks was the heart. Frank was the soul.*
> *McNally, Mike, and Palmer were his Orioles,*
> *Winning with Weaver, winning for Baltimore.*
> *The men in blue, oh he drove them wild.*
> *The fight and the fire, that leprechaun smile.*
> *We'll always remember the Earl of Baltimore.*

At the memorial service, players spoke of their stormy relationships. "Yeah, he probably did yell at me more than anybody because I probably made more mistakes than a lot of them did," said Dempsey. "Oh my God, what a relationship I had with him, always yelling and screaming, but you know what? Like a lot of these players have said, he never gave up on me. He made every single one of us a better player. One thing about Earl, we hated him a lot of the time, but at the end of the day you loved him because he was a winner."

Palmer's voice cracked. "Earl gave me the opportunity to get to the Hall of Fame," he said. "What more can you ask of anybody?" After listening to Dempsey's recollections of Weaver, he added, "I feel like we had a love affair."

35

THE MANAGER'S CARDS

Managing is getting paid for home runs someone else hits.

—Casey Stengel

Managers who followed Earl Weaver preached his commandments. As twenty-first-century baseball teams adopted the analytics-based approaches Weaver prophesized, they hired managers who bunted less, prioritized walks and home runs, and orchestrated favorable pitcher-batter matchups.

To be sure, the context of the job has changed, along with baseball, and America. Teams are now billion-dollar entertainment corporations that accumulate data as if they were the U.S. Census Bureau, and place their managers at the center of sprawling org charts that informally include private trainers and agents. Big-league teams travel with more than double the number of people they did in Weaver's day, including seventy-five or so ballplayers, coaches, analysts, nutritionists, trainers, psychologists, and public relations officials. Teams manipulate transaction rules to field far bigger rosters, and use many more pitchers, over each season.

Players are more international, technically skilled, and financially ambitious. Young American prospects apprentice on private for-profit "travel" clubs instead of playing with their dads in city parks like Earl Weaver did. The best teenagers get signing bonuses worth more than Earl Weaver made in forty years of professional baseball. They're far more demanding and, empowered by a powerful union and free agency, don't tolerate autocratic managers. Fans, equipped with computers, phones, cameras, data, and information networks, post millions of pictures and social media comments a season, making managers feel like they're in a fishbowl.

All this has made the job of the modern manager more difficult in many ways than it was in Weaver's day, with more money at stake, more exposure via the internet, and more people to deal with. You have to wonder if Earl Weaver and Billy Martin would even want to learn to navigate bossy front offices, social media, the expansion of coaching staffs, the rise of powerful player agents, Japanese- and Spanish-speaking clubhouses, the computerization of a game they learned to play as little boys, and teams' increasing investment in chiropractors, nutritionists, and other specialized trainers and coaches.

By necessity, the typical modern manager is capable of reading and writing modern corporate memos, understanding at least parts of multiple languages, and directing ambitious, self-centered elite athletes. "There's a lot more people behind the scenes studying things, and it's a lot more computer-driven," said A. J. Hinch, manager of the Diamondbacks, Astros, and Tigers starting in 2009. Hinch was handpicked by Astros general manager Jeff Luhnow and won a World Series in 2017, but was fired because of a sign-stealing scheme orchestrated by players. Hinch, a classic modern manager, said he was powerless to stop it.

And yet, managers still matter, and they still look to the story of Earl Weaver for inspiration, because he stands for qualities that will always have value and can never be quantified: leadership, passion, and motivation. They're still the ones who are blamed for losses, and many still hit the hotel bar after games to drown their sorrows. "You have to be the leader and have to have the pulse of your team," said Ron Washington, the former Texas Rangers skipper the Anaheim Angels hired after the 2023 season. "You have to let them know what you expect in how they play the game of baseball. That's not being a hardass. That's being correct. There's right and wrong. The guys like Earl Weaver and Billy Martin, that's the way you play the game. What you're doing is right or what you're doing is wrong, and I won't accept anything less."

Weaver had "command, and control of the game and his players," said Derek Shelton, manager of the Pittsburgh Pirates, reared as an Orioles fan because his dad played in the Orioles' minor-league system. "It stood out as, this is what a leader looks like." How would Earl, Billy Martin, or Sparky Anderson fare today? "They would be great in the modern game," said Shelton. "Those guys led." Weaver "believed that at the end of the day, you were going to have a good day if you won and a bad day if you lost, and that sort of matter-of-fact attitude is awesome," said Hinch.

There have been powerful star managers since Weaver. Tommy Lasorda pioneered a cuddly, cheerleading leadership style with the Dodgers from 1976 to 1996. Joe Torre managed the Yankees' 1996–2001 dynasty as a cool CEO. Bobby Cox was a more passionate Earl Weaver–style leader and won fourteen division titles with the Braves. Tony La Russa, profiled by George Will in *Men at Work* and Buzz Bissinger in *Three Nights in August*, was a shrewd tactician. In 2004, Terry Francona led the Red Sox to their first title since 1918, and then won a second World Series three years later.

Their names don't echo through baseball history quite like Weaver's. Fans, players, and managers call a three-run homer an "Earl Weaver special." Whenever a manager goes berserk, he's compared to Earl. Online, fans still share clips of the 1980 Bill Haller hot mic incident. "I made no bones about it when I first got the job: I always wanted the next Earl Weaver as manager," said former Oakland A's executive and *Moneyball* hero Billy Beane. "Consciously or not, he understood mathematics and probability." The name Earl Weaver "means passion, it means winner," said ex–White Sox manager Pedro Grifol, who watched Weaver manage spring training games when he was a boy growing up in Miami in the 1980s.

And somebody still has to lead the team during the game. "You still have to empower the field manager who's with the players," said Dave Roberts, manager of the Padres and Dodgers starting in 2015 and World Series champion with the Dodgers in 2020. "If a person is making decisions who's not there with the players every day, you completely lose credibility within the organization, it's not going to end well."

In several high-profile instances, notably Tampa Bay Rays manager Kevin Cash's decision to remove Blake Snell in game 6 of the 2020 World Series against the Dodgers even though he had a 1–0 lead, had struck out 9, and had surrendered only 2 hits and walked none, the manager was blamed for following orders. The Rays lost the game, and the Dodgers won the World Series. The Rays were acting on data showing that Snell struggled against lineups the third time through the order. The formula had proven successful during the regular season, but this was the World Series, and baseball fans were deprived of the thrill of seeing a starting pitcher carry his team into the late innings. However, keeping Snell in was not a decision Cash felt he had the power to make. He had to stick to the plan.

Plans are laid out in the "Manager's Card," a sophisticated modern version of the pregame data Earl assembled. The Manager's Card, prepared by front offices in advance of each day's game, scores the desirability of all possible batter-pitcher matchups and offers data and suggestions relevant to all decisions a manager might have to make that day. The metrics vary by organization. Some favor a scale from −20 to +20, some from 0 to 100. To make things easier, they often use colors from green to red.

Managers still pass on Weaverian theology.

As a rookie manager with the Texas Rangers in 1986, Bobby Valentine asked Weaver for a pearl. "Just remember you only have twenty-seven outs," Weaver told him. "Don't waste any of them." Valentine said he remembered that years later when a front-office analyst handed him a paper using data to make the exact same case. Weaver "was way ahead of his time, and anybody can learn from how Earl Weaver went about it," said Giants manager Bob Melvin, who met Weaver when he tried out with the Orioles out of high school.

The manager with the best combination of old-school pedigree and new-age style might be David Bell, manager of the Cincinnati Reds from 2019 to 2024. I talked to Bell during the 2023 season as he guided an inexperienced Reds team to a surprising 82-80 record. The team was in contention for a playoff spot in September. In an illustration of the job's fragility, the Reds fired Bell toward the end of a disappointing 2024 season.

Like Weaver, Bell signed out of high school, and didn't attend college. His father, Buddy, and grandfather Gus had played Major League Baseball. Buddy managed nine seasons in the major leagues for Detroit, Colorado, and Kansas City. Unlike Earl, David Bell played twelve seasons in the big leagues, notching over 5,000 plate appearances in 1,403 games. After he retired, he felt compelled to catch up by reading voraciously. After our first meeting at PNC Park, Bell texted me a picture of his well-stocked bookshelves, which included Jim Collins's business classic about what makes great companies, *Good to Great*; Nate Silver's guide to interpreting data, *The Signal and the Noise*; and Nobel Prize winner Daniel Kahneman's classic about decision-making, *Thinking, Fast and Slow*. "I spent a lot of time reading, thinking, and getting very organized," Bell said. "I had to go through many different jobs to be really qualified to do this."

Bell framed his job as an executive position where he worked as part of the front office's team. "The environment I work in is very collaborative, working with the general manager, and ownership, but they allow me to do my job," said Bell. "They never tell me the lineup to play, or a strategy I have to use." And even with sophisticated data, the meat of modern managing is wise human leadership. "You can get all the odds right, but you need to understand the psychology of your players," said Bell. For example, he said, he often hated pinch-hitting even when it makes statistical sense, because it deflated the morale of the player he was taking out of the game.

Bell loved the information and data front offices generated. He would have loved to have had access to spin rates and digital spray charts when he was playing. But managers also need to triage and protect their players from drowning in data offering marginal improvements and diminishing returns. Baseball players still need to focus most of their energy and skill on executing core tasks. All the data in the world can't change the fact that pitchers since the nineteenth century have known that they need to try to hit corners and change speeds. Defenses still need to execute pickoffs, double plays, and relays. Hitters need to get the ball out of the infield with a runner on third and less than two out. The physical, practical game still humbles young men and requires the bulk of a manager's focus. "Too much information can paralyze a player," said Bell. "It's still important to compete and not overthink things."

In motivating players, managers can no longer scream like Weaver did at Rick Dempsey. "There are just too many games, and after a certain point, players will lose respect for you," said Bell, who professed a love for the television show about a new-age touchy-feely soccer coach Ted Lasso. "It's a question of what it takes to motivate each player." The goal of the manager is to "tap the inner motivation, the inner drive, for each of these players," said Bell. At the beginning of the season, Bell talked to each of his players. "On the first day of spring training, I ask each player if they understand why they're doing this. And there's no right or wrong. Ideally, it's to win a championship, but we all have our personal motivations." Does he bring money into the conversation? "I acknowledge it, I don't run away from it," he said. "At times, it's such a given. That's kind of there, so we can focus on the motivation of doing it together as a team."

One reason managers can't resort to threats anymore is because they'd have the players' union and the player's agent howling. "Before, you had that hammer as a leader and you could say it's my way or the highway, and the highway is life in the minor leagues," said Valentine. "You can't do that anymore." Valentine recalled that he was once demoted to the minor leagues "because the manager didn't like the way I gave the underhand feed to the second baseman." In Japan, where Valentine managed, baseball culture is more hierarchical. The boss is boss.

In America, managers can no longer threaten their players with insults, demotion to the minor leagues, or their fists, as Earl Weaver did. The table-flipping days "are over," said Melvin. "My first year in the minors, Jim Leyland was the manager, and he took things very seriously. We lost three or four games in a row and he lost it, in front of everybody." As we watched the Atlanta Braves take batting practice on a gentle summer evening, I asked manager Brian Snitker if he ever yelled at players. Snitker, who took over the Braves in 2016 and won a World Series in 2021, huffed as he looked out at his players warming up. "These guys ain't ever had anybody yell at them," he said. "These players were raised differently. When I played high school football, a coach kicked me."

All the managers I talked to said that what unites them with their predecessors is a love of and care for players. "The relationship might even be stronger now," said Hinch. "We know so much more about our players now, and the love of the players never goes away."

Bell played for larger-than-life leaders Tony La Russa, Lou Piniella, and

Dusty Baker. "I watched them very closely, and they knew every stat. I don't think that part has changed. Lou had high, high expectations, and he spent time in New York and he knew what it looked like to be a winner," said Bell. "His greatest strength was the attitude, 'this is the major leagues,' and he held people to that standard of winning." The Seattle Mariners in 2001 won 116 games, tied with the 1906 Cubs for most wins ever in a regular season.

Like Weaver, managers still preach honesty. Baseball players "respond to authenticity," said Bell. "You cannot do something that's not true to yourself, because they won't believe you ever again." That's what made playing for managers like Weaver, Martin, and Leyland so enjoyable. "They knew who they were, they knew what to expect, and they knew how much they cared," said Bell. "It worked because they were just being themselves. If I ever tried to be like Earl or Tony or any of the managers I played for, they wouldn't have responded to me. I try to not do anything that's not true to myself."

Managers can still make a big difference in how they structure practices. Major-league teams used to follow a rigid, pre-scripted routine of general fielding and batting practice. As I was talking to Bell in the visiting team dugout at PNC Park in Pittsburgh, we watched his Reds hit off a live pitcher throwing much harder than a typical soft-tossing batting practice pitcher. Off to the side, catchers practiced framing off a pitching machine. A coach hit tricky ground balls to infielders practicing double plays. "Practice has really evolved," said Bell. He made sure everybody on the team practiced their bunt defense. "Nobody bunts anymore, so when it comes up during a game, you have to be ready for it," he said.

With the authority of managers shrinking, one of those things front offices look for in modern players is leadership. "Front offices look for players who have talent and like other people doing well," said Valentine, naming the Orioles' Adley Rutschman and the Yankees' Aaron Judge as good examples. The mantle of leadership has shifted to star players. The mentality of the team becomes "if that's the way he does things, that's the way we're going to do things," said Valentine.

Bell said he prioritized empowering his players to be team leaders. "Getting to know each of these players as people, building that trust, is everything," said Bell. With his then–first baseman Joey Votto, "you couldn't ask for a better player who is really talented and whose heart is in the right place." Managers have to develop a trust, he added, "so that when you go to a player and ask them to do something, they'll listen."

Players still struggle with the same battles that consumed young Earl Weaver. "Players coming to the big leagues have the same dreams and fears as players coming to the big leagues twenty or thirty years ago," said Craig Counsell, considered the best young manager in big-league baseball. "A large part of the manager's job is still people. That hasn't changed." After the 2023 season, the Chicago Cubs hired Counsell away from the Milwaukee Brewers, giving him a five-year, $40 million contract. The $8 million a year was a fortune for a citizen but equivalent to an average free agent reliever.

When Dan Duquette ran the Montreal Expos (1991–1994), Boston Red Sox (1994–2002), and Orioles (2011–2018) as a general manager, he started every season by making his manager read *Weaver on Strategy*. "Nobody understood percentage baseball better than Earl Weaver. Nobody," he said. "Players liked him because they knew that he could help them. They knew that he knew his shit, and that he was on them to get the best out of them as a ballplayer. He was a crusty bastard, but I believe his only intent was to make the ballplayers as good as they could be."

EPILOGUE

THE PLAYERS

Baltimore, 1991

God moves the player as he the pieces
But what god behind God plots the advent
Of dust and time and dreams and agonies?

—Jorge Luis Borges, *The Game of Chess*

In 1988, the Orioles announced the construction of a new baseball stadium by Baltimore's inner harbor—Camden Yards—to open in 1992. That meant that the last Orioles game in the history of Memorial Stadium would be October 6, 1991, against the Detroit Tigers.

The Orioles planned a secret ceremony following the game. "If a Broadway play ran for thirty-eight years and was coming to an end, you'd want the opportunity to savor it one last time," said Charles Steinberg, who helped plan it. "We viewed this as the ultimate curtain call to a thirty-eight-year performance."

Alas, the chilly Sunday afternoon contest was a bore, except for franchise legend Mike Flanagan striking out two batters in the top of the ninth, a memory that's been bittersweet for Orioles fans since Flanagan's death by suicide in 2011. The Tigers beat the Orioles, 7–1. Cal Ripken Jr. was the last man to bat in Memorial Stadium. He grounded into a double play to end the game. The loss was typical for those years. In the five seasons after Weaver retired, the Orioles had only one winning season. Their three worst seasons since 1955 had been in 1988, 1990, and 1991.

Despite the humdrum ballgame, a sadness hung over Memorial Stadium. "Don't call any errors today," somebody quipped to official scorekeeper Bill Stetka. "How can I see errors when I'm crying?" said Stetka. The field cleared. The players gathered in the dugout. Just as they had on the last day of the 1982 season, Orioles fans stayed to pay tribute to something bigger than the game they had just watched.

The stadium loudspeaker played James Earl Jones's quote from *Field of Dreams*, the one about the constant of America being baseball that could also be about Earl Weaver's two urban homes, St. Louis and Baltimore: "America has rolled by like an army of steamrollers. It has been erased like a blackboard, rebuilt and erased again. But baseball has marked the time."

Then Brooks Robinson emerged from the first-base dugout and ran to third base. Then Frank Robinson, who trotted to right field. Then Boog to first base. Palmer to the mound. And so on. Don Baylor. Rick Dempsey. Davey Johnson. Bobby Grich. Rich Dauer. Mark Belanger. Billy Hunter. Lee May. Pat Kelly. Ellie Hendricks. Dave McNally. Pat Dobson. Mike Cuellar. Doug DeCinces. Jim Gentile. Scott McGregor. Terry Crowley. All these ballplayers.

"I wonder who's last," said Keith Mills, broadcasting on Channel 2.

"What a love affair," said Scott Garceau.

"The fan reaction is incredible."

"Here comes Cal."

The last man out: Earl. The Orioles picked him.

The little manager stood in the dugout tunnel listening to the cheers for Cal. Weaver fought back tears. "I don't know if I can do this," he said to public relations director Rick Vaughn.

He steeled himself and ran out into the sun. The crowd went crazy. Earl grinned. He shook hands with all the catchers and coaches at home plate. He walked over to the plate and kicked dirt on it. The players, coaches, and managers formed a giant circle around the infield.

Dempsey waved the towel and, with the Oriole Bird, spelled the letters: O-R-I-O-L-E-S. The players threw baseballs into the stands. Frank Robinson ran home from third and scored the final run. The grounds crew dug up home plate and put it in a stretch limo to carry it downtown under police escorts. The video board showed a live feed of the crew installing it at Camden Yards. The stadium played "Auld Lang Syne." The tears flowed.

"Everything came back to me in one big rush," said a red-eyed Weaver. "I knew this was the last time." After the ceremony, he smoked cigarettes and talked to his former players. He pointed around the room, at Brooks, Frank, Boog, Palmer, Aparicio, Dempsey, Baylor, Grich, and the rest. "The people in here, this is what it all comes down to," he said. "The people in here are the reason there is such a great sense of history about this stadium. We've got four Hall of Famers in this room. Four 20-game winners. We just had so many great players and teams here. That's what today was all about. I couldn't imagine not being here."

He recalled what it was like to get a major-league managing job at age thirty-seven. "Sheer panic," he said. "I knew the average life of a major league manager was two and a half years. And I wondered if there would still be an opening in the minors when the ax falls." And yes, there were fights, he admitted, "but after it was all said and done it was enjoyable, and each and every year you started, you had to put enough wins on the board so the owners would ask you back next year."

Fans had cheered Earl Weaver, but his players had felt more conflicted. Loving him was complicated. The years away from him, in retirement or playing for less successful managers and teams, had given them perspective. On this day, big-league ballplayers, the athletes whose respect Earl Weaver had craved since he was a little boy in St. Louis, finally loved him back. "Our common denominator may have been hating Earl," said Flanagan, who thanked Weaver for caring so deeply, and for driving his teams to master their craft. "There's nobody like him left."

ACKNOWLEDGMENTS

On the day Earl Weaver died in 2013, Kevin Helliker, an editor at the *Wall Street Journal*, invited me to write his obituary. Another editor, Tom Mudd, an Orioles fan from Towson, Maryland, who died in 2020, excitedly kept the Weaver obit atop the *WSJ* home page for almost the entire day. I'm grateful to them for getting this project started.

Backing up a bit, it was my uncle Steve Miller and my father, David Miller, who took me to my first baseball game at Memorial Stadium in 1985, right after Earl Weaver had returned to the dugout. That summer, my uncle Jimmy pitched to me in the backyard, and baseball became my first escape from the Belgian rain and my long days at the *école communale*. Thank you, Mom and Dad, and my siblings, Emily, Libby, Eleanor, Jacob, and Moe, for your cheer, pluck, and bookishness. In my twenties, I coached Jacob and Moe, and our fourth brother, Davey Nielsen, on youth teams, part of a lifetime of thinking about baseball.

That journey accelerated when I moved to Maryland at age seventeen to attend college and play baseball at Mount Saint Mary's in Emmitsburg. Theologians make great baseball critics, and I'm grateful to George Weigel, Bill Portier, and Bill Collinge for reading drafts and offering feedback. George, biographer of Pope John Paul II, gave detailed and generous notes about the entire manuscript.

In Maryland, my uncle Earl and his family, Jan, Daniel, and Rachel, and my uncle Steve, and his family Marianne, Ben, and Stephanie, treated me like a son and brother. In college I rode the bench for the Mountaineers and talked baseball into the night with our shortstop-philosopher Jaime Cevallos. In 1997, with Irene Cuyun, we attended a crab feast at the Ripkens'.

In my twenties, I caught and coached for the Brussels Kangaroos, and I am grateful to my players and teammates, especially Chris Blackbee, Matt Brown, Ryan Burr (who became a big-league pitcher), Jean-Michel De Rede, Jean-Michel Depasse, Kevin Desmedt, Cedric Desmedt, Manu Roggen, Eric McKay, Matt Oppenheim, Rick Prindle, Leander Schaerlaeckens, and Olivier Troussart. *Merci, les mecs.* Go Roos. Leander is an accomplished sportswriter who generously read the manuscript and offered feedback.

During those years, I worked with great baseball coaches. Thank you, Tim Casale, Lucas Fogarty, Sean Gilbert, Sam Faeder, Cameron Forbes (formerly a minor-league pitcher for the Orioles), JR Jacoby, Tim McClean, Tom McMahon, Frank Pericolosi, Jon Whalen, and Joe Vladeck. Tim, now a player agent, introduced me to Reds manager David Bell and many others who helped me understand the job of the modern manager.

Thank you to Brigid Grauman at the *Bulletin* and Jamie Graff at *Time* for giving me my first jobs in journalism. I learned to write and report during my thirteen years at the *Wall Street Journal*, under Bill Echikson, Peter Fritsch, Marc Champion, Stephen Fidler (who valiantly tried to teach me cricket), Clare Ansberry, and Elena Cherney. It was Peter who taught me to think harder, report more, and wait for the right pitch. Better to write nothing at all than derivative pablum. In Brussels, Peter, Charles Forelle, and I used to head to Kangaroo Field for *WSJ* bureau batting practice after work. We bashed one three-run homer after another. I've grateful for those years, and all the conversations about journalism, writing, and baseball that have followed.

I miss my incredible colleagues and friends at the *Journal*, notably Reed Albergotti, Mike Allen, Rachel Bachman, Joe Barrett, Ali Berzon, Matt Dalton, Ken Gepfert, Bryan Gruley, Bob Hagerty, Drew Hinshaw, Dan Michaels, Kris Maher, Adam Najberg, Laurence Norman, Bruce Orwall, Scott Patterson, Joe Parkinson, Mike Ramsey, Geoffrey Rogow, Justin Scheck, Joe White, William Westbrook, Jeanne Whalen, and Robbie Whelan. Neil King was the best fellow traveler in sharing his wisdom about book writing. Jonathan Eig, a *WSJ* alum and Pulitzer Prize–winning biographer, was incredibly generous in helping me recraft my book proposal.

Literary agent Eric Lupfer believed in the idea, and introduced me to Jofie Ferrari-Adler at Simon & Schuster's Avid Reader Press. I loved working with Eric, Jofie and Avid Reader's ace editor Carolyn Kelly. Thank you.

I'm lucky to have found a new professional home at *America*, and their wonderful editors James Martin SJ, Sam Sawyer SJ, Jim Keane, Tim Reidy, and Kerry Weber, and Trade Data Monitor, where founder and CEO Don Brasher has supported my work on this book, and my PBS film with David Bernabo, *Moundsville*. Mike Laskey and his brilliant team at the Jesuit Media Lab have offered me a writing community and welcomed me at annual creative retreats. I beg forgiveness for interrupting silence and prayer to interview Cal Ripken Jr. from my sparse room at the convent.

I'm grateful to the coaches I worked with during my four years coaching for a private travel baseball club in Pittsburgh, Derrick Wood, Brian Herb, and Sammy Sibeto, and to my favorite baseball dads, Chris Eifler, Travis Rice, Tom Sommer, and Adam Stickle.

Writers in and near Pittsburgh have helped me with conversation and reading, notably Mike Elk, Will Graves, Beth Kracklauer, Steve Novotney, Matt Smith, and Anne Trubek. Mick Landaiche, my therapist, talked me through how to be faithful in this project to myself, and Earl Weaver, as human beings. I chewed the fat with *Post-Gazette* food critic Hal Klein.

Dan Hart and Jim Trdinich of the Pirates helped coordinate interviews with active MLB managers David Bell, Craig Counsell, A. J. Hinch, Bob Melvin, Dave Roberts, Derek Shelton, Brian Snitker, and Ron Washington. In Chicago, Scott Reifert set up time with Pedro Grifol.

Mike Sowers, my father-in-law, read many early drafts and provided essential feedback. Christine Long, Geoff Rogow, and Matthew Strauss also read early versions. Thank you also to Will Bardenwerper, Jamey Caroll, Nelson Cooper, Brian Jacobson, Art Lindsey, Patrick Lutz, Jonathan Mayo, Sherry Rhodes, Kolin Smith, Rob Stewart, and Mike Vargo.

The baseball-writing community is extremely generous. Cassidy Lent and the staff at the Hall of Fame in Cooperstown welcomed me warmly. MLB historian John Thorn hosted me at his charming book-lined house in Catskill, New York. Tom Gilbert offered feedback on a draft and welcomed me to his warm home in Brooklyn for dinner, cigars, and long conversations about nineteenth-century baseball, the 1980s Yankees, and Belgian detective novels. Rob Neyer threw two immaculate innings of middle relief, digging up extra Weaver data and catching mistakes. Lee Kluck, author of a 2024 Harry Dalton biography, provided a solid fact-check. Mark Simon offered incredibly sharp, smart notes and feedback.

The ex-Orioles who helped me the most were Rick Dempsey, Bobby Grich, and Ken Singleton. Thanks, guys. Two veteran baseball writers have my infinite gratitude: Terry Pluto, author of the excellent first biography of my subject, the *Earl of Baltimore*, and Tom Boswell, the inimitable *Washington Post* beat writer, and my hero as a young reader. Ron Shelton, the king of baseball in Hollywood, shared his experience as an Orioles minor leaguer. All answered my questions. Thank you.

Earl's daughter Terry Leahy welcomed me twice in St. Louis, and answered all my questions about her dad. ("What would my dad make of what you're trying to do?" she once said, pointing at my chest like her dad would have done. "He would have said: If you feel that this is something that *you* have to do, well *you* go ahead and do it, but you make sure it's *good*." Even from the grave, Earl pushes people to do better.)

Michele Soulli, an all-pro researcher and genealogist, dug into the history of the Weaver family and their neighborhood. In St. Louis, Tim Metcalf guided me on a tour of St. Louis and the world of Uncle Bud's 1940s criminal underworld. Ed Wheatley and Pat Elliott, the son of Earl Weaver's high school coach, answered question about the history of baseball in St. Louis. Marty Chalk showed me around Elmira, New York. Dan Mason and Naomi Silver welcomed me in Rochester. In Baltimore, Mike Gibbons welcomed me at the Orioles archives. Orioles alumni director Bill Stetka introduced me to ex-Oriole players. In Baltimore, Nestor Aparicio, Bill Birrane, Stan Charles, Jim Henneman, Tom and Brendan Marr, Mike Olesker, Greg Schwalenberg, Gregg Wilhelm, and Charlie Vascarello shared their recollections of the old days.

Mike Woodham, Ephraim Ritter, and Ken Nelson showed me around Thomasville, Georgia. Rob Fitts and Ryan Holmberg helped me understand Weaver and the Orioles' 1971 trip to Japan.

Thank you to my Orioles Club Pittsburgh pals: Bob Ross, Dave Matlin,

Ethan Frier, Matt McDermit, and Andrew Gibson. Andrew is a talented analyst for major-league front offices, now with the Athletics, and I'm grateful for all of his patient explanations of modern baseball scouting, analysis, and strategy. Same for Katie Krall and Mike Snyder, a friend in the Orioles front office. I talked Earl Weaver on bike rides and during adult morning batting practice with Josh Friedman, and over drinks and playing and watching hoops with Andy Moore and Ad Yeomans.

My latest baseball coaching adventure led me to Pittsburgh's Allderdice High School, alma mater of former Orioles president Larry Lucchino. Thanks to coaches Brad Hoffer, Mike and Mark Pfleger, and Quinn McGrath. Talking baseball never gets old. Miraculously, that's what happened after an alert truck driver named Darryl Smith slammed on his brakes and possibly saved Meri's and my life after our car veered out of control after a tire blowout in 2023 on the Pennsylvania turnpike. Darryl is a Yankees fan.

And finally, thank you to Meri, my partner in talk and travel, books, and love.

NOTES ON SOURCES

The lifeblood of a biography is the subject's own words. Earl Weaver authored two memoirs, *Winning!* and *It's What You Learn After You Know It All That Counts*, and a first-person strategy guide, *Weaver on Strategy*, and was the cooperative subject of a 1981 biography by Terry Pluto, *The Earl of Baltimore*. He also gabbed with baseball writers like Roger Angell, Tom Boswell, and Peter Gammons for over five decades. In addition, John Eisenberg's remarkable oral history of the Orioles, *From 33rd Street to Camden Yards*, includes long interviews of and about Weaver. Weaver's own account of his journey from the streets of Depression-era St. Louis to Memorial Stadium and Cooperstown was my starting point.

I then, on my own, researched and reported his life from cradle to grave, conducting over 200 interviews with family members, former players, major-league umpires, team officials, minor-league officials, historians, MLB managers, general managers and players, and baseball writers and historians. In describing scenes, I've relied on firsthand sources, and, when possible, interviewed somebody who was present.

Thanks to online newspaper archives, especially newspapers.com, I was able to search and read thousands of newspapers. I'm indebted to the men and women who wrote and edited all those stories. YouTube has an impressive collection of old base-ballgames, and Weaver arguments with umpires.

I traveled on reporting trips to St. Louis, Baltimore, Ft. Lauderdale, Cooperstown, Elmira, and Rochester, and Albany, Thomasville, Fitzgerald, and Dublin in southern Georgia. I visited the state archives of Maryland and Missouri. At my request, genealogist Michele Soulli researched Earl Weaver's family tree. Tim Metcalf, a researcher in St. Louis dug up newspaper and police records on Uncle Bud Bochert's criminal career.

I interviewed Earl's three children, Mike, Rhonda, and Terry, stepdaughter Kim, and cousin Joyce Hale multiple times, and Marianna Weaver, Earl's widow, once.

The following Orioles minor- and major-league players spoke with me on the record: Benny Ayala, Bobby Bonner, Don Buford, Doug DeCinces, Dave Criscione,

Rick Dempsey, Ken Dixon, Dan Ford, Kiko Garcia, Bobby Grich, Glenn Gulliver, Fred Lynn, Dennis Martinez, Tippy Martinez, Dyar Miller, Boog Powell, Cal Ripken Jr., Merv Rettenmund, Gary Roenicke, Ron Shelton, Ken Singleton, Tim Sommer, John Stefero, Tim Stoddard, Ron Stone, and Steve Stone. Jim Palmer answered questions by email.

Three retired umpires, Dave Phillips, Larry Barnett, and Jim Evans, spoke at length with me about Weaver's tormenting of American League officials.

For the history of the manager, I relied on Chris Jaffe's *Evaluating Baseball's Managers*, Bill James's *Guide to Baseball Managers*, Harvey Frommer's *Baseball's Best Managers*, and Leonard Koppett's *The Man in the Dugout*.

The Society for American Baseball Research's amazing collection of biographical sketches helped me understand various baseball characters. Tom Gilbert's *How Baseball Happened* and John Thorn's *Baseball in the Garden of Eden* grounded my understanding of early baseball history.

NOTES

CHAPTER 1: PART WIZARD, PART GENERAL, PART CLOWN

Primary sources include newspaper accounts, baseball writer Tom Boswell's "Bred to a Harder Thing Than Triumph," in his book, *Why Time Begins on Opening Day*, and tape of full games, televised originally by ABC Sports, on YouTube. I used Baseball-Reference.com to compile Orioles win-loss records during different eras.

3 *"All life is six-to-five against"*: Damon Runyon, "A Nice Price," *Evening Standard*, September 20, 1937.

3 *Earl Weaver was crying*: Thomas Boswell, *Why Time Begins on Opening Day*, 60.

3 *On top of the pitcher's mound*: Ibid.

4 *Up in the TV booth*: Howard Cosell, "1982 10 03 ABC Brewers at Orioles," Classic MLB1, February 7, 2019, YouTube video, 3:08:55, https://www.you tube.com/watch?v=-qNR_wC_6Qo.

5 *"Each manager, his ball club, it was* his *team"*: Dave Roberts, author interview, April 26, 2023.

6 *Here's how the Orioles have done in their franchise history*: https://www.baseball -reference.com/teams/BAL/index.shtml.

7 *who likened Earl Weaver*: Weigel, *Not Forgotten*, 201.

8 *"For people in Baltimore, Earl was one of us"*: Greg Schwalenberg, author interview, October 15, 2023.

8 *Here's how Cosell wrapped up the scene*: Cosell, "1982 10 03 ABC Brewers at Orioles."

CHAPTER 2: BRAT VS. BRAT

Primary sources include Weaver's memoirs, interviews with family members, and newspaper accounts. I relied on the biographical sketch by SABR's Alexander Edelman to describe Stanky.

9 *"Not making the baseball team at West Point"*: Seymour, *The People's Game*, 322.

9 *The hot ticket in St. Pete on March 8*: Martin J. Haley, "Cards' Boots Lift Yanks Over, 11-5," *St. Louis Globe-Democrat*, March 9, 1952.

10 *there were 43 minor leagues with 378 teams*: Lloyd Johnson and Miles Wolff, eds., *The Encyclopedia of Minor League Baseball*, 263.

10 *Weaver had graduated from Beaumont High School*: Weaver, *It's What You Learn After You Know It All That Counts*, 1982.

10 *A "nice little jewel"*: Forrest Wonneman, "Movie Camera Snaps Mexican in Action at Cardinal Camp," *Mexico Ledger*, March, 27, 1952.

11 *100 Per Cent*: Neal Russo, "Weaver Talks About His Twin City Days," *Sentinel*, February 12, 1952.

11 *the great Harry Caray broadcast the game:* Dial Doings, *Hannibal Courier-Post*, March 3, 1952.

11 *Eddie "The Brat" Stanky was a tough Polish kid*: Alexander Edelman, "Eddy Stanky," SABR, January, 4, 2012, https://sabr.org/bioproj/person/eddie -stanky/.

11 *"another Eddie Stanky"*: Bill Beck, "He's Certain to Stick, Providing He Beats Out Schoendienst, Stanky," *Tampa Bay Times*, February 27, 1952.

11 *"If I find out it will help the club"*: Bill Beck, "City Greets Yankees with Fanfare Tomorrow but We Like Cards, Too," *Tampa Bay Times*, February 20, 1952.

11 *"Our scouts are high on a kid called Earl Weaver"*: Eddie Stanky, "Stanky Predicts Four-Team Fight," Associated Press, February 21, 1952.

12 *"Stanky simply could not accept"*: Weaver, *It's What You Learn*, 90.

12 *"If the records are correct"*: Eddie Stanky, "Stanky Says Spring Training," Associated Press, February 21, 1952.

13 *When Cardinals right fielder Enos Slaughter*: Weaver, *It's What Your Learn*, 90.

13 *"The more I see of him, the more I like"*: Bill Beck, "Stanky Still Looking For Answers," *Tampa Bay Times*, March 19, 1952.

13 *"Stanky Keeping Fans Guessing on Infield"*: "Stanky Keeping Fans Guessing on Infield," Associated Press, March 21, 1952.

13 *Here's how the paper reported it*: "Redbird Notes," *St. Louis Post-Dispatch*, March 31, 1952.

14 *"When you're a twenty-one-year-old kid"*: Weaver, *It's What Your Learn*, 92.

14 *"The only thing Earl knows"*: Peter Gammons, "Is He a Genius?" *Boston Globe*, October 16, 1979.

15 *"My dad was so proud"*: Terry Weaver, author interview, February 8, 2023.

CHAPTER 3: MOUND CITY

Primary sources include Earl Weaver's memoirs, interviews with family members, James McDonald's paper on the Gashouse Gang's cowboy band, Leonard Koppett's *The Man in the Dugout*, Walter Johnson's *The Broken Heart of America*, and SABR's *Sportsman's Park in St. Louis*. Researcher and historian Tim Metcalf guided me on several tours of Earl Weaver's birthplace site, Sportsman's Park, and surrounding neighborhoods. Genealogist Michele Soulli did a deep dive into the Weaver family tree, going back to eighteenth-century England.

19 *"Your Holiness, I'm Joseph Medwick"*: Whitey Gruhler, "Coverin' Ground," *Press of Atlantic City*, July 19, 1954.

19 *Earl Sr. ran dry-cleaning businesses*: Weaver, *It's What You Learn*, 79–80.

20 *"And I wasn't so good at first grade either"*: Curt Smith, "Dizzy Dean's Greatness: He Was Americana and a Man of the People," *New York Times*, June 18, 1978.

20 *"Sure, I heard it"*: John Heidenry, *The Gashouse Gang*, 55.

20 *replica Cardinals uniform*: Weaver, *It's What You Learn*, 79.

20 *The rest of the Cardinals matched Dizzy*: Heidenry, *The Gashouse Gang*.

21 *started a cowboy band*: James McDonald, *The Marvelous Musical Mississippi Mudcat Band*.

21 *"the only manager that carried an orchestra"*: Bill Christine, "Briles Hears Roar of a Different Crowd," *Pittsburgh Press*, October 27, 1971.

21 *"garish, county fair"*: Scott Ferkovich, "Sportsman's Park (St. Louis)," SABR, March 4, 2013.

22 *since the modern version of the sport arrived*: Gilbert, *How Baseball Happened*.

22 *they took over Sportsman's Park*: Wolf, *Sportsman's Park in St. Louis*.

22 *He was born in St. Louis in 1901*: Ancestry.com, World War II draft card.

23 *Her dad died when she was a child*: Joyce Hale, author interview, March 15, 2023.

23 *when the family referred to Uncle Red*: Weaver, *It's What You Learn*, 122.

23 *"When he died"*: Doug Brown, "The Earl Weaver You Don't Know," *Baltimore Sun*, April 28, 1974.

23 *"First in booze, first in shoes"*: Dennis Pajot and Greg Erion, "St. Louis Browns Team Ownership History," SABR, https://sabr.org/bioproj/topic/st-louis-browns-team-ownership-history/#_edn2.

24 *"The City Surrounded by the United States"*: 1940 St. Louis phone book.

24 *a plant that made TNT explosives*: Ancestry.com, World War II draft card.

24 *Mike Weaver, Earl's son*: Mike Weaver, author interview, November 15, 2021.

24 *Phone books from the 1930s*: St. Louis phone books, Missouri State Archives, St. Louis.

24 *Four employees sued him*: "Suit Asks Receiver for Cleaning Concern," *St. Louis Globe-Democrat*, July 25, 1934.

24 *"It was my job to deliver them"*: Pluto, *The Earl of Baltimore*, 12.

25   *The* Post-Dispatch *described him*: "Twentieth Ward," *St. Louis Post-Dispatch,* March 28, 1951.

25   *"That was me at the ballpark"*: Bob Rubin, "Fiery Weaver Aging but Not Mellowing," *Miami Herald,* February 25, 1979.

25   *Joe Medwick signed a scorecard for Earl*: Weaver, *It's What You Learn,* 80.

25   *Managers fascinated young Earl*: Ibid.

26   *"Our Captain is a goodly man"*: Stephen Guschov, *The Red Stockings of Cincinnati,* 18.

26   *"Harry Wright in a poetic sense"*: Thomas W. Gilbert, author interview. March 4, 2024.

26   *"eat hearty—Roast Beef rare will do"*: Harold Seymour, *The Early Years,* 67.

27   *young Earl studied Southworth*: Weaver, *It's What You Learn.*

27   *"Did Southworth Blunder"*: "Did Southworth Blunder When He Called on Stan Musial to Bunt?," *St. Louis Star and Times,* October 4, 1944.

28   *Irene married a small-time mobster*: Ancestry.com, Indiana marriage licenses, 1810–2001.

CHAPTER 4: GANG OF ST. LOUIS

Primary sources include Weaver's memoirs, police records, old gambling guides, Daniel Waugh's chronicles of St. Louis gangs, and contemporary St. Louis newspaper accounts.

29   *"The gambling known as business"*: Ambrose Bierce, *The Devil's Dictionary.*

29   *Earl usually attended games at Sportsman's Park with his favorite uncle*: Weaver, *It's What You Learn,* 80.

31   *Bud hooked up with a powerful St. Louis gang*: Daniel Waugh, author interview, February 1, 2023.

31   *The Cuckoos, violent gangsters who drove a maroon automobile*: Walter Fontane, "Baseball to Bullets," *Gateway,* vol. 27, 2007.

31   *"An elastic bunch of punks"*: Ibid.

31   *Earl admired Bud*: Weaver, *It's What You Learn,* 80.

31   *"Uncle Bud was the well-to-do"*: Ibid.

31   *"He was always handing out cash"*: Mike Weaver, author interview, November 15, 2022.

32   *"When I was just big enough to crawl"*: Will Grimsley, "Orioles Earl Weaver Sorry for Misconduct," Associated Press, March 18, 1982.

32   *Americans wagered as much as $5 billion a year*: "Betting on Baseball Declared Huge Figure," Associated Press, August 22, 1949.

32   *The first game to charge admission*: Gilbert, *How Baseball Happened.*

32   *"People think the NFL invented sports betting"*: Raphael Esparza, author interview, January 15, 2024.

32   *"You will see them everywhere"*: John Lardner, "Money to Burn," *Newsweek,* August 21, 1944.

32   *In 1949, casinos in Los Angeles*: "Baseball Television Betting Is Popular Racket in L.A.," Associated Press, July 2, 1949.

33   *Cardinals owner Sam Breadon hung a sign*: Sid Keener, "Sid Keener's Column," *St. Louis Star and Times*, May 11, 1940.

33   *Bud taught him golf*: Weaver, *It's What You Learn*.

33   *Irene was riding in the passenger seat*: "Woman Hurt in Crash," *St. Louis Globe-Democrat*, November 8, 1937.

33   *Bud and an accomplice roughed up*: "Ex-Congressman Drops Charge," *St. Louis Post-Dispatch*, December 27, 1941.

34   *A cousin recalled him as a docile old man*: Joyce Hale, author interview, March 14, 2023.

34   *Baseball, John Davenport reported in* Esquire *in 1956*: John Davenport, "How to Bet on Baseball," *Esquire*, May 1956.

34   Pitchers Record Guide: Samuel J. Georgeson, *Pitchers Record Guide*.

34   *"It can be of extreme value"*: Ibid.

35   *betting system based on a 1–10 rating system*: Ibid.

35   *Jim Jasper, a bookie*: Jasper, *Sports Betting*, 83.

35   *"the idea is* not *to make an out"*: Ibid.

35   *"Your most precious possession"*: Weaver, *Weaver on Strategy*, 39.

36   *"This is the first time"*: Davenport, "How to Bet on Baseball."

36   *"You look at the daily gambling odds"*: Thomas Boswell, "Earl Weaver," *Washington Post*, April 6, 1979.

36   *"I'm a conservative man"*: Edwin Pope, "Weaver: No Desire to Return," *Knight-Ridder*, September 17, 1983.

36   *"Earl talked like a bookmaker"*: Dan Duquette, author interview, November 16, 2023.

36   *"Sometimes the ground decides the game"*: Randy Schultz, "Longshots Not Earl's Long Suit," *Palm Beach Post*, March 17, 1949.

36   *"If we had been at a crap table tonight"*: Randy Minkoff, "Sox Have Earl Shaking His Head," United Press International, August 11, 1982.

37   *"All the time people tell me"*: Steve Jacobson, "Whatever Became of Earl Weaver?" *Newsday*, January 13, 1970.

CHAPTER 5: COACH WEAVER

Primary sources for this chapter include Weaver's memoirs, newspaper accounts, and interviews with family members of his contemporaries, notably Pat Elliott, son of Earl's high school coach Ray Elliott, who shared his dad's practice plans.

39   *"Throw to second, not first"*: Andrew Rosenthal, "In Baseball, Soviets Are Still Minor Leaguers," *New York Times*, April 12, 1989.

39   *Earl Sr., Grandpa Zastrow, or Uncle Bud*: Weaver, *It's What You Learn*.

40   *eighty-nine public baseball fields*: 1944 St. Louis phone book, Missouri State Archives.

40   *an "average" boy*: Weaver, *Winning!*, 3.

40   *Earl Sr. coached a team*: "Woltman Champs Honored for Perennial Muny Feats," *St. Louis Globe-Democrat*, December 14, 1947.

40   *Weaver Sr. recruited the best players*: "Baseball Tryouts Today for Jeweler Team," *St. Louis Globe-Democrat*, March 22, 1946.

40   *The team won three straight city titles*: "Woltman Champs Honored for Perennial Muny Feats," *St. Louis Globe-Democrat*, December 14, 1947.

40   *fifteen-year-old Earl blasted a home run*: Pluto, *The Earl of Baltimore*, 13.

40   *"It's the old hustle"*: "Woltman Champs Honored for Perennial Muny Feats," *St. Louis Globe-Democrat*, December 14, 1947.

40   *"He was a real scrapper"*: Mike Drew, "Timeout with Mike Drew," *Post-Crescent*, July 28, 1961.

41   *threw a party at the Fairground Hotel*: "Woltman Nine Feted with Banquet, Gifts," October 31, 1946.

41   *the league suspended Earl Sr.*: Marion Milton, "Weaver, Shain Request Action by Muny Body," *St. Louis Star and Times*, August 21, 1948.

41   *"Pitchers be careful"*: Beaumont High School 1948 yearbook.

41   *"He taught my dad to say 'cocksucker'"*: Author interview, Doug Siedel.

42   *"A hard-hitting second baseman"*: Bill Kerch, "Stockham Gains Legion Honors with 11–5 Victory," *St. Louis Globe-Democrat*, July 26, 1947.

42   *"He was a stud"*: Bob Hardcastle, author interview, August 18, 2023.

42   *"The first thing I remember"*: Larry Willard, "Natural Bridge & Vandeventer," *St. Louis Globe-Democrat*, August 21, 1980.

42   *The coach made players do 50 or 100 push-ups*: Pat Elliott, author interview, August 10, 2023.

42   *"A fighter all the way"*: Willard, "Natural Bridge & Vandeventer."

43   *"I looked over at my dad"*: Ibid.

43   *Earl wrote up the 1946 season*: 1947 Beaumont High School yearbook.

43   *"Would your son Earl be interested"*: Weaver, *It's What You Learn*, 81.

44   *"juggling baseballs"*: "My Favorite Pastime!" *Prom*, December, 1947.

45   *"Earl, as far as we're concerned"*: Ibid.

45   *led him to the Cardinals' office*: Ibid, 83.

45   *"You'll be playing here"*: Ibid.

46   *They arrived at Albany's*: Weaver, *Winning!*, 6.

47   *"Weaver and Beavers, your stop"*: Ibid.

47   *"My God, Harley"*: Weaver, *It's What You Learn*, 84.

CHAPTER 6: LETTUCE DAYS

Primary sources include Weaver's memoirs, newspaper accounts, and *Season of Change*, a book by Toby Brooks about the 1948–1949 West Frankfort Cardinals. Paul Hemphill's 1979 novel, *Long Gone*, helped me understand minor-league life in the late 1940s.

51   *"Mr. President, you can tell those Russians"*: Bob Verdi, "Dempsey Keeps Things Light," *Chicago Tribune*, October 17, 1983.

51   *first pitch of the first at-bat of his pro career*: Weaver, *It's What You Learn*, 85.

52   *On his first day in Albany*: Ibid.

52   *The fear of getting cut*: Weaver, *Winning!*, 8.

53   *"Come on, you jerk"*: Ibid.

53   *Once settled in West Frankfort*: Weaver, *It's What You Learn*, 85.

53   *he ordered two eggs, bacon*: Ibid.

54   *"Before television, before air conditioning"*: White, *Left on Base in the Bush Leagues*, xx.

55   *"Earl and Jane Ann planned the wedding"*: "Earl Weaver, Card Second Baseman, Weds Jane Johnston," *St. Joseph News-Press*, May 8, 1949.

56   *"I was only eighteen"*: Weaver, *Winning!*, 13.

57   *"Things won't be the same"*: Bill Kerch, "Stars in the Making," *St. Louis Globe-Democrat*, August 11, 1950.

57   *"He could teach a snake to box"*: Warren Corbett, "George Kissell," SABR, https://sabr.org/bioproj/person/george-kissell/.

57   *"I went to school with George Kissell"*: Weaver, *It's What You Learn*, 89.

58   *"Omaha's Stanky"*: Robert Phipps, "Bunts Help as Omaha Rolls, 6–2," *Omaha World-Herald*, May 8, 1951.

58   *"probably the league's finest competitor"*: Robert Phipps, "Omaha Sweep Features One-Hitter by Coffman," *Omaha World-Herald*, August 16, 1951.

59   *"What is happening to the Earl"*: "Arrival of Eddie Stanky Complicates Future of Cards' Rookie Second Sacker," Associated Press, December 12, 1951.

59   *"After all"*: Ibid.

CHAPTER 7: THE BUFF GOAT

Primary sources include Weaver's memoirs, newspaper accounts, Howard Megdal's book *The Cardinal Way*, the Missouri State Archives, and interviews with current and former minor-league baseball players.

61   *"Oh, Lord, give me a bastard with talent"*: Lesley Visser, "Howard Cosell, with His Exclusive View of Himself, Is Returning," *Boston Globe*, January 23, 1988.

61   *"I reported to Houston with bitterness"*: Weaver, *It's What You Learn*, 92.

62   *"The Buff second baseman"*: "Tribe Wins, 9–7," United Press, April 14, 1952.

62   *"Little Earl Weaver"*: "Sportsbriefs," *Sentinel*, August 5, 1952.

62   *In denial and angry*: Pluto, *The Earl of Baltimore*, 22.

62   *he wore a sad, tired face*: "Sky Sox Nine Here Tonight," *Omaha World-Herald*, June 21, 1952.

62   *"a steady, poised second baseman"*: Robert Phipps, "Rain Washes Out Last Tilt with Wichita," *Evening World-Herald*, June 21, 1952.

62   *"the best player in the Western League"*: Robert Phipps, "Onrushing Omaha," *Omaha World-Herald*, August 2, 1952.

62   *"guys in their late twenties"*: Weaver, *It's What You Learn*, 92.

63   *"Can Weaver reach the top rung"*: "Sure Loss," *Evening World-Herald*, September 24, 1953.

64   *"Andy was a genius"*: Earl Weaver, interview with Dan Austin for National Baseball Hall of Fame, July 3, 1990.

64   *"Man, I love baseball!"*: Career minor leaguer, author interview, March 19, 2023.

64   *"get your ass in the clubhouse"*: Weaver, *It's What You Learn*, 93–94.

64   *"When you swung the bat"*: Ibid., 94.

65   *"Now I had to deal"*: Ibid., 95.

65   *Uncle Bud got Weaver a soft job*: Ibid., 98.

66   *"I was empathetic to everyone"*: Ibid, 99.

66   *"I was a definite menace"*: Ibid.

66   *Earl lived part-time in an apartment*: 1955 St. Louis city phone book.

CHAPTER 8: THE EARL OF KNOXVILLE

Primary sources include Weaver's memoirs, newspaper accounts, Dick Bartell's memoir, *Rowdy Richard*, and an interview with former congressman John J. Duncan, whose father owned the Knoxville Smokies.

69   *"A baseball manager is a necessary evil"*: John Egan, "Lookin' In," *Argus-Leader*, October 22, 1974.

70   *Dick Bartell was a small, quick infielder*: Bartell, *Rowdy Richard*.

70   *Weaver had thought about quitting*: Weaver, *It's What You Learn*.

71   *"for the good of the team and for the fans"*: Ed Harris, "Bartell Out—Weaver New Smokies Pilot," *Knoxville Journal*, August 9, 1956.

71   *"My dad realized they could save"*: Jimmy Duncan, author interview, July 10, 2023.

71   *"We have appointed Earl Weaver"*: Ibid.

71   *"Earl is the best possible choice"*: "Weaver Replaces Dick Bartell as Smoky Manager," *Knoxville News-Sentinel*, August 9, 1956.

71   *"I am quite sure that in making this change"*: Ibid.

71   *"Dick Bartell is a good baseball man"*: Ibid.

72 *"It's hard to get Weaver to tell you"*: Harris, "Bartell Out."

72 *he posed for a picture*: "Weaver Replaces Dick Bartell as Smoky Manager," *Knoxville News-Sentinel*.

72 *"The new Smoky skipper looks like a youngster"*: Ibid.

72 *the Smokies got a visit*: Weaver, *It's What You Learn*, 100.

73 *He invented a circle graph*: Corbett, *Wizard of Waxahachie*, 173.

73 *it was "horseshit"*: Ibid.

74 *"I wanted to see how I could do"*: Weaver, *It's What You Learn*, 100.

74 *"Each man is an individual"*: Marvin West, "Weaver's Future Not as Pilot—Yet," *Knoxville News-Sentinel*, August 10, 1956.

74 *In St. Louis phone books*: St. Louis phone books, Missouri State Archives, St. Louis.

75 *"I expected to be a player"*: Ibid.

CHAPTER 9: BIRD'S NEST

Primary sources include Weaver's memoirs, newspaper accounts, a reporting trip to Thomasville, and a CBS broadcast from 1961 I purchased from Rare Sportsfilms.

77 *"I'm superstitious, and every night"*: Bruce Newman, "Scorecard," *Sports Illustrated*, September 14, 1987.

77 *Earl Weaver reported in March 1957*: Weaver, *It's What You Learn*, 101.

78 *earning him the nickname*: Ibid.

79 *the backbone of any baseball team*: Richards, *Modern Baseball Strategy*, 11.

79 *"If we expect to improve our player strength"*: Harry Dalton memo at National Baseball Hall of Fame.

80 *the young Orioles ate, practiced, and played together*: Eisenberg, *From 33rd Street*.

80 *"to illustrate [that] if you slid the proper way"*: Jim Palmer, email to author, March 13, 2023.

81 *"Little Hitler"*: Norm Miller, "Key to O's Success? Bauer," *Daily News*, July 15, 1964.

81 *The Orioles gave Weaver a house*: Terry Leahy, author interview, February 10, 2023.

81 *"Daddy also put in two fridges"*: Ken Coram, author interview, October 12, 2023.

81 *"Let's have today's nominations"*: Weaver, *It's What You Learn*, 101.

81 *"After eating, will the following"*: Ibid., 102.

82 *"The decision had been made"*: Ibid., 103.

82 *"You're always going to be"*: Thomas Boswell, "Earl Weaver," *Washington Post*, March 27, 1982.

82 *"Get rid of that SOB"*: Weaver, *It's What You Learn*, 103.

82 *players crept under the window*: Sommer, *Beating Around the Bushes*, 234.

82 *Weaver and his buddies also drank*: Weaver, *It's What You Learn*, 127–28.

CHAPTER 10: CLIMB THE FLAGPOLE

Primary sources include Weaver's memoirs, newspaper accounts, and a reporting trip I took through southern Georgia to Albany, Thomasville, Dublin, and Fitzgerald.

85 *"I'd rather ride the buses in Triple A"*: Peter Gammons, "Between the Lines the Firing Squad," *Sports Illustrated*, July 21, 1986.

85 *favored a restaurant, the Spotted Pig*: Weaver, *Winning!*, 35.

86 *"My club had a hell of a first half"*: Ibid.

86 *"Players in their second"*: Weaver, *It's What You Know*, 105.

86 *"Nice hit, clown"*: Weaver, *Winning!*, 37.

86 *"Watermelon Head"*: Pluto, *The Earl of Baltimore*, 32.

87 *"Hey, Weaver, pull up a wheelchair"*: Weaver, *Winning!*, 38.

87 *"one of the biggest and most colorful little men"*: George Landy, "Dublin Opens 1958 Season at Home Tonight," *Macon News*, April 22, 1958.

87 *5-7, 175 pounds "of baseball energy"*: Sam Glassman Jr., "Dublin Manager Earl Weaver Described as Colorful, Dynamic and Fiery Leader," *Macon Telegraph*, March 28, 1958.

87 *Weaver pitched four shutout innings*: "Albany Leaps to Fast Start in 2nd Half," Associated Press, June 28, 1957.

87 *"We have a good manager"*: "Dublin Seeks to Up Crowds," *Macon Telegraph*, May 16, 1958.

88 *"The deal's off"*: Al Thomy, "When Dublin Went to Bat, Weaver Stayed at 'Home,'" *Atlanta Constitution*, May 24, 1958.

88 *W. T. Anderson, the president of the Georgia-Florida League*: Eisenberg, *From 33rd Street*, 194.

88 *Earl got so mad at an umpire*: Pascarelli, *The Toughest Job in Baseball*, 89.

89 *"big, full-faced kid"*: Mike Klingaman, "Roots of Iron," *Baltimore Sun*, September 3, 1995.

89 *"I remember Earl Sidney Weaver"*: Pluto, *The Earl of Baltimore*, 34.

89 *The hurler threw the ball into Earl's chest*: Eisenberg, *From 33rd Street*, 193.

CHAPTER 11: *BULL DURHAM*

Primary sources include Weaver's memoirs, newspaper accounts, two reporting trips to Elmira, New York (Marty Chalk, a former public address announcer for the Pioneers, gave me a detailed tour of the town), and *Beating the Bushes*, Tim Sommer's self-published memoir about playing minor-league baseball for the Orioles.

91 *"I could manage Adolf Hitler"*: Gary Ronberg, "A Hideout Here for Billy the Kid," *Philadelphia Inquirer*, August 1, 1978.

91 *The Pioneers ran promotions*: "Pioneers Glad to Get Out of Springfield," *Star-Gazette*, September 5, 1962.

92 *"Put some zookum"*: Sommer, *Beating About the Bushes*, 119.

93 *"That is what haunts us"*: Ron Shelton, "Stuff of Legends," *Los Angeles Times*, July 19, 2009.

93 *"As forty years go by"*: Pete McEntegart, "The Wild One," *Sports Illustrated*, June 30, 2003.

93 *"He had long arms, big hands"*: John Eisenberg, "Lost Phenom Finds His Way," *Baltimore Sun*, February 16, 2003.

94 *Weaver bailed Dalkowski*: Weaver, *Winning!*, 39.

94 *"that friggin' midget"*: Sommer, *Beating About the Bushes*, 238.

94 *"He handled me with tough love"*: Eisenberg, "Lost Phenom."

94 *"finally made Dalkowski understand"*: Weaver, *It's What You Learn*, 129.

94 *"I wish I knew"*: Al Mallette, "Dalkowski's Changed—He's Not Sure How," *Star-Gazette*, July 10, 1962.

94 *"I feel great, great, great"*: "Elmira Wins EL Title," Associated Press, September 17, 1962.

95 *"I started keeping the box scores"*: Al Mallette, "'Book' Gives Facts on Elmira vs. Charleston," *Star-Gazette*, September 6, 1962.

95 *"But can I trust a Yankees fan?"*: Martin Chalk, email to author, December 18, 2023.

95 *"He helped Earl Weaver"*: "Obituaries: John Morris (Jack) Crandall," *Star-Gazette*, October 6, 2021.

95 *"like a fugitive"*: Weaver, *It's What You Learn*, 130.

95 *"After the game"*: George Vecsey, "A Hall of Fame for a Legendary Fastball Pitcher," *New York Times*, July 18, 2009.

95 *"Let it suffice"*: Al Mallette, "Won't Need Scorecard to Recognize '64 Pioneers," *Star-Gazette*, March 29, 1964.

96 *down the drain emotionally*: Weaver, *It's What You Learn*, 132.

96 *"You must remember"*: Thomas Boswell, "Earl Weaver," *Washington Post*, March 27, 1982.

96 *Earl gave baseball a break*: Weaver, *It's What You Learn*, 133.

97 *"You know, I think we're gonna"*: Ibid., 134.

97 *"He was very persuasive"*: Martin Chalk, author interview, November 15, 2021.

97 *"The fellow who's hollering encouragement"*: Tracy, *The Psychologist at Bat*, 89.

97 *"I have tried to reach the subconscious"*: Weaver, *It's What You Learn*, 124.

98 *In one successful month*: Ibid., 134.

98 *"Weaver would stand in the dugout"*: Ron Stone, author interview, January 4, 2024.

98 *"Never in all my travels"*: Al Mallette, "Letter from Earl," *Star-Gazette*, December 4, 1965.

99 *One night in Elmira*: Eisenberg, *From 33rd Street*, 194.

99 *yanked third base*: Shelley Rolfe, "DeMars Follows Weaver," *Richmond Times-Dispatch*, April 28, 1968.

99 *"You just can't keep badgering"*: Eisenberg, *From 33rd Street*, 194.

99   *"Make it to Triple-A Rochester"*: Frank Peters, author interview, January 19, 2024.

99   *"guys who, in some cases"*: Eisenberg, *From 33rd Street*, 195.

CHAPTER 12: PRINCE HAL

Primary sources include Weaver's and Palmer's memoirs, newspaper accounts, interviews with former players, and a reporting trip to Rochester, New York.

101   *Born in New York City, he was adopted*: Palmer, *Palmer and Weaver*.

102   *Palmer learned to play baseball*: Palmer, *Palmer and Weaver*, 1.

102   *"I learned a lot"*: Palmer, *Palmer and Weaver*, 15.

103   *"sit in the bullpen and wager"*: Jim Mandelaro and Scott Pitoniak, *Silver Seasons*, 122.

103   *When pitcher Jerry Herron*: Pluto, *The Earl of Baltimore*, 43.

103   *"The ideal manager for us"*: Dan Mason, author interview, February 24, 2023.

103   *"Earl Weaver Music Appreciation Night"*: Shelly Rolfe, "Tone Set for Weaver's Night," *Richmond Times-Dispatch*, July 10, 1968.

103   *"The noisiest night"*: Lou Hatter, "Loved in Richmond," *Baltimore Sun*, August 4, 1968.

104   *"When I stepped out"*: Weaver, *It's What You Learn*, 136.

104   *"For God's sake, draft him, Harry"*: Weaver, *It's What You Learn*, 138.

104   *"This was Earl's first chance"*: Van Hyning, *The Santurce Crabbers*, 104.

105   *Over 10,000 fans watched Silver*: "I Am the Luckiest Man Alive," *Democrat and Chronicle*, September 5, 1967.

105   *After losing money in 1965*: Jim Castor, "Red Wings in the Black," *Democrat and Chronicle*, December 15, 1970.

105   *"not in good physical condition"*: Pluto, *The Earl of Baltimore*, 52.

105   *"I'm finally going"*: Weaver, *It's What You Learn*, 140.

CHAPTER 13: BIG LEAGUER

109   *"There comes a time"*: Galyn Wilkins, column, *Fort Worth Star-Telegram*, July 8, 1974.

109   *Earl rented an apartment*: Weaver, *Winning!*, 62.

110   *"American piety, stupidity, tin-pot morality"*: Mark Kram, "A Wink at a Homely Girl," *Sports Illustrated*, October 10, 1966.

110   *Baltimore exploded on April 6*: Michael Yockel, "The Riots of 1968," *Baltimore*, May 2007.

110   *only 22,050 fans*: Doug Brown, "Buford: Birds' New Whippet," *Evening Sun*, April 11, 1968.

111   *baseball's first collective bargaining agreement*: Miller, *A Whole Different Ballgame*.

112   *"Best job I ever had"*: Pluto, *The Earl of Baltimore*, 53.

112   *"big enough to stand"*: Richmond, *Ballpark*, 23.

113   *"The neighborhoods lapped up"*: Ibid., 28.

113   *He called Weaver*: Weaver, *Winning!*, 62.
113   *"There is no happiness"*: Transcript of press conference, Harry Dalton papers, National Baseball of Hall of Fame.
114   *"I plan to scramble"*: Ibid.
114   *"Weaver Won't Wait for Big Inning"*: Phil Jackman, "Weaver Won't Wait for Big Inning," *Evening Sun*, July 12, 1968.
114   *"It's what you learn"*: Weaver, *It's What You Learn*, 148.

CHAPTER 14: FRANK
Primary sources include Weaver's and Robinson's memoirs, newspaper accounts, and player interviews.

115   *"I think it's a tragedy"*: Milton Richman, "Says Looting 'Completely Wrong,'" United Press International, April 10, 1968.
115   *As a young man, racial slurs*: Terry Leahy, author interview, February 10, 2023.
115   *"I came into baseball"*: Weaver, *It's What You Learn*, 126.
116   *Ken Dixon, a Black pitcher for the Orioles*: Ken Dixon, author interview, January 20, 2024.
117   *Robinson's wife lost an apartment*: Mike Klingaman, "Fifty Years Ago, Frank Robinson's Search for Housing in Baltimore Helped in 'Opening the Doors for Others,'" *Baltimore Sun*, January 22, 2016.
117   *"The prejudice against Negroes in baseball"*: "O's Slugger Taking Aim on Baseball Manager Post," Associated Press, February 5, 1967.
117   *Weaver put in a crucial call*: Van Hyning, *The Santurce Crabbers*, 110.
117   *"Williams' coming back is great for baseball"*: Lou Hatter, "Weaver Plugs Frank as Pilot," *Baltimore Sun*, March 3, 1969.
118   *"The man made it a complete club"*: Alfred Wright, "The Birds Hop for a Lively Bantam," *Sports Illustrated*, April 13, 1970.
118   *"By scrambling more"*: Lou Hatter, "Weaver's Debut Is Big Success," *Baltimore Sun*, July 12, 1968.
119   *"The main thing"*: Wright, "The Birds Hop."
119   *"Earl Weaver doesn't look like a magician"*: Dick Young, New York News Service, July 19, 1968.
119   *Earl paid $28,000*: Property records, Maryland State Archives.

CHAPTER 15: MIRACLE WAY
Primary sources include Weaver's memoirs, newspaper accounts, player interviews, and Harry Dalton's papers at the National Baseball Hall of Fame.

121   *"The greatest feeling"*: Bob McCoy, "Insiders Say," *Sporting News*, July 15, 1985.
121   *"Believe it or not"*: Al Mallette, "Weaver's Woes," *Star-Gazette*, February 2, 1969.

123 *"Programming the Orioles"*: "Some Computing . . . Runs a Game!," Associated Press, February 16, 1969.

124 *"THIS MANUAL IS PREPARED"*: Harry Dalton papers, National Baseball Hall of Fame.

124 *The Oriole Way manual*: Ibid.

125 *"Hank was from the Yankee school"*: Eisenberg, *From 33rd Street*, 233.

126 *credits Weaver for accelerating*: Schwartz, *The Numbers Game*, 135.

126 *"Probably more than any other manager"*: James, *Guide to Baseball Managers*, 244.

126 *The Sodfather carried out his boss's orders*: Weaver, *Winning!*, 78.

127 *"I got permission long ago"*: Jim Elliot, "Haller Saw Smoke, Heard Words and Chased Weaver," *Baltimore Sun*, August 3, 1969.

127 *"Chances are some fans"*: Doug Brown, "Unprincely Earl," *Evening Sun*, August 5, 1970.

128 *the Orioles rebooted the Kangaroo Court*: Weaver, *Winning!*, 81.

128 *"Some of the guys made funny speeches"*: Wright, "The Birds Hop."

129 *"By the time I came back, in '69"*: Palmer, *Palmer and Weaver*, 43.

129 *"deep in pitching and strong up the middle"*: William Leggett, "An Idea Team in Harm's Way," *Sports Illustrated*, October 6, 1969.

130 *"Shut your mouth"*: Pluto, *The Earl of Baltimore*, 71.

CHAPTER 16: BUS LEAGUE NAPOLEONS

Primary sources for this chapter include Weaver's and Palmer's memoirs, newspaper accounts, and player interviews. Rob Neyer conducted a special research project on managers in one-run games.

133 *"sudden realization"*: Stephenson, *Is Baseball Holy?*, 17.

133 *"I had a very, very happy childhood"*: Neal Russo, "Home-Town Salute No. 1 to Weaver," *St. Louis Post-Dispatch*, January 27, 1970.

133 *never stopped calling him Sonny*: Kim Benson, interview, January 15, 2023.

133 *"If we lose opening day"*: Phil Jackman, "Earl's Tantrum Heats Orioles Bats," *Baltimore Sun*, March 18, 1970.

134 *"I'm not worried"*: "And Once Again the Superlative Orioles," *Sports Illustrated*, April 13, 1970.

134 *"The operation lowered"*: "Weaver Loses, Wins Arguments with Handicap," Associated Press, April 17, 1970.

134 *When former Oriole Curt Blefary*: "Super Jest," *Baltimore Sun*, September 11, 1970.

134 *"I don't believe"*: Anthony Cotton, "Platoon, For-r-r-d Harch!" *Sports Illustrated*, July 21, 1980.

135 *"bus league Napoleon"*: Melvin Durslag, "A Grad of Bus Leagues," *Sporting News*, September 26, 1970.

135 *"He didn't overmanage"*: Pluto, *The Earl of Baltimore*, 67.

135 *"one of the last frontiers"*: John Thorn, author interview, November 22, 2022.

136 *"The Orioles made me"*: Bill Tanton, "Birds Weaver Hits Award Winning Trail," *Evening Sun*, October 29, 1970.

136 *"this ain't like football"*: Gerald Ensley, "Only Apple Pie Is More American than Baseball," *Tallahassee Democrat*, July 4, 1983.

137 *the Orioles went 40-15*: Research conducted on behalf of the author by Rob Neyer.

137 *Bill James found*: Bill James, "One-Run Records as a Basis for Managerial Evaluation," Bill James Online, September 19, 2007, https://www.billjamesonline .com/article154/.

137 *"a little round man"*: "World Series Hangover," *Sporting News*, November 7, 1970.

137 *"You made all the right moves"*: Larry Greybill, "Give Credit to Weaver," *Lancaster New Era*, October 16, 1970.

138 *"Earl doesn't get nearly the credit"*: Ibid.

138 *"It's time Earl got the credit"*: Bob Maisel, "Morning After," *Baltimore Sun*, October 16, 1970.

138 *"Everything has been easy for me"*: Greybill, "Give Credit to Weaver."

138 *"If I run second"*: Phil Jackman, "Billy Set to Fire," *Evening Sun*, October 7, 1970.

CHAPTER 17: PITCHING

Primary sources include newspaper accounts, Palmer's and Weaver's memoirs, and player interviews.

139 *"When I pick up the ball"*: Dickson, *Baseball's Greatest Quotations*, 132.

141 *"If you don't get the ball"*: Weaver, *It's What You Learn*, 161.

142 *"Earl gets coaches"*: Thomas Boswell, "Earl Weaver," *Washington Post*, March 27, 1982.

142 *"When you pitch"*: Doug Brown, "Oriole Hurlers Please Note: Bauer Is Sick of Sore Arms," *Sporting News*, March 2, 1968.

142 *"The most amazing thing"*: James, *Guide to Baseball Managers*, 247.

142 *Managers switched from a plurality*: Frank Vaccaro, "Origins of the Pitching Rotation," *Baseball Research Journal*, Fall 2011, https://sabr.org/journal/article /origins-of-the-pitching-rotation/.

143 *"Me and Palmer don't like"*: "Slugging Match Goes to Boston," Associated Press, June 29, 1976.

144 *"He was like an artist"*: Adam Ulrey, "Mike Cuellar," SABR, https://sabr.org /bioproj/person/mike-cuellar/.

144 *"The Orioles became truly inhuman"*: "Alas, It Will Be a Shambles," *Sports Illustrated*, April 12, 1971.

145   *Phil Rizzuto "couldn't make this team"*: "Orioles vs. Yankees," Associated Press, October 13, 1971.

145   *"has no weaknesses"*: Fred Tharp, "Consistent with a Bat," *News-Journal*, October 19, 1971.

146   *"The President said"*: Lou Hatter, "Weaver Cites Bucs' Blass," *Baltimore Sun*, October 18, 1971.

146   *"Ten years ago"*: Al Mallette, "The Call," *Star-Gazette*, October 20, 1971.

147   *"I'm really looking forward"*: Ibid.

CHAPTER 18: STRIKE ONE

Primary sources include newspaper accounts, Weaver's memoirs, and unpublished interviews with Weaver. Historian Ryan Holmberg researched and translated Japanese newspapers and magazines.

149   *"Even Napoleon"*: Hal Bodley, "Two Championships Later Ozark Still Fighting for Respect," *Morning News*, May 7, 1978.

149   *"Who'll follow me?"*: "Weaver Claims Orioles Will Defy Strike Edict," Associated Press, April 5, 1972.

149   *"What's the sense in us getting 'em fat"*: "Birds Can't Ham It Up," *Morning News*, March 17, 1972.

150   *"There's a fine point in labor laws"*: "Miller Accuses Weaver of Coercion in Strike," Associated Press, April 6, 1972.

150   *"dead without Frank Robinson"*: Bill Tanton, "Weaver Welcomes Martin's Cockiness," *Evening Sun*, April 18, 1972.

151   *"wine and champagne"*: Weaver, *It's What You Learn*, 196.

151   *According to Japanese press*: Survey of Japanese media compiled and translated by Ryan Holmberg.

151   *"The most interesting place"*: Clif Keane, "Tokyo Tranquility Moves Weaver," *Boston Globe*, November 30, 1971.

152   *"Weaver says 'statistics' dictate"*: Jim Elliot, "Weaver Says 'Statistics' Dictate His Moves," *Baltimore Sun*, February 29, 1972.

152   *"Grandstand managers"*: "Winning!," book review, *Kirkus Reviews*, https:// www.kirkusreviews.com/book-reviews/a/earl-weaver-2/winning-2/.

152   *"I've managed to develop"*: Weaver, *Winning!*, 78.

152   *"All I'm trying to do"*: Ibid., 79.

152   *"Baseball, while it is called a team sport"*: Ibid., 184.

153   *"If you've got a third baseman"*: Ibid., 148.

153   *"Really the only time"*: Ibid., 154.

153   *"You only get three outs"*: Ibid.

153   *"in dire need"*: Weaver, *It's What You Learn*, 202.

153 *"I don't enjoy going places"*: "Brooks Objects to Weaver's 'Over-the-Hill' Comments," Associated Press, June 13, 1972.

153 *"There's no rhyme"*: Ken Nigro, "Weaver Warns Oriole Batters," *Baltimore Sun*, August 2, 1972.

154 *"nothing more than scrub tomatoes"*: "Orioles Tomatoes: A Smelly Subject," Associated Press, August 19, 1979.

155 *The* Sun *printed his recipes*: Francis Rackemann, "Earl Weaver Gardens, Preserves, Cooks," *Evening Sun*, September 2, 1971.

155 *"packages of diced peppers"*: Ibid.

155 *"In the morning"*: Earl Weaver, interview with Mike Gibbons, 1991.

155 *"I'd see that snorkel"*: Kim Benson, author interview, January 15, 2023.

156 *"I'm sure people who read"*: Frank Deford, "Marianna and Earl Weaver," *Sports Illustrated*, June 30, 1980.

156 *"To my everlasting shame"*: Weaver, *It's What You Learn*, 227.

156 *"I don't think the brother umpire"*: Lou Hatter, "Weaver Wants Ump Out," *Baltimore Sun*, July 24, 1972.

156 *"The proper response"*: Leonard Koppett, "Revival of the Haller Case," *Sporting News*, September 16, 1972.

CHAPTER 19: CLAP FOR THE CLOWN

Primary sources include interviews with retired umpires Larry Barnett, Dave Phillips, and Jim Evans, newspaper accounts, Weaver's memoirs, and online databases.

157 *"I never questioned"*: Durocher, *Nice Guys Finish Last*, 180.

157 *"Nobody recognized me"*: Steve Summers, "Siegel Wins Kirchner Award," *Intelligencer Journal*, February 1, 1973.

158 *once faked a heart attack*: Luciano, *The Umpire Strikes Back*, 46.

158 *"If you umpired the Yankees"*: Larry Barnett, author interview, August 28, 2023.

158 *"like watching Hulk Hogan"*: Bill Burr, "Bill Burr—Earl Weaver Umpire Fight," November 29, 2016, YouTube video, 5:29, https://www.youtube.com/watch?v=psxmsJaMC_o.

158 *"He lit up the night"*: Mike Olesker, author interview, November 28, 2023.

158 *"Weaver played Memorial Stadium"*: Pascarelli, *The Toughest Job in Baseball*, 91.

159 *Here's the top ten*: https://www.baseball-reference.com/leaders/mgr_ejections_career.shtml.

159 *"Watch this!"*: Palmer, *Nine Innings to Success*, 104.

159 *"I'd like to read your rule book"*: Bill Vanderschmidt, "Wings Blanked Again," *Democrat and Chronicle*, June 6, 1967.

160 *"I'm sorry, Hank"*: Jim Evans, author interview, September 8, 2023.

160 *"If you don't get off the field"*: Ibid.

161   *"What are you doing"*: Thomas Boswell, "Umps Return Venom on Weaver," *Washington Post*, May 20, 1981.

161   *"I don't think that it will be dropped"*: Jim Elliot, "Weaver to Keep Oriole Pitchers in Batting Cage," *Baltimore Sun*, February 12, 1973.

162   *until his death in 2024*: "Fritz Peterson . . . Dies at Age 81," Associated Press, April 16, 2024.

162   *"O's Won't Rattle Yanks' Swappers"*: Doug Brown, "O's Won't Rattle Yanks' Swappers," *Evening Sun*, March 12, 1973.

162   *"It would only make them mad"*: Ibid.

162   *"I'm not sure it would be effective"*: Ibid.

162   *"They're my personal friends"*: Ibid.

CHAPTER 20: . . . AND DEFENSE

Primary sources include Weaver's memoirs, newspaper accounts, and player interviews. Bobby Grich gave me a wonderful two-hour seminar on the Orioles' defensive philosophy.

163   *"Baseball is the only sport"*: *Sports Illustrated*, September 6, 1976.

163   *Here are the top five teams*: fangraphs.com.

164   *Weaver managed* three of the top four: https://www.baseball-reference.com/leaders/WAR_def_career.shtml.

164   *FanGraphs ranks the 1973 Orioles*: fangraphs.com.

164   *Four of the top twenty-five teams by runs saved*: Ibid.

164   *"I never left"*: Eisenberg, *From 33rd Street*, 206–7.

165   *"Like trying to throw a hamburger"*: Bill Tanton, "Mayo Smith Warns Twins Can Beat O's," *Evening Sun*, September 17, 1969.

165   *He wore a small glove and never dove*: Frank Vaccaro, "Mark Belanger," SABR, https://sabr.org/bioproj/person/mark-belanger/.

166   *"Belanger's got unbelievable range"*: Luther Evans, "Weaver Playing It Safe on Calling Belanger Best," *Miami Herald*, March 1, 1973.

166   *"never threw a ball without"*: Falkner, *Nines Side of the Diamond*, 18.

166   *"like he's playing on roller skates"*: Doug Brown, "Belanger Army Call Could Help Birds," *Sporting News*, March 16, 1963.

166   *"My wife's really been getting on me"*: Evans, "Weaver Playing It Safe."

167   *"Jesus Fucking Christ"*: Rick Dempsey, author interview, August 18, 2023.

167   *"How the hell"*: Bobby Grich, author interview, July 31, 2023.

167   *"The Orioles had their own way"*: Ibid.

167   *"As the ball is on its way"*: Ibid.

168   *"Patient Earl Weaver"*: "Patient Earl Weaver," Associated Press, October 30, 1973.

CHAPTER 21: SUPERNATURAL MANAGER

Primary sources include Weaver's memoirs, newspaper accounts, *True* magazine's 1974 profile of Weaver, and player interviews.

170   *"he took it all so seriously"*: Thomas Boswell, "Baseball's Rock of Sages," *Washington Post*, March 6, 1996.

170   *"I hope you get hit by a truck"*: Baylor, *Don Baylor*, 71.

170   *"He didn't give a shit"*: Dan Ford, author interview, August 7, 2023.

170   *"He treated you like a man"*: Ken Singleton, author interview, January 20, 2023.

170   *"That whole coaching staff drank"*: Terry Pluto, author interview, October 21, 2023.

171   *Bill James once estimated*: James, *Guide to Baseball Managers*.

171   *he and his coaches were waiting*: Palmer, *Palmer and Weaver*, 48.

171   *"You lose a tough one"*: Ibid.

171   *"I got a good voice"*: Myron Cope, "The Earl of Rasp," *Sports Illustrated*, July 7, 1975.

171   *Singleton flew to Las Vegas*: Ken Singleton, author interview, March 20, 2023.

171   *Maryland State Police trooper Jim Slocum*: Jim Hawkins, "Well I'll Be a No-Good Rock Sucker," *True*, June 1974.

171   *"If you're a teetotaler"*: Kerry Dougherty and Thomas Boswell, "Weaver Charge: Drunk Driving," *Washington Post*, August 31, 1981.

172   True *magazine reported*: Hawkins, "Well I'll Be a No-Good Rock Sucker."

172   *"Earl, you gotta stop drinking"*: Rick Dempsey, author interview, February 1, 2023.

172   *"that everybody needs a crutch"*: Terry Leahy, author interview February 10, 2023.

172   *a roast in 2000 where Jim Palmer made fun*: "Palmer, Weaver Burn Roast," *Baltimore Sun*, November 4, 2000.

172   *"is the exact opposite of his personal deportment"*: Hawkins, "Well I'll Be a No-Good Rock Sucker."

173   *"No promises to anybody"*: Thom Greer, "O's Weaver Has Staying Power," *Philadelphia Daily News*, June 11, 1979.

173   *"The insurrection of 1974"*: Baylor, *Don Baylor*, 79.

173   *"Deep down inside"*: Ibid.

173   *"You had better be glad"*: Ibid., 80.

173   *"Knowing Earl"*: Ibid.

174   *"If Earl had put his foot down"*: Palmer, *Nine Innings to Success*, 124.

174   *"If you couldn't handle"*: Doug DeCinces, author interview, August 10, 2023.

174   *"Go fuck yourself"*: Dyar Miller, author interview, January 11, 2024.

174 *Orioles resumed their Kangaroo Court*: Ray Buck, "Kangaroo Court Helps Orioles," Gannett, October 1, 1974.

175 *"was a manager for all seasons"*: Eisenberg, *From 33rd Street*, 360.

CHAPTER 22: SPRING OF THE GUN

Primary sources include newspaper accounts, Weaver's memoirs, player interviews, and Danny Litwhiler's memoir, *Living the Baseball Dream*.

177 *"We forgot about"*: Jim Henneman, "Would Birds Gamble and Put Aase on Disabled List?" *Evening Sun*, August 5, 1986.

177 *"radar gun"*: Bill Tanton, "New 'Toy' Brings Out Little Boy in Weaver," *Evening Sun*, March 19, 1975.

177 *"Scouting was imprecise"*: Weaver, *It's What You Learn*, 234.

178 *Litwhiler was born in 1916*: Litwhiler, *Living the Baseball Dream*, 13.

178 *In a charming memoir*: Ibid.

178 *"If Litwhiler had lived"*: Robert Creamer, "With Mirrors, Flat Gloves and Sawed-Up Bats," *Sports Illustrated*, June 3, 1963.

179 *he saw a photo*: Litwhiler, *Living the Baseball Dream*, 220.

179 *Litwhiler bought a used gun*: Ibid., 221.

180 *"In 1975, I took it"*: Ibid., 223.

180 *"We could get a lot of use"*: Tanton, "New 'Toy' Brings Out Little Boy in Weaver."

180 *He also discovered*: Weaver, *It's What You Learn*, 234.

180 *"only looking at the radar gun"*: Ibid.

181 *The technology was another tool*: Ibid., 328.

181 *"the first guy to use the radar guns"*: Dan Duquette, author interview, November 16, 2023.

181 *who had used a corked bat*: Weaver, *It's What Your Learn*, 94.

181 *Pat Santarone to experiment with bats*: Alan Goldstein, "Orioles' Santarone Says Players Who Swear by Cork Truly Are Batty," *Baltimore Sun*, August 16, 1987.

182 *"BP ONLY!"*: Ken Singleton, text message with author, May 15, 2023.

182 *"That's why I still enjoy"*: Thomas Boswell, "Sammy Stewart," *Washington Post*, May 15, 1982.

182 *"if you know how to cheat"*: Thomas Boswell, "Pastime Still 'Agreeably Free of Chivalry,'" *Washington Post*, August 6, 1987.

182 *the Orioles had used amphetamines*: Lawrence Linderman, "Baseball's Rowdy Genius," *Playboy*, July 1983.

183 *"Orioles manager Earl Weaver hasn't lost his mind"*: Larry Bump, "A Shortstop Who Isn't," *Democrat and Chronicle*, September 16, 1975.

184 *"It's obvious"*: Michael Janofsky, "Boog Warm to Trade, If He Plays Regularly," *Evening Sun*, February 25, 1975.

184 *"I don't steal bases"*: Ken Singleton, author interview, March 20, 2023.

184   *"He was more intense"*: Ibid.

184   *"So far he has been every place"*: Milton Richman, "Oriole's Weaver Gets Respect of His Players," United Press International, March 10, 1975.

CHAPTER 23: FREE REGGIE
Primary sources include Weaver's, Palmer's, and Jackson's memoirs, player interviews, and newspaper accounts.

187   *"Ballplayers should get"*: John Steadman, "Players Want Ball Fans on Their Side," *Evening Sun*, August 9, 1994.

187   *"Suddenly we were all underpaid"*: Palmer, *Palmer and Weaver*, 61.

188   *Orioles were the oldest*: "1976 Major League Team Statistics," https://www .baseball-reference.com/leagues/majors/1976.shtml.

188   *"We fit in very nicely"*: Ken Nigro, "Old Age Is Stalking Oriole Starters," *Baltimore Sun*, March 25, 1976.

188   *"You still pay only 85 cents"*: Ray Fitzgerald, "How Long Can a Man Wait," *Boston Globe*, March 26, 1976.

188   *"Earl gave Brooks every opportunity"*: Doug DeCinces, author interview, August 10, 2023.

188   *"To Earl Weaver and team"*: Michael Janofsky, "Birds Win, No Thanks to Reggie," *Evening Sun*, April 10, 1976.

188   *"half-expecting him to parachute in"*: Ken Nigro, "Orioles Start Season Against Red Sox Today," *Baltimore Sun*, April 9, 1976.

188   *"Reggie Jackson Agrees to Join Orioles Tonight"*: *Baltimore Sun*, April 30, 1976.

189   *"It's hard"*: Lou Hatter, "Chisox Defeat Orioles," *Baltimore Sun*, May 5, 1976.

189   *"I gave Mike Cuellar"*: Edwin Pope, "O's Armed for Raid on Pitching History," *Miami Herald*, March 19, 1981.

189   *"You have no idea"*: Mike DeArmond, "Royals Push Orioles to Brink of '58 Disaster," *Kansas City Star*, June 14, 1976.

189   *"We feel that all of the players"*: Jim Henneman, "5-for-5 Deal Hardly a 10-Strike for Orioles," *Sporting News*, July 3, 1976.

190   *"If you don't put on a tie"*: Pluto, *The Earl of Baltimore*, 1.

190   *"This dress code is ridiculous"*: Palmer, *Palmer and Weaver*, 64.

191   *"I loved the little Weave"*: Thomas Boswell, "Earl Weaver: Words from a Baseball Master," *Washington Post*, January 19, 2013.

191   *"He's the smartest guy"*: Gordon Beard, "Bean War Mars Orioles' 4-1 Victory," Associated Press, July 28, 1976.

191   *"If I'm going to sit all year"*: Michael Janofsky, "Grich Says He May Leave Birds," *Evening Sun*, May 4, 1976.

191   *"When Reggie came here"*: Andrew Culberston, "Unenchanted Interlude: Reggie Jackson's Lost Season in Baltimore," *Hardball Times*, March 27, 2012.

192 *"If the club persists in its policy"*: "Earl Weaver May Leave Orioles," United Press International, August 11, 1976.

192 *"something you have to accept"*: Sandra McKee, "Rumors Don't Faze Bird Manager's Wife Marianna," *Evening Sun*, July 10, 1976.

192 *"I made up my mind"*: Ken Nigro, "Birds Sign Weaver for '77 Season," *Baltimore Sun*, September 29, 1976.

CHAPTER 24: FAVORITE SON

Primary sources include Weaver's memoirs, newspaper accounts, player interviews, Baseball-Reference.com, and Kevin Kerrane's classic book about baseball scouting, *Dollar Sign on the Muscle*.

194 *"Baltimore has no chance"*: *Sports Illustrated*, April 11, 1977.

194 *It was the year*: Bryan Soderholm-Difatte, "1977: When Earl Weaver Became Earl Weaver," *Baseball Research Journal*, Fall 2011.

195 *"well above professional average"*: Kerrane, *Dollar Sign on the Muscle*, 149–50.

195 *"Who's this kid?"*: Ken Singleton, author interview, March 20, 2023.

196 *"This man fought for me"*: Mike Klingman and Peter Schmuck, "The Earl of Baltimore," *Baltimore Sun*, January 20, 2013.

196 *"Brooks and Frank and Boog"*: Thomas Boswell, "Orioles Are Having Fun While Shocking Fans, Foes," *Washington Post*, July 23, 1977.

196 *"Catch the fucking ball"*: Rick Dempsey, author interview, August 18, 2023.

197 *One day in the urinals*: Palmer, *Palmer and Weaver*, 81.

197 *"You got more hits"*: Charles Steinberg, author interview, October 12, 2023.

197 *In the bottom of the tenth*: Bill Tanton, "Brooks Provides an All Time Thrill," *Baltimore Evening Sun*, April 20, 1977.

199 *"when he was a superstar"*: Thomas Boswell, "Robinson's 'Day' Sad, Jubilant," *Washington Post*, September 18, 1977.

CHAPTER 25: SON OF SAM

Primary sources include Weaver's memoirs, newspaper accounts, player interviews, and John Eisenberg's oral history of the Orioles.

201 *"Earl took the abuse because"*: Rick Dempsey, author interview, August 18, 2023.

203 *"Can't somebody make"*: Ibid.

203 *"He saw guys pulling together"*: Palmer, *Palmer and Weaver*.

203 *"We were very tight"*: Eisenberg, *From 33rd Street*, 335.

203 *"He's about 3-foot-1"*: "Umps Want Their Share," United Press International, February 16, 1979.

203 *"That's when Earl started"*: Larry Barnett, author interview, August 28, 2023.

204 *"There ain't no rule"*: Terry Pluto, "Ump's Call Leaves Earl Ripping Mad," *Evening Sun*, June 19, 1979.

204 *"If I didn't respect the umpire's uniform"*: Thomas Boswell, "Umps Return Venom on Weaver," *Washington Post*, May 20, 1981.

204 *"You got to do what you think is right"*: Edwin Pope, "Forsooth! Bard and Birds Will Prevail," *Miami Herald*, March 28, 1982.

205 *"He's just the best"*: Alan Goldstein, "Palmer's 2-Hitter in '78 Debut Leads Orioles' 7–0 Romp," *Baltimore Sun*, April 16, 1978.

205 *"Earl, I've been here twelve years"*: Palmer, *Palmer and Weaver*, 102.

206 *"I'm the boss around here"*: Rick Dempsey, author interview, August 18, 2023.

206 *One year, Dempsey grew his hair long*: Boswell, *Why Time Begins on Opening Day*, 36.

206 *"My dad used to get up at six a.m."*: Rick Dempsey, author interview, August 18, 2023.

207 *"I didn't pick you off"*: Ibid.

CHAPTER 26: THREE-RUN HOMERS

Primary sources include Weaver's memoirs, newspaper accounts, and interviews with writers and players. Terry Pluto and Tom Boswell responded to my questions.

209 *"The baseball mania has run its course"*: Editorial, *Detroit Free Press*, March 31, 2011.

210 *"Pluto, I always read your crap"*: Terry Pluto, author interview, October 21, 2023.

210 *"That pad you're carrying"*: Pascarelli, *The Toughest Job in Baseball*, 114.

210 *"If the thing goes long"*: Ibid., 114–15.

211 *"The Chinese tell time"*: Phil Jackman, "Mutt & Jeff," *Evening Sun*, July 3, 1979.

211 *"Don't worry, the fans don't start booing until July"*: "Angel Notes," *Los Angeles Times*, May 7, 1980.

211 *"crawled out of more coffins than Bela Lugosi"*: Ray Fitzgerald, "TV Missed the Jewel," *Boston Globe*, September 17, 1975.

211 *"This ain't a football game"*: "Earl Weaver Quotes to Thomas Boswell," *Washington Post*, January 19, 2013.

211 *"A baseball manager has no chance"*: Thomas Boswell, "Earl Weaver," *Washington Post*, April 6, 1979.

211 *"We're so bad right now"*: "They Said It," *Sports Illustrated*, May 29, 1972.

211 *"The judge gave me custody"*: Palmer, *Palmer and Weaver*, 141.

211 *"If baseball can germinate genius"*: Boswell, "Earl Weaver."

211 *"Few things are harder"*: Thomas Boswell, email to author, January 11, 2023.

212 *Weaver and Orioles team officials*: Charles Steinberg, interview with author, October 12, 2023.

212 *"It was devastating"*: Susan Reimer, author interview, January 17, 2024.

212   *"Susan, I have to give you credit"*: Susan Fornoff, author interview, May 6, 2024.

213   *"I'm tired of hearing Earl"*: Steve Stone, author interview, July 17, 2023.

214   *"Earl, this is the way I feel"*: Ibid.

214   *"I think Earl innately knew"*: Ibid.

215   *"The Orioles are not prone to panic"*: Kupfer, *Something Magic*, 66.

215   *"We've got a much better club"*: Thom Greer, "O's Weaver Has Staying Power," *Philadelphia Daily News*, June 11, 1979.

215   *"I don't give a damn"*: "Palmer, Weaver Feud," Associated Press, June 19, 1979.

216   *"The man's a genius"*: Lawrence Linderman, "Baseball's Rowdy Genius," *Playboy*, July 1983.

216   *"Mr. Sunshine" versus "Mr. Computer"*: Will Grimsley, "Series Matches Mr. Computer Against Mr. Sunshine," Associated Press, October 8, 1979.

217   *"We won 102 ballgames"*: Mike Tully, "'Pops' Is Tops for Bucs," *Herald*, October 18, 1979.

CHAPTER 27: YOU'RE HERE FOR ONE REASON

Primary sources include Weaver's memoirs, newspaper accounts, interviews with umpires and players, participants in the hot-mic incident, Ron Shelton, and of course many viewings of the hot-mic tape on YouTube.

219   *"Billy Martin makes the game"*: Mike Downey, "Billy's Not a Kid, but He Acts Like One," *Honolulu Advertiser*, May 5, 1983.

219   *"We spent three weeks"*: Murray Schweitzer, author interview, November 23, 2022.

220   *"I've umpired games with Earl"*: Lou Hatter, "Weaver Wants Ump Out," *Baltimore Sun*, July 24, 1972.

220   *"Weaver: That's bullshit!"*: Earl Weaver and Bill Haller, "Earl Weaver's Legendary Tirade at Bill Haller," Derek Wood, January 19, 2013, YouTube video, https://www.youtube.com/watch?v=f6cmqUTPn08.

220   *"We were trying to get off"*: Murray Schweitzer, author interview, November 23, 2022.

220   *"The crowd was so loud"*: Rick Armstrong, author interview, November 25, 2022.

221   *Here are the ten causes*: "Earl Weaver," Retrosheet, https://www.retrosheet.org/boxesetc/W/Pweave801.htm.

222   *"We could see"*: John Blake, author interview, April 10, 2023.

222   *"Cheeseman said"*: Rick Armstrong, author interview, November 25, 2022.

223   *"Dumb luck they called that balk"*: Rick Armstrong, author interview, November 25, 2022.

223   *"Each guy is baiting"*: Ron Shelton, author interview, January 9, 2023.

223 *Shelton based the famous scene*: Ron Shelton, *Bull Durham.*
223 *"I was inspired by the rhythms"*: Ron Shelton, author interview, January 9, 2023.
224 *"If they took that word"*: Larry Barnett, author interview, August 28, 2023.
224 *"my dad ran him all the time"*: Dave Phillips, author interview, May 15, 2023.
225 *"Ya know, Jim"*: Jim Evans, author interview, September 8, 2023.
226 *"This counts to me"*: "Hot Weaver Lines Up Forfeit for Orioles," Associated Press, March 20, 1981.

CHAPTER 28: THE CHOSEN

Primary sources include interviews with Cal Ripken and Bobby Bonner, Weaver's and Ripken's memoirs, and newspaper accounts.

227 *"I found a delivery"*: Mike McKenzie, "Leonard and Quisenberry Bend, but Red Sox Break," *Kansas City Star*, May 18, 1981.
227 *As a freshman, Cal hit .065*: Mike Klingaman, "Ripken's Childhood in Aberdeen," *Baltimore Sun*, September 3, 1995.
228 *He had once scooped him up*: Milton Richman, "Orioles' Rookie Is 'Family,'" United Press International, March 16, 1981.
228 *If it ever did come to that point*: Ibid.
228 *"I've always had a good rapport with Cal"*: Jim Henneman, "Orioles Hope to Get Mileage from Car-Pooling by Ripkens," *Evening Sun*, August 10, 1981.
228 *"If I do well in baseball"*: Milton Richman, "Oriole Coach's Son Has Bright Future," United Press International, March 15, 1981.
228 *Weaver fought with Peters*: Weaver, *It's What You Learn.*
229 *The first time they met*: Bobby Bonner, author interview, August 7, 2023.
230 *On a flight to Seattle during the 1982 season*: Ibid.
230 *"walk with the Lord"*: Terry Pluto, "Victory 1,000 Makes Weaver Pause," *Evening Sun*, April 7, 1979.
230 *"What about that poor sonuvabitch"*: Frank Deford, "Earl Weaver," *Sports Illustrated*, June 30, 1980.
230 *"I can't live with hatred inside of me"*: Ibid.
230 *He told Playboy*: Lawrence Linderman, "Baseball's Rowdy Genius," *Playboy*, July 1983.
231 *"Take your bat"*: Thomas Boswell, "Stranger in Paradox," June 15, 1985.
231 *"You're taking this Jesus thing too far"*: Bobby Bonner, author interview, August 7, 2023.
231 *"Earl just destroyed that kid"*: Eisenberg, *From 33rd Street*, 356.
231 *"a really good shortstop"*: Cal Ripken, author interview, August 22, 2023.
231 *Bobby walked over to Earl*: Bobby Bonner, author interview, August 7, 2023.
232 *"Take the fucking pitch down the middle"*: Ripken, *The Only Way I Know*, 82.

232   *"I didn't know if he was talking to me"*: Cal Ripken, author interview, August 22, 2023.

232   *Cal Sr. was born in Stepney, Maryland*: Jimmy Keenan, "Cal Ripken Sr.," SABR.

233   *"Practice doesn't make perfect"*: Mark Muske, "Ex-Manager Cal Ripken Sr. Dies," *Washington Post*, March 26, 1999.

233   *"my dad wasn't there for me a lot"*: Ibid.

233   *fourteen towns in ten states*: Ripken, *The Only Way I Know*.

233   *Not fucking likely*: Ripken, *The Only Way I Know*, 68.

233   *"He would reassure me"*: Cal Ripken, author interview, August 22, 2023.

234   *"You're standing too far"*: Ibid.

234   *"When the ball's hit to you"*: Ibid.

CHAPTER 29: THANKS, EARL

Primary sources include newspaper accounts and player interviews.

237   *"Managing is like holding a dove"*: Bill Braucher, "A Quick Glance at Sports and Such," *Cincinnati Enquirer*, July 3, 1978.

237   *"It rips your heart"*: Weaver, *It's What You Learn*, 10.

237   *"Just once"*: Thomas Boswell, "Strangers in Paradox," *Washington Post*, June 15, 1983.

238   *"everything that people"*: Gary Pomerantz, "Leaving Baseball to Stop Hurting People," *Washington Post*, October 10, 1982.

238   *"If there was physical contact"*: Kent Baker, "Weaver Smiling After Recent Suspension," Field News Service, July 21, 1982.

238   *"You take the bad"*: Thomas Boswell, "Weaver, Not Cooney, Is the Bruised Party," *Washington Post*, July 21, 1982.

238   *"The Toronto management"*: Steve Wulf, "Hoping to Bring In One Last Big Harvest," *Sports Illustrated*, September 13, 1982.

238   *"He has fought with all the umpires"*: Mike Lupica, "Weaver Kept Learning After He Knew It All," New York *Daily News*, June 20, 1982.

239   *"We're gonna miss The Weave"*: Thomas Boswell, "Is There Life After Weaver?" *Washington Post*, May 23, 1982.

239   *"that I never got to play in the big leagues"*: Mike Lupica, "Feisty Weaver Never Led Orioles to Losing Season," New York *Daily News*, June 24, 1982.

239   *"Go to Vegas. Take a cruise"*: Ibid.

239   *"the best talk we've ever had"*: Ibid.

240   *"Earl told me I was going to bat second"*: Glenn Gulliver, author interview, October 19, 2023.

240   *"I fit into his mold"*: Ibid.

240   *The introduction*: Earl Weaver and Tom Marr, "Managers Corner," eskay-izezy, November 28, 2006, YouTube video, 2:38, https://www.youtube.com/watch?v=QWQbN0jFo_k.

241 *"Little did I know fifteen years ago"*: Kent Baker, "41,127 See Orioles Retire an Awed Earl Weaver's No. 4," *Baltimore Sun*, September 20, 1982.

242 *"putting up with a mind"*: Ibid.

242 *"As far as I'm concerned"*: "Earl Weaver Retires," Associated Press, September 20, 1982.

243 *"Who knows"*: Phil Pepe, "Earl Weaver's Last Day as Manager," New York *Daily News*, October 4, 1982.

243 *Weaver watched* The Dirty Dozen: Jim Henneman, "The Final Day Near Perfect for Weaver," *Baltimore Sun*, October 4, 1982.

243 *"Earl told me"*: Dave Anderson, "Well, It's Over With," *New York Times*, October 4, 1982.

243 *"It was probably the most dramatic"*: Eisenberg, *From 33rd Street*, 358.

244 *"In twelve of the fifteen seasons as manager here"*: Keith Jackson, "1982 10 03 ABC Brewers at Orioles," Classic MLB1, February 7, 2019, YouTube video, 3:08:55, https://www.youtube.com/watch?v=-qNR_wC_6Qo.

244 *"remind me of my playing days"*: Greg Boeck, "Earl Relinquishes His Kingdom," *Democrat and Chronicle*, October 4, 1982.

244 *"That's hypothetical"*: Dave Anderson, "Earl of Baltimore Takes Curtain Call on Final Day," *New York Times*, October 4, 1982.

244 *"They're still out there?"*: Henneman, "The Final Day Near Perfect for Weaver."

CHAPTER 30: DE-WEAVERIZATION

Primary sources include newspaper accounts, player interviews, and Eisenberg's oral history.

245 *"Baseball and malaria"*: Dick Young, "In L.A. or Oz, There's No Place Like Home," *The Record*, May 10, 1982.

245 *"The first time Joe said hello"*: Thomas Boswell, "The Sad-Happy Passing of Weaver's Reign," *Washington Post*, February 23, 1983.

246 *"I'm always asked"*: Ibid.

246 *"Hope it stays just like it is"*: Thomas Boswell, "The Earl in Retirement," *Washington Post*, March 8, 1983.

246 *"People were thinking"*: Eisenberg, *From 33rd Street*, 366.

246 *Al Michaels recalled Weaver*: Al Michaels with L. Jon Wertheim, "Al Michaels Reflects on His Time with Howard Cosell," *Sports Illustrated*, October 31, 2014.

247 *"I should have jumped up"*: Boswell, "The Earl in Retirement."

247 *"For a little fella, at 82 pounds"*: Earl Weaver, "1983 Little League World Series," Jeff Whitehead, January 13, 2020, YouTube video, https://youtube.com/watch?v=TmWzUur7aWM.

247 *"a sense of humor about himself"*: Lawrence Linderman, "Baseball's Rowdy Genius," *Playboy*, July 1983.

248   *"I wouldn't swap my lifestyle"*: Ibid.

248   *"The cream will come to the top"*: Earl Weaver, "Except for White Sox, Pennant Races Still in Doubt," *Evening Sun*, September 9, 1983.

248   *"When it came to me"*: Jeff Neuman, author interview, November 3, 2023.

249   *"His ability to focus"*: Terry Pluto, author interview, October 21, 2023.

249   the *"Loss in Daytona Beach theory"*: Weaver, *Weaver on Strategy*, 17.

250   *"Altobelli let the engine run"*: Cal Ripken, author interview, August 22, 2023.

250   *"Are you satisfied now?"*: "Sports Entrepreneur, Noted Criminal Lawyer Williams Is Dead at 68," Associated Press, August 14, 1988.

251   *"I couldn't make myself"*: "Weaver Says He's Rejected Six Clubs, Is Off ABC," Associated Press, November 15, 1984.

CHAPTER 31: THINGS FALL APART

Primary sources include interviews with ex-players, newspaper accounts, and Eisenberg's oral history.

253   *"I managed a team that was so bad"*: "Insiders Say," *Sporting News*, May 29, 1989.

254   *"In the past, when the Orioles required"*: Ron Fimrite, "These Movers Are Shakers," *Sports Illustrated*, March 18, 1985.

254   *"Earl just can't stand it that I'm back"*: Thomas Boswell, "Martin 'n' Weaver: Peaches 'n' Cream," *Washington Post*, June 18, 1985.

254   *"Does anybody know if I've been fired?"*: Melody Simmons, "Who's the Manager? Asks Angry Altobelli," *Evening Sun*, June 13, 1985.

254   *Weaver's reinstatement thrilled many fans*: Paul McMullen and Mike Klingaman, "Baseball Fans on Weaver," *Evening Sun*, June 13, 1985.

255   *"I haven't seen a big-league pitch up that close"*: Thomas Boswell, "Stranger in Paradox," *Washington Post*, June 15, 1985.

255   *"He says he might sing to them at night"*: Craig Neff, "A Weaver of Dreams Returns to Baltimore," *Sports Illustrated*, June 24, 1985.

255   *"I'm putting a reputation on the line here"*: Ibid.

256   *"We're not going anywhere"*: Eisenberg, *From 33rd Street*, 384.

256   *"Unless the stock market"*: Thomas Boswell, "Weaver Is Free, Orioles Are in Free Fall," *Washington Post*, October 5, 1986.

256   *"Earl should have never come back"*: Eisenberg, *From 33rd Street*, 383.

256   *"The new guys were nonbelievers"*: Ibid., 381.

256   *"he was a little more tame"*: Fred Lynn, author interview, April 26, 2023.

257   *"He didn't have the weapons"*: Cal Ripken, author interview, August 22, 2023.

257   *"Things couldn't be the same"*: Eisenberg, *From 33rd Street*, 382–83.

257   *"My dad and my mom"*: Terry Leahy, author interview, February 11, 2023.

257   *"I remember when"*: Kim Benson, author interview, January 15, 2023.

258   *"wasn't there to rebel against"*: Mike Weaver, author interview, November 15, 2022.

258   *" 'Do it this way' "*: Ibid.

CHAPTER 32: VIDEOGAME

Primary sources include interviews with Trip Hawkins, Eddie Dombrower, and Don Daglow, newspaper accounts, and Patrick Hickey's *The Minds Behind Sports Games*. I also bought and played the game.

262   *"I learned how Bayesian"*: Trip Hawkins, author interview, November 24, 2021.

262   *"the records, the statistics, the peculiar balances"*: Coover, *The Universal Baseball Association*, 45.

263   *"Pretty soon I was doing a lot of ballet"*: Eddie Dombrower, author interview, October 15, 2021.

263   *"I started with a hand"*: Ibid.

263   *"I came here to work"*: Trip Hawkins, author interview, November 24, 2021.

264   *"may not be the sharpest tool in the box"*: Don Daglow, author interview, October 19, 2021.

264   *"He didn't sound like an intellectual"*: Trip Hawkins, author interview, November 24, 2021.

264   *"He said I don't like it"*: Don Daglow, author interview, October 19, 2021.

264   *"We wanted the doubles to look different"*: Eddie Dombrower, author interview, October 15, 2021.

264   *"There would be wind in Chicago"*: Don Daglow, author interview, October 19, 2021.

264   *"Don came to me with this algorithm"*: Eddie Dombrower, author interview, October 15, 2021.

265   *"Thank God you're here"*: Don Daglow, author interview, October 19, 2021.

265   *"We had to educate him"*: Ibid.

265   *"During events"*: Eddie Dombrower, author interview, October 15, 2021.

265   *"best computer game of all time"*: Nate Silver (@Natesilver538), "Annoyed that we couldn't get Earl Weaver Baseball, the best computer game of all time, onto the list," X, May 6, 2014.

266   *"Earl Weaver Baseball was the first game"*: John Delia, author interview, November 15, 2021.

266   *"My dad knew exactly who Earl Weaver was"*: Bryan Stroh, author interview, March 13, 2023.

266   *"I don't feel like going"*: Don Daglow, author interview, October 19, 2021.

CHAPTER 33: COOPERSTOWN

Primary sources include newspaper accounts and a YouTube recording of Weaver's 1996 Hall of Fame induction speech.

267　*"Earl is baseball"*: Frank Deford, "Marianna and Earl Weaver," *Sports Illustrated*, June 30, 1980.

267　*Earl Weaver was playing golf*: Mike Klingaman, "Another Title for Weaver," *Baltimore Sun*, March 6, 1996.

269　*"When they sit down"*: Mike Klingaman, "Weaver Teed Up for Vote," *Baltimore Sun*, March 5, 1996.

269　*"He was always pulling something fast"*: Klingaman, "Another Title for Weaver."

269　*"the best manager of his era"*: Ibid.

269　*"Those boys are the ones that put me in"*: *Baltimore Sun*, March 7, 1996.

269　*"If I could play now, I'd play"*: "Weaver Leads Hall Inductees," Associated Press, August 4, 1996.

270　*"How could any baseball fan"*: "Earl Weaver 1996 Hall of Fame Induction Speech," National Baseball Hall of Fame, January 6, 2015, https://www.you tube.com/watch?v=OVWBne272t8.

271　*"No manager belongs there more"*: Thomas Boswell, "Baseball's Rock of Sages," *Washington Post*, March 6, 1996.

CHAPTER 34: THE EARL OF BALTIMORE

Primary sources include newspaper accounts and interviews with players and family.

273　*"If you don't think baseball"*: Jordan, *The Suitors of Spring*.

273　*"I paid attention to how he stood"*: Toby Mendez, author interview, December 15, 2022.

274　*"Tell the boys I love 'em"*: Ken Singleton, author interview, March 20, 2023.

274　*"the Copernicus of baseball"*: Tom Verducci, "Earl Weaver," *Sports Illustrated*, July 13, 2009.

274　*"People talk about Moneyball"*: Dan Connolly, "A Fond Farewell," January 20, 2013.

274　*"better than Earl"*: *Baltimore Sun*, January 20, 2013.

274　*"scholar's familiarity with the rule book"*: Bruce Weber, "Earl Weaver, a Volatile, Visionary Manager, Dies at 82," *New York Times*, January 19, 2013.

274　*"the best naked talker"*: Roger Angell, "Postscript: Earl Weaver, 1930–2013," *New Yorker*, January 20, 2013.

275　*"was in many ways the team's brightest star"*: Bart Barnes and Matt Schudel, "Earl Weaver, Hall of Fame Orioles Manager, Dies at 82," *Washington Post*, January 19, 2013.

275　*"He wasn't too happy with Clownvis"*: Aimee Levitt, "Earl Weaver Remembered by His Grandson Mike Leahy, aka Clownvis Presley," January 20, 2013.

275 *"Whatever you think he was"*: Thomas Boswell, "Earl Weaver: Words from a Baseball Master," *Washington Post*, January 19, 2013.

275 *Agent Dick Gordon led*: Juan C. Rodriguez, "Gathering to Share Stories of 'a Winner,'" *Baltimore Sun*, January 27, 2013.

276 *Terry Cashman appeared*: Ibid.

276 *"Yeah, he probably did yell at me more"*: Ibid.

276 *"Earl gave me the opportunity"*: Ibid.

CHAPTER 35: THE MANAGER'S CARDS

Primary sources include interviews with current and former MLB managers and general managers. Reds manager David Bell stayed in touch and answered questions throughout the year.

277 *"Managing is getting paid"*: Chip Ainsworth, "Happy Birthday, Old Professor," *Recorder*, July 30, 2016.

278 *"There's a lot more people behind the scenes"*: A. J. Hinch, author interview, August 2, 2023.

279 *"command, and control of the game"*: Derek Shelton, author interview, September 30, 2023.

279 *"believed that at the end of the day"*: A. J. Hinch, author interview, August 2, 2023.

279 *"I made no bones about it"*: Tom Verducci, "Earl Weaver," *Sports Illustrated*, July 13, 2009.

279 *"means passion, it means winner"*: Pedro Grifol, author interview, July 7, 2023.

279 *"You still have to empower the field manager"*: Dave Roberts, author interview, April 26, 2023.

280 *"Just remember"*: Bobby Valentine, author interview, April 11, 2023.

280 *"way ahead of his time"*: Bob Melvin, author interview, June 28, 2023.

281 *"I spent a lot of time"*: David Bell, author interview, April 21, 2023.

282 *"Before, you had that hammer"*: Bobby Valentine, author interview, April 11, 2023.

282 *The table-flipping days*: Bob Melvin, author interview, June 28, 2023.

282 *"These guys ain't ever"*: Brian Snitker, author interview, August 8, 2023.

283 *"His greatest strength"*: David Bell, author interview, April 21, 2023.

283 *"Front offices look"*: Bobby Valentine, author interview, April 11, 2023.

284 *"Players coming to the big leagues"*: Craig Counsell, author interview, June 30, 2023.

284 *"Nobody understood percentage baseball"*: Dan Duquette, author interview, November 16, 2023.

EPILOGUE: THE PLAYERS

Primary sources include newspaper accounts, a video recording available on YouTube of Memorial Stadium's closing ceremony, and unpublished interviews kindly shared by Mike Gibbons of the Orioles archives at the Babe Ruth Museum.

285   *"God moves the player"*: Jorge Luis Borges, *Chess.*

285   *"If a Broadway play"*: Milton Kent, "A Good 'Bye," *Evening Sun*, October 8, 1991.

286   *"Don't call any errors today"*: Michael Olesker, "Baseball's Gone from 33d Street," *Baltimore Sun*, October 7, 1991.

286   *"I wonder who's last"*: "Last Game at Memorial Stadium 10 6 1991," BASH953, May 3, 2023, https://www.youtube.com/watch?v=S35d2e2kcRg.

286   *"I don't know if I can do this"*: Ken Rosenthal, "For Boyd, 65, 2,600-Mile Drive Was Most Satisfying Ever," *Baltimore Sun*, October 10, 1991.

287   *"Everything came back to me"*: Mike Littwin, "No Introductions, Just Cheers, Tears Needed for This Famous Final Scene," *Baltimore Sun*, October 7, 1991.

287   *"The people in here"*: John Eisenberg, "O's Leave Stadium; Memories Remain," *Baltimore Sun*, October 8, 1991.

287   *"Sheer panic"*: Unpublished interview with Mike Gibbons, October 6, 1991.

287   *"Our common denominator"*: Thomas Boswell, "Occasion Builds to Proper Pitch," *Washington Post*, October 7, 1991.

BIBLIOGRAPHY

Angell, Roger. *Five Seasons: A Baseball Companion.* New York: Popular Library, 1982.

———. *Once More Around the Park.* New York: Ballantine, 1991.

Armour, Mark, and Malcolm Allen, eds. *Pitching, Defense and Three-Run Homers.* Lincoln: University of Nebraska Press, 2012.

Armour, Mark, and Daniel Levitt. *In Pursuit of Pennants.* Lincoln: University of Nebraska Press, 2015.

Barney, Rex, and Norman L. Macht. *Rex Barney's Orioles Memories.* Woodbury, CT: Goodwood Press, 1994.

Bartell, Richard. *Rowdy Richard.* Berkeley, CA: North Atlantic Books, 1987.

Bloss, Bob. *Baseball Managers.* Philadelphia: Temple University Press, 1999.

Boswell, Thomas. *How Life Imitates the World Series.* New York: Penguin Books, 1982.

———. *Why Time Begins on Opening Day.* New York: Penguin Books, 1984.

Bouton, Jim. *Ball Four.* New York: Dell, 1970.

Brooks, Toby. *Season of Change.* Lubbock, TX: Chaplain, 2011.

Bryan, Mike. *Baseball Lives.* New York: Ballantine, 1989.

Cashen, J. Frank. *Winning in Both Leagues.* Lincoln: University of Nebraska Press, 2014.

Coover, Robert. *The Universal Baseball Association, Inc.* New York: Penguin Books, 1968.

Dewey, Donald. *The 10th Man.* New York: Avalon, 2004.

Dickson, Paul. *Baseball's Greatest Quotations.* New York: HarperCollins, 1991.

———. *The Dickson Baseball Dictionary.* 3rd ed. New York: Norton, 2009.

Durocher, Leo. *Nice Guys Finish Last.* New York: Simon & Schuster, 1975.

Eisenberg, John. *From 33rd Street to Camden Yards.* New York: McGraw-Hill, 2001.

Falkner, David. *Nine Sides of the Diamond.* New York: Simon & Schuster, 1990.

———. *The Short Season.* New York: Times Books, 1986.

Frommer, Harvey. *Baseball's Greatest Managers.* Lanham, MD: Rowman & Littlefield, 1985.

Georgeson, Samuel J. *Picking the Winners*. Youngstown, OH, 1947.

———. *The Pitchers Record Guide*. Youngstown, OH, 1942.

Gesker, Mike: *The Orioles Encyclopedia*. Baltimore: Johns Hopkins University Press, 2009.

Gilbert, Thomas W. *How Baseball Happened*. Boston: Godine, 2020.

Ginsberg, Daniel E. *The Fix Is In*. Jefferson, NC: McFarland, 1995.

Golenbock, Peter. *The Spirit of St. Louis*. New York: HarperCollins, 2000.

Heidenry, John. *The Gashouse Gang*. New York: PublicAffairs, 1982.

Hemphill, Paul. *Long Gone*. New York: Viking, 1979.

Herzog, Whitey. *You're Missing a Great Game*. New York: Simon & Schuster, 1999.

Hickey, Patrick, Jr. *The Minds Behind Sports Games*. Jefferson, NC: McFarland, 2020.

Honig, Donald. *The Man in the Dugout*. Chicago: Follett, 1977.

Jackson, Reggie, and Mike Lupica: *Reggie*. New York: Ballantine, 1984.

Jaffe, Chris. *Evaluating Baseball's Managers*. Jefferson, NC: McFarland, 2010.

James, Bill. *The Bill James Guide to Baseball Managers*. New York: Scribner, 1997.

———. *The New Bill James Historical Baseball Abstract*. New York: Simon & Schuster, 2001.

Johnson, Lloyd, and Miles Wolff, eds. *The Encyclopedia of Minor League Baseball*. Durham, NC: Baseball America, 1995.

Johnson, Walter. *The Broken Heart of America*. New York: Basic Books, 2020.

Kerrane, Kevin. *Dollar Sign on the Muscle*. New York: Simon & Schuster, 1984.

Kluck, Lee. *Leave While the Party's Good*. Lincoln: University of Nebraska Press, 2024.

Koppett, Leonard. *The Man in the Dugout*. New York: Crown, 1993.

Lewis, Michael. *Moneyball*. New York: Norton, 2003.

Litwhiler, Danny, and Jim Sargent. *Living the Baseball Dream*. Philadelphia: Temple University Press, 2006.

Lowenfish, Lee. *Branch Rickey*. Lincoln: University of Nebraska Press, 2007.

———. *The Imperfect Diamond*. New York: Da Capo, 1980.

Luciano, Ron, and David Fisher. *The Umpire Strikes Back*. New York: Bantam, 1982.

Madden, W. C., and Patrick J. Stewart. *The Western League*. Jefferson, NC: McFarland, 2002.

Mandelaro, Jim, and Scott Pitoniak. *Silver Seasons*. Syracuse, NY: Syracuse University Press, 1996.

Mead, William. *Even the Browns*. Chicago: Temporary Books, 1978.

Morris, Peter. *A Game of Inches*. Chicago: Ivan R. Dee, 2006.

Nuwer, Hank. *Strategies of the Great Baseball Managers*. New York: Franklin Watts, 1988.

Oboski, Robert. *Bush League*. New York: Macmillan, 1975.

Okrent, Daniel. *Nine Innings*. New York: Ticknor & Fields, 1985.

Palmer, Jim, and Jim Dale. *Palmer and Weaver*. Kansas City, MO: Andrews & McMeel, 1996.

Palmer, Jim, and Alan Maimon. *Nine Innings to Success.* Chicago: Triumph Books, 2016.

Pascarelli, Peter. *The Toughest Job in Baseball.* New York: Simon & Schuster, 1993.

Pluto, Terry. *The Earl of Baltimore.* Piscataway, NJ: New Century, 1982.

Richards, Paul. *Modern Baseball Strategy.* New York: Prentice-Hall, 1955.

Richmond, Peter. *Ballpark.* New York: Simon & Schuster, 1993.

Ripken, Cal, Jr., and Mike Bryan. *The Only Way I Know.* New York: Penguin, 1997.

Robinson, Frank, and Berry Stainback. *Extra Innings.* New York: McGraw-Hill, 1988.

Russo, Jim, and Bob Hammel. *Super Scout.* Carrol Stream, IL: Bonus Books, 1992.

Schwarz, Alan. *The Numbers Game.* New York: St. Martin's, 2004.

Seymour, Harold. *Baseball: The Golden Age. New York:* Oxford, 1971.

———. *Baseball: The People's Game.* New York: Oxford, 1990.

Shelton, Ron. *The Church of Baseball.* New York: Knopf, 2022.

Silberstang, Edwin. *Playboy's Guide to Baseball Betting.* New York: PEI Books, 1982.

Skipper, James. *Baseball Nicknames.* Jefferson, NC: McFarland, 1992.

Smith, Curt. *Storied Stadiums.* New York: Carroll & Graf, 2003.

Stainback, Robert D. *Alcohol and Sport.* Champaign, IL: Human Kinetics, 1997.

Stein, Fred. *And the Skipper Bats Cleanup.* Jefferson, NC: McFarland, 2002.

Stephenson, Gregory. *Is Baseball Holy?* Heidelberg: Ober-Limbo Verlag, 2021.

Stockton, J. Roy. *The Gashouse Gang.* New York: A. S. Barnes, 1945.

Sullivan, Neil J. *The Minors.* New York: St. Martin's, 1990.

Thomas, Evan. *The Man to See.* New York: Simon & Schuster, 1991.

Van Hyning, Thomas E. *Puerto Rico's Winter League.* Jefferson, NC: McFarland, 1995.

———. *The Santurce Crabbers.* Jefferson, NC: McFarland, 1999.

Weaver, Earl, and Terry Pluto. *Weaver on Strategy.* New York: Collier, 1984.

Weaver, Earl, and John Sammis. *Winning!* New York: William Morrow, 1972.

Weaver, Earl, and Berry Stainback. *It's What You Learn After You Know It All That Counts.* New York: Doubleday, 1982.

Weigel, George. *Not Forgotten.* San Francisco: Ignatius Press, 2020.

Wendel, Tim. *Summer of '68.* Boston: Perseus Books, 2012.

Will, George. *Men at Work.* New York: HarperCollins, 1990.

Wilson, Doug. *Brooks.* New York: St. Martin's, 2014.

Wolf, Gregory, ed. *Sportsman's Park in St. Louis.* Phoenix: SABR, 2017.

INDEX

PHOTO CREDITS

ABOUT THE AUTHOR

JOHN W. MILLER is a writer and baseball coach from Brussels. He is a contributor at *America* magazine and chief economic analyst at Trade Data Monitor. For thirteen years he was an award-winning correspondent for the *Wall Street Journal* from forty countries. He has played and coached baseball for forty years, scouted for the Baltimore Orioles, and managed teams from Brussels to the under-15 and under-17 Little League World Series. Codirector of the 2020 PBS film *Moundsville,* he lives with his wife, Meri, in Pittsburgh.